W9-AFR-522

Kafka: The Definitive Guide
Real-Time Data and Stream Processing at Scale

Neha Narkhede, Gwen Shapira, and Todd Palino

Beijing · Boston · Farnham · Sebastopol · Tokyo

Kafka: The Definitive Guide

by Neha Narkhede, Gwen Shapira, and Todd Palino

Copyright © 2017 Neha Narkhede, Gwen Shapira, Todd Palino. All rights reserved.

Printed in the United States of America.

Published by O'Reilly Media, Inc., 1005 Gravenstein Highway North, Sebastopol, CA 95472.

O'Reilly books may be purchased for educational, business, or sales promotional use. Online editions are also available for most titles (*http://oreilly.com/safari*). For more information, contact our corporate/institutional sales department: 800-998-9938 or *corporate@oreilly.com*.

Editor: Shannon Cutt	**Indexer:** WordCo Indexing Services, Inc.
Production Editor: Shiny Kalapurakkel	**Interior Designer:** David Futato
Copyeditor: Christina Edwards	**Cover Designer:** Karen Montgomery
Proofreader: Amanda Kersey	**Illustrator:** Rebecca Demarest

July 2017:   First Edition

Revision History for the First Edition

2017-07-07:   First Release

See *http://oreilly.com/catalog/errata.csp?isbn=9781491936160* for release details.

The O'Reilly logo is a registered trademark of O'Reilly Media, Inc. *Kafka: The Definitive Guide*, the cover image, and related trade dress are trademarks of O'Reilly Media, Inc.

978-1-491-93616-0

[M]

Table of Contents

Foreword

It's an exciting time for Apache Kafka. Kafka is being used by tens of thousands of organizations, including over a third of the Fortune 500 companies. It's among the fastest growing open source projects and has spawned an immense ecosystem around it. It's at the heart of a movement towards managing and processing streams of data.

So where did Kafka come from? Why did we build it? And what exactly is it?

Kafka got its start as an internal infrastructure system we built at LinkedIn. Our observation was really simple: there were lots of databases and other systems built to *store* data, but what was missing in our architecture was something that would help us to handle the continuous *flow* of data. Prior to building Kafka, we experimented with all kinds of off the shelf options; from messaging systems to log aggregation and ETL tools, but none of them gave us what we wanted.

We eventually decided to build something from scratch. Our idea was that instead of focusing on holding piles of data like our relational databases, key-value stores, search indexes, or caches, we would focus on treating data as a continually evolving and ever growing stream, and build a data system—and indeed a data architecture—oriented around that idea.

This idea turned out to be even more broadly applicable than we expected. Though Kafka got its start powering real-time applications and data flow behind the scenes of a social network, you can now see it at the heart of next-generation architectures in every industry imaginable. Big retailers are re-working their fundamental business processes around continuous data streams; car companies are collecting and processing real-time data streams from internet-connected cars; and banks are rethinking their fundamental processes and systems around Kafka as well.

So what is this Kafka thing all about? How does it compare to the systems you already know and use?

We've come to think of Kafka as a *streaming platform*: a system that lets you publish and subscribe to streams of data, store them, and process them, and that is exactly what Apache Kafka is built to be. Getting used to this way of thinking about data might be a little different than what you're used to, but it turns out to be an incredibly powerful abstraction for building applications and architectures. Kafka is often compared to a couple of existing technology categories: enterprise messaging systems, big data systems like Hadoop, and data integration or ETL tools. Each of these comparisons has some validity but also falls a little short.

Kafka is like a messaging system in that it lets you publish and subscribe to streams of messages. In this way, it is similar to products like ActiveMQ, RabbitMQ, IBM's MQSeries, and other products. But even with these similarities, Kafka has a number of core differences from traditional messaging systems that make it another kind of animal entirely. Here are the big three differences: first, it works as a modern distributed system that runs as a cluster and can scale to handle all the applications in even the most massive of companies. Rather than running dozens of individual messaging brokers, hand wired to different apps, this lets you have a central platform that can scale elastically to handle all the streams of data in a company. Secondly, Kafka is a true storage system built to store data for as long as you might like. This has huge advantages in using it as a connecting layer as it provides real delivery guarantees—its data is replicated, persistent, and can be kept around as long as you like. Finally, the world of stream processing raises the level of abstraction quite significantly. Messaging systems mostly just hand out messages. The stream processing capabilities in Kafka let you compute derived streams and datasets dynamically off of your streams with far less code. These differences make Kafka enough of its own thing that it doesn't really make sense to think of it as "yet another queue."

Another view on Kafka—and one of our motivating lenses in designing and building it—was to think of it as a kind of real-time version of Hadoop. Hadoop lets you store and periodically process file data at a very large scale. Kafka lets you store and continuously process streams of data, also at a large scale. At a technical level, there are definitely similarities, and many people see the emerging area of stream processing as a superset of the kind of batch processing people have done with Hadoop and its various processing layers. What this comparison misses is that the use cases that continuous, low-latency processing opens up are quite different from those that naturally fall on a batch processing system. Whereas Hadoop and big data targeted analytics applications, often in the data warehousing space, the low latency nature of Kafka makes it applicable for the kind of core applications that directly power a business. This makes sense: events in a business are happening all the time and the ability to react to them as they occur makes it much easier to build services that directly power the operation of the business, feed back into customer experiences, and so on.

The final area Kafka gets compared to is ETL or data integration tools. After all, these tools move data around, and Kafka moves data around. There is some validity to this as well, but I think the core difference is that Kafka has inverted the problem. Rather than a tool for scraping data out of one system and inserting it into another, Kafka is a platform oriented around real-time streams of events. This means that not only can it connect off-the-shelf applications and data systems, it can power custom applications built to trigger off of these same data streams. We think this architecture centered around streams of events is a really important thing. In some ways these flows of data are the most central aspect of a modern digital company, as important as the cash flows you'd see in a financial statement.

The ability to combine these three areas—to bring all the streams of data together across all the use cases—is what makes the idea of a streaming platform so appealing to people.

Still, all of this is a bit different, and learning how to think and build applications oriented around continuous streams of data is quite a mindshift if you are coming from the world of request/response style applications and relational databases. This book is absolutely the best way to learn about Kafka; from internals to APIs, written by some of the people who know it best. I hope you enjoy reading it as much as I have!

— *Jay Kreps*
Cofounder and CEO at Confluent

Preface

The greatest compliment you can give an author of a technical book is "This is the book I wish I had when I got started with this subject." This is the goal we set for ourselves when we started writing this book. We looked back at our experience writing Kafka, running Kafka in production, and helping many companies use Kafka to build software architectures and manage their data pipelines and we asked ourselves, "What are the most useful things we can share with new users to take them from beginner to experts?" This book is a reflection of the work we do every day: run Apache Kafka and help others use it in the best ways.

We included what we believe you need to know in order to successfully run Apache Kafka in production and build robust and performant applications on top of it. We highlighted the popular use cases: message bus for event-driven microservices, stream-processing applications, and large-scale data pipelines. We also focused on making the book general and comprehensive enough so it will be useful to anyone using Kafka, no matter the use case or architecture. We cover practical matters such as how to install and configure Kafka and how to use the Kafka APIs, and we also dedicated space to Kafka's design principles and reliability guarantees, and explore several of Kafka's delightful architecture details: the replication protocol, controller, and storage layer. We believe that knowledge of Kafka's design and internals is not only a fun read for those interested in distributed systems, but it is also incredibly useful for those who are seeking to make informed decisions when they deploy Kafka in production and design applications that use Kafka. The better you understand how Kafka works, the more you can make informed decisions regarding the many trade-offs that are involved in engineering.

One of the problems in software engineering is that there is always more than one way to do anything. Platforms such as Apache Kafka provide plenty of flexibility, which is great for experts but makes for a steep learning curve for beginners. Very often, Apache Kafka tells you how to use a feature but not why you should or shouldn't use it. Whenever possible, we try to clarify the existing choices, the trade-offs involved, and when you should and shouldn't use the different options presented by Apache Kafka.

Who Should Read This Book

Kafka: The Definitive Guide was written for software engineers who develop applications that use Kafka's APIs and for production engineers (also called SREs, devops, or sysadmins) who install, configure, tune, and monitor Kafka in production. We also wrote the book with data architects and data engineers in mind—those responsible for designing and building an organization's entire data infrastructure. Some of the chapters, especially chapters 3, 4, and 11 are geared toward Java developers. Those chapters assume that the reader is familiar with the basics of the Java programming language, including topics such as exception handling and concurrency. Other chapters, especially chapters 2, 8, 9, and 10, assume the reader has some experience running Linux and some familiarity with storage and network configuration in Linux. The rest of the book discusses Kafka and software architectures in more general terms and does not assume special knowledge.

Another category of people who may find this book interesting are the managers and architects who don't work directly with Kafka but work with the people who do. It is just as important that they understand the guarantees that Kafka provides and the trade-offs that their employees and coworkers will need to make while building Kafka-based systems. The book can provide ammunition to managers who would like to get their staff trained in Apache Kafka or ensure that their teams know what they need to know.

Conventions Used in This Book

The following typographical conventions are used in this book:

Italic
:   Indicates new terms, URLs, email addresses, filenames, and file extensions.

`Constant width`
:   Used for program listings, as well as within paragraphs to refer to program elements such as variable or function names, databases, data types, environment variables, statements, and keywords.

`Constant width bold`
:   Shows commands or other text that should be typed literally by the user.

`Constant width italic`
:   Shows text that should be replaced with user-supplied values or by values determined by context.

This element signifies a tip or suggestion.

This element signifies a general note.

This element indicates a warning or caution.

Using Code Examples

This book is here to help you get your job done. In general, if example code is offered with this book, you may use it in your programs and documentation. You do not need to contact us for permission unless you're reproducing a significant portion of the code. For example, writing a program that uses several chunks of code from this book does not require permission. Selling or distributing a CD-ROM of examples from O'Reilly books does require permission. Answering a question by citing this book and quoting example code does not require permission. Incorporating a significant amount of example code from this book into your product's documentation does require permission.

We appreciate, but do not require, attribution. An attribution usually includes the title, author, publisher, and ISBN. For example: "*Kafka: The Definitive Guide* by Neha Narkhede, Gwen Shapira, and Todd Palino (O'Reilly). Copyright 2017 Neha Narkhede, Gwen Shapira, and Todd Palino, 978-1-491-93616-0."

If you feel your use of code examples falls outside fair use or the permission given above, feel free to contact us at *permissions@oreilly.com*.

O'Reilly Safari

Safari (formerly Safari Books Online) is a membership-based training and reference platform for enterprise, government, educators, and individuals.

Members have access to thousands of books, training videos, Learning Paths, interactive tutorials, and curated playlists from over 250 publishers, including O'Reilly Media, Harvard Business Review, Prentice Hall Professional, Addison-Wesley Professional, Microsoft Press, Sams, Que, Peachpit Press, Adobe, Focal Press, Cisco Press, John Wiley & Sons, Syngress, Morgan Kaufmann, IBM Redbooks, Packt, Adobe Press, FT Press, Apress, Manning, New Riders, McGraw-Hill, Jones & Bartlett, and Course Technology, among others.

For more information, please visit *http://oreilly.com/safari*.

How to Contact Us

Please address comments and questions concerning this book to the publisher:

O'Reilly Media, Inc.
1005 Gravenstein Highway North
Sebastopol, CA 95472
800-998-9938 (in the United States or Canada)
707-829-0515 (international or local)
707-829-0104 (fax)

We have a web page for this book, where we list errata, examples, and any additional information. You can access this page at *http://oreil.ly/2tVmYjk*.

To comment or ask technical questions about this book, send email to *bookquestions@oreilly.com*.

For more information about our books, courses, conferences, and news, see our website at *http://www.oreilly.com*.

Find us on Facebook: *http://facebook.com/oreilly*

Follow us on Twitter: *http://twitter.com/oreillymedia*

Watch us on YouTube: *http://www.youtube.com/oreillymedia*

Acknowledgments

We would like to thank the many contributors to Apache Kafka and its ecosystem. Without their work, this book would not exist. Special thanks to Jay Kreps, Neha Narkhede, and Jun Rao, as well as their colleagues and the leadership at LinkedIn, for cocreating Kafka and contributing it to the Apache Software Foundation.

Many people provided valuable feedback on early versions of the book and we appreciate their time and expertise: Apurva Mehta, Arseniy Tashoyan, Dylan Scott, Ewen Cheslack-Postava, Grant Henke, Ismael Juma, James Cheng, Jason Gustafson, Jeff

Holoman, Joel Koshy, Jonathan Seidman, Matthias Sax, Michael Noll, Paolo Castagna, and Jesse Anderson. We also want to thank the many readers who left comments and feedback via the rough-cuts feedback site.

Many reviewers helped us out and greatly improved the quality of this book, so any mistakes left are our own.

We'd like to thank our O'Reilly editor Shannon Cutt for her encouragement and patience, and for being far more on top of things than we were. Working with O'Reilly is a great experience for an author—the support they provide, from tools to book signings is unparallel. We are grateful to everyone involved in making this happen and we appreciate their choice to work with us.

And we'd like to thank our managers and colleagues for enabling and encouraging us while writing the book.

Gwen wants to thank her husband, Omer Shapira, for his support and patience during the many months spent writing yet another book; her cats, Luke and Lea for being cuddly; and her dad, Lior Shapira, for teaching her to always say yes to opportunities, even when it seems daunting.

Todd would be nowhere without his wife, Marcy, and daughters, Bella and Kaylee, behind him all the way. Their support for all the extra time writing, and long hours running to clear his head, keeps him going.

## CHAPTER 1

Meet Kafka

Every enterprise is powered by data. We take information in, analyze it, manipulate it, and create more as output. Every application creates data, whether it is log messages, metrics, user activity, outgoing messages, or something else. Every byte of data has a story to tell, something of importance that will inform the next thing to be done. In order to know what that is, we need to get the data from where it is created to where it can be analyzed. We see this every day on websites like Amazon, where our clicks on items of interest to us are turned into recommendations that are shown to us a little later.

The faster we can do this, the more agile and responsive our organizations can be. The less effort we spend on moving data around, the more we can focus on the core business at hand. This is why the pipeline is a critical component in the data-driven enterprise. How we move the data becomes nearly as important as the data itself.

> Any time scientists disagree, it's because we have insufficient data. Then we can agree on what kind of data to get; we get the data; and the data solves the problem. Either I'm right, or you're right, or we're both wrong. And we move on.
>
> —Neil deGrasse Tyson

Publish/Subscribe Messaging

Before discussing the specifics of Apache Kafka, it is important for us to understand the concept of publish/subscribe messaging and why it is important. *Publish/subscribe messaging* is a pattern that is characterized by the sender (publisher) of a piece of data (message) not specifically directing it to a receiver. Instead, the publisher classifies the message somehow, and that receiver (subscriber) subscribes to receive certain classes of messages. Pub/sub systems often have a broker, a central point where messages are published, to facilitate this.

How It Starts

Many use cases for publish/subscribe start out the same way: with a simple message queue or interprocess communication channel. For example, you create an application that needs to send monitoring information somewhere, so you write in a direct connection from your application to an app that displays your metrics on a dashboard, and push metrics over that connection, as seen in Figure 1-1.

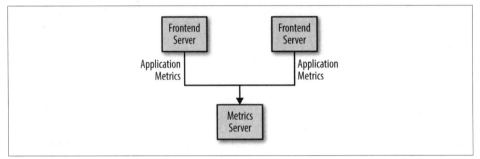

Figure 1-1. A single, direct metrics publisher

This is a simple solution to a simple problem that works when you are getting started with monitoring. Before long, you decide you would like to analyze your metrics over a longer term, and that doesn't work well in the dashboard. You start a new service that can receive metrics, store them, and analyze them. In order to support this, you modify your application to write metrics to both systems. By now you have three more applications that are generating metrics, and they all make the same connections to these two services. Your coworker thinks it would be a good idea to do active polling of the services for alerting as well, so you add a server on each of the applications to provide metrics on request. After a while, you have more applications that are using those servers to get individual metrics and use them for various purposes. This architecture can look much like Figure 1-2, with connections that are even harder to trace.

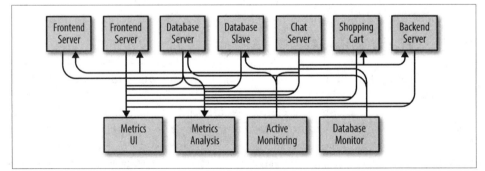

Figure 1-2. Many metrics publishers, using direct connections

The technical debt built up here is obvious, so you decide to pay some of it back. You set up a single application that receives metrics from all the applications out there, and provide a server to query those metrics for any system that needs them. This reduces the complexity of the architecture to something similar to Figure 1-3. Congratulations, you have built a publish-subscribe messaging system!

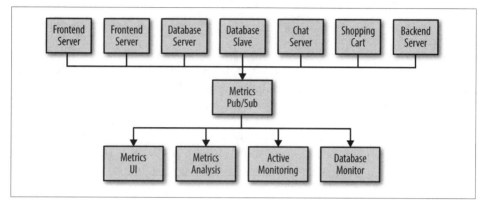

Figure 1-3. A metrics publish/subscribe system

Individual Queue Systems

At the same time that you have been waging this war with metrics, one of your coworkers has been doing similar work with log messages. Another has been working on tracking user behavior on the frontend website and providing that information to developers who are working on machine learning, as well as creating some reports for management. You have all followed a similar path of building out systems that decouple the publishers of the information from the subscribers to that information. Figure 1-4 shows such an infrastructure, with three separate pub/sub systems.

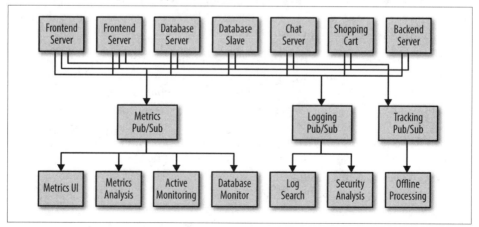

Figure 1-4. Multiple publish/subscribe systems

This is certainly a lot better than utilizing point-to-point connections (as in Figure 1-2), but there is a lot of duplication. Your company is maintaining multiple systems for queuing data, all of which have their own individual bugs and limitations. You also know that there will be more use cases for messaging coming soon. What you would like to have is a single centralized system that allows for publishing generic types of data, which will grow as your business grows.

Enter Kafka

Apache Kafka is a publish/subscribe messaging system designed to solve this problem. It is often described as a "distributed commit log" or more recently as a "distributing streaming platform." A filesystem or database commit log is designed to provide a durable record of all transactions so that they can be replayed to consistently build the state of a system. Similarly, data within Kafka is stored durably, in order, and can be read deterministically. In addition, the data can be distributed within the system to provide additional protections against failures, as well as significant opportunities for scaling performance.

Messages and Batches

The unit of data within Kafka is called a *message*. If you are approaching Kafka from a database background, you can think of this as similar to a *row* or a *record*. A message is simply an array of bytes as far as Kafka is concerned, so the data contained within it does not have a specific format or meaning to Kafka. A message can have an optional bit of metadata, which is referred to as a *key*. The key is also a byte array and, as with the message, has no specific meaning to Kafka. Keys are used when messages are to be written to partitions in a more controlled manner. The simplest such scheme is to generate a consistent hash of the key, and then select the partition number for that message by taking the result of the hash modulo, the total number of partitions in the topic. This assures that messages with the same key are always written to the same partition. Keys are discussed in more detail in Chapter 3.

For efficiency, messages are written into Kafka in batches. A *batch* is just a collection of messages, all of which are being produced to the same topic and partition. An individual roundtrip across the network for each message would result in excessive overhead, and collecting messages together into a batch reduces this. Of course, this is a tradeoff between latency and throughput: the larger the batches, the more messages that can be handled per unit of time, but the longer it takes an individual message to propagate. Batches are also typically compressed, providing more efficient data transfer and storage at the cost of some processing power.

Schemas

While messages are opaque byte arrays to Kafka itself, it is recommended that additional structure, or schema, be imposed on the message content so that it can be easily understood. There are many options available for message *schema*, depending on your application's individual needs. Simplistic systems, such as Javascript Object Notation (JSON) and Extensible Markup Language (XML), are easy to use and human-readable. However, they lack features such as robust type handling and compatibility between schema versions. Many Kafka developers favor the use of Apache Avro, which is a serialization framework originally developed for Hadoop. Avro provides a compact serialization format; schemas that are separate from the message payloads and that do not require code to be generated when they change; and strong data typing and schema evolution, with both backward and forward compatibility.

A consistent data format is important in Kafka, as it allows writing and reading messages to be decoupled. When these tasks are tightly coupled, applications that subscribe to messages must be updated to handle the new data format, in parallel with the old format. Only then can the applications that publish the messages be updated to utilize the new format. By using well-defined schemas and storing them in a common repository, the messages in Kafka can be understood without coordination. Schemas and serialization are covered in more detail in Chapter 3.

Topics and Partitions

Messages in Kafka are categorized into *topics*. The closest analogies for a topic are a database table or a folder in a filesystem. Topics are additionally broken down into a number of *partitions*. Going back to the "commit log" description, a partition is a single log. Messages are written to it in an append-only fashion, and are read in order from beginning to end. Note that as a topic typically has multiple partitions, there is no guarantee of message time-ordering across the entire topic, just within a single partition. Figure 1-5 shows a topic with four partitions, with writes being appended to the end of each one. Partitions are also the way that Kafka provides redundancy and scalability. Each partition can be hosted on a different server, which means that a single topic can be scaled horizontally across multiple servers to provide performance far beyond the ability of a single server.

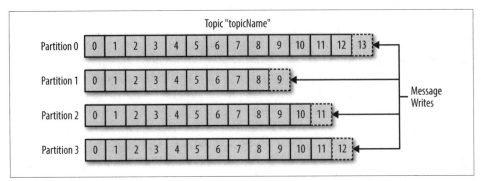

Figure 1-5. Representation of a topic with multiple partitions

The term *stream* is often used when discussing data within systems like Kafka. Most often, a stream is considered to be a single topic of data, regardless of the number of partitions. This represents a single stream of data moving from the producers to the consumers. This way of referring to messages is most common when discussing stream processing, which is when frameworks—some of which are Kafka Streams, Apache Samza, and Storm—operate on the messages in real time. This method of operation can be compared to the way offline frameworks, namely Hadoop, are designed to work on bulk data at a later time. An overview of stream processing is provided in Chapter 11.

Producers and Consumers

Kafka clients are users of the system, and there are two basic types: producers and consumers. There are also advanced client APIs—Kafka Connect API for data integration and Kafka Streams for stream processing. The advanced clients use producers and consumers as building blocks and provide higher-level functionality on top.

Producers create new messages. In other publish/subscribe systems, these may be called *publishers* or *writers*. In general, a message will be produced to a specific topic. By default, the producer does not care what partition a specific message is written to and will balance messages over all partitions of a topic evenly. In some cases, the producer will direct messages to specific partitions. This is typically done using the message key and a partitioner that will generate a hash of the key and map it to a specific partition. This assures that all messages produced with a given key will get written to the same partition. The producer could also use a custom partitioner that follows other business rules for mapping messages to partitions. Producers are covered in more detail in Chapter 3.

Consumers read messages. In other publish/subscribe systems, these clients may be called *subscribers* or *readers*. The consumer subscribes to one or more topics and reads the messages in the order in which they were produced. The consumer keeps track of which messages it has already consumed by keeping track of the offset of messages. The *offset* is another bit of metadata—an integer value that continually increases—that Kafka adds to each message as it is produced. Each message in a given partition has a unique offset. By storing the offset of the last consumed message for each partition, either in Zookeeper or in Kafka itself, a consumer can stop and restart without losing its place.

Consumers work as part of a *consumer group*, which is one or more consumers that work together to consume a topic. The group assures that each partition is only consumed by one member. In Figure 1-6, there are three consumers in a single group consuming a topic. Two of the consumers are working from one partition each, while the third consumer is working from two partitions. The mapping of a consumer to a partition is often called *ownership* of the partition by the consumer.

In this way, consumers can horizontally scale to consume topics with a large number of messages. Additionally, if a single consumer fails, the remaining members of the group will rebalance the partitions being consumed to take over for the missing member. Consumers and consumer groups are discussed in more detail in Chapter 4.

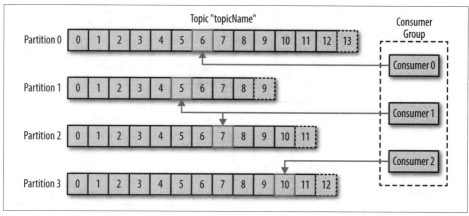

Figure 1-6. A consumer group reading from a topic

Brokers and Clusters

A single Kafka server is called a *broker*. The broker receives messages from producers, assigns offsets to them, and commits the messages to storage on disk. It also services consumers, responding to fetch requests for partitions and responding with the messages that have been committed to disk. Depending on the specific hardware and its performance characteristics, a single broker can easily handle thousands of partitions and millions of messages per second.

Kafka brokers are designed to operate as part of a *cluster*. Within a cluster of brokers, one broker will also function as the cluster *controller* (elected automatically from the live members of the cluster). The controller is responsible for administrative operations, including assigning partitions to brokers and monitoring for broker failures. A partition is owned by a single broker in the cluster, and that broker is called the *leader* of the partition. A partition may be assigned to multiple brokers, which will result in the partition being replicated (as seen in Figure 1-7). This provides redundancy of messages in the partition, such that another broker can take over leadership if there is a broker failure. However, all consumers and producers operating on that partition must connect to the leader. Cluster operations, including partition replication, are covered in detail in Chapter 6.

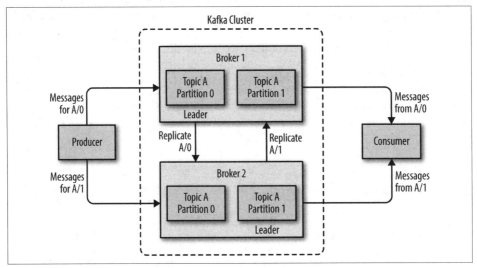

Figure 1-7. Replication of partitions in a cluster

A key feature of Apache Kafka is that of *retention*, which is the durable storage of messages for some period of time. Kafka brokers are configured with a default retention setting for topics, either retaining messages for some period of time (e.g., 7 days) or until the topic reaches a certain size in bytes (e.g., 1 GB). Once these limits are reached, messages are expired and deleted so that the retention configuration is a minimum amount of data available at any time. Individual topics can also be configured with their own retention settings so that messages are stored for only as long as they are useful. For example, a tracking topic might be retained for several days, whereas application metrics might be retained for only a few hours. Topics can also be configured as *log compacted*, which means that Kafka will retain only the last message produced with a specific key. This can be useful for changelog-type data, where only the last update is interesting.

Multiple Clusters

As Kafka deployments grow, it is often advantageous to have multiple clusters. There are several reasons why this can be useful:

- Segregation of types of data
- Isolation for security requirements
- Multiple datacenters (disaster recovery)

When working with multiple datacenters in particular, it is often required that messages be copied between them. In this way, online applications can have access to user activity at both sites. For example, if a user changes public information in their profile, that change will need to be visible regardless of the datacenter in which search results are displayed. Or, monitoring data can be collected from many sites into a single central location where the analysis and alerting systems are hosted. The replication mechanisms within the Kafka clusters are designed only to work within a single cluster, not between multiple clusters.

The Kafka project includes a tool called *MirrorMaker*, used for this purpose. At its core, MirrorMaker is simply a Kafka consumer and producer, linked together with a queue. Messages are consumed from one Kafka cluster and produced for another. Figure 1-8 shows an example of an architecture that uses MirrorMaker, aggregating messages from two local clusters into an aggregate cluster, and then copying that cluster to other datacenters. The simple nature of the application belies its power in creating sophisticated data pipelines, which will be detailed further in Chapter 7.

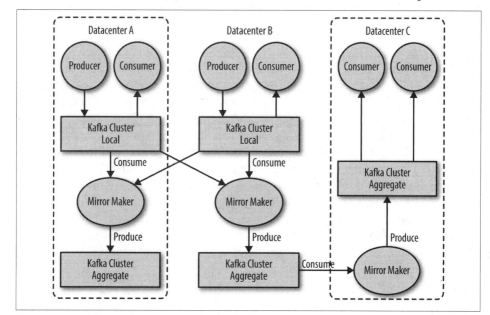

Figure 1-8. Multiple datacenter architecture

Why Kafka?

There are many choices for publish/subscribe messaging systems, so what makes Apache Kafka a good choice?

Multiple Producers

Kafka is able to seamlessly handle multiple producers, whether those clients are using many topics or the same topic. This makes the system ideal for aggregating data from many frontend systems and making it consistent. For example, a site that serves content to users via a number of microservices can have a single topic for page views that all services can write to using a common format. Consumer applications can then receive a single stream of page views for all applications on the site without having to coordinate consuming from multiple topics, one for each application.

Multiple Consumers

In addition to multiple producers, Kafka is designed for multiple consumers to read any single stream of messages without interfering with each other. This is in contrast to many queuing systems where once a message is consumed by one client, it is not available to any other. Multiple Kafka consumers can choose to operate as part of a group and share a stream, assuring that the entire group processes a given message only once.

Disk-Based Retention

Not only can Kafka handle multiple consumers, but durable message retention means that consumers do not always need to work in real time. Messages are committed to disk, and will be stored with configurable retention rules. These options can be selected on a per-topic basis, allowing for different streams of messages to have different amounts of retention depending on the consumer needs. Durable retention means that if a consumer falls behind, either due to slow processing or a burst in traffic, there is no danger of losing data. It also means that maintenance can be performed on consumers, taking applications offline for a short period of time, with no concern about messages backing up on the producer or getting lost. Consumers can be stopped, and the messages will be retained in Kafka. This allows them to restart and pick up processing messages where they left off with no data loss.

Scalable

Kafka's flexible scalability makes it easy to handle any amount of data. Users can start with a single broker as a proof of concept, expand to a small development cluster of three brokers, and move into production with a larger cluster of tens or even hundreds of brokers that grows over time as the data scales up. Expansions can be performed while the cluster is online, with no impact on the availability of the system as a whole. This also means that a cluster of multiple brokers can handle the failure of an individual broker, and continue servicing clients. Clusters that need to tolerate more simultaneous failures can be configured with higher replication factors. Replication is discussed in more detail in Chapter 6.

High Performance

All of these features come together to make Apache Kafka a publish/subscribe messaging system with excellent performance under high load. Producers, consumers, and brokers can all be scaled out to handle very large message streams with ease. This can be done while still providing subsecond message latency from producing a message to availability to consumers.

The Data Ecosystem

Many applications participate in the environments we build for data processing. We have defined inputs in the form of applications that create data or otherwise introduce it to the system. We have defined outputs in the form of metrics, reports, and other data products. We create loops, with some components reading data from the system, transforming it using data from other sources, and then introducing it back into the data infrastructure to be used elsewhere. This is done for numerous types of data, with each having unique qualities of content, size, and usage.

Apache Kafka provides the circulatory system for the data ecosystem, as shown in Figure 1-9. It carries messages between the various members of the infrastructure, providing a consistent interface for all clients. When coupled with a system to provide message schemas, producers and consumers no longer require tight coupling or direct connections of any sort. Components can be added and removed as business cases are created and dissolved, and producers do not need to be concerned about who is using the data or the number of consuming applications.

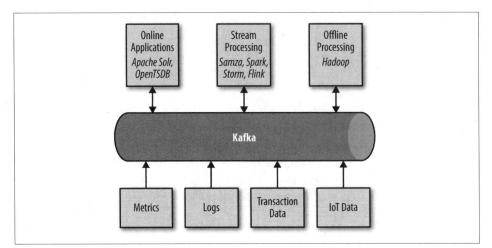

Figure 1-9. A big data ecosystem

Use Cases

Activity tracking

The original use case for Kafka, as it was designed at LinkedIn, is that of user activity tracking. A website's users interact with frontend applications, which generate messages regarding actions the user is taking. This can be passive information, such as page views and click tracking, or it can be more complex actions, such as information that a user adds to their profile. The messages are published to one or more topics, which are then consumed by applications on the backend. These applications may be generating reports, feeding machine learning systems, updating search results, or performing other operations that are necessary to provide a rich user experience.

Messaging

Kafka is also used for messaging, where applications need to send notifications (such as emails) to users. Those applications can produce messages without needing to be concerned about formatting or how the messages will actually be sent. A single application can then read all the messages to be sent and handle them consistently, including:

- Formatting the messages (also known as decorating) using a common look and feel
- Collecting multiple messages into a single notification to be sent
- Applying a user's preferences for how they want to receive messages

Using a single application for this avoids the need to duplicate functionality in multiple applications, as well as allows operations like aggregation which would not otherwise be possible.

Metrics and logging

Kafka is also ideal for collecting application and system metrics and logs. This is a use case in which the ability to have multiple applications producing the same type of message shines. Applications publish metrics on a regular basis to a Kafka topic, and those metrics can be consumed by systems for monitoring and alerting. They can also be used in an offline system like Hadoop to perform longer-term analysis, such as growth projections. Log messages can be published in the same way, and can be routed to dedicated log search systems like Elastisearch or security analysis applications. Another added benefit of Kafka is that when the destination system needs to change (e.g., it's time to update the log storage system), there is no need to alter the frontend applications or the means of aggregation.

Commit log

Since Kafka is based on the concept of a commit log, database changes can be published to Kafka and applications can easily monitor this stream to receive live updates as they happen. This changelog stream can also be used for replicating database updates to a remote system, or for consolidating changes from multiple applications into a single database view. Durable retention is useful here for providing a buffer for the changelog, meaning it can be replayed in the event of a failure of the consuming applications. Alternately, log-compacted topics can be used to provide longer retention by only retaining a single change per key.

Stream processing

Another area that provides numerous types of applications is stream processing. While almost all usage of Kafka can be thought of as stream processing, the term is typically used to refer to applications that provide similar functionality to map/reduce processing in Hadoop. Hadoop usually relies on aggregation of data over a long time frame, either hours or days. Stream processing operates on data in real time, as quickly as messages are produced. Stream frameworks allow users to write small applications to operate on Kafka messages, performing tasks such as counting metrics, partitioning messages for efficient processing by other applications, or transforming messages using data from multiple sources. Stream processing is covered in Chapter 11.

Kafka's Origin

Kafka was created to address the data pipeline problem at LinkedIn. It was designed to provide a high-performance messaging system that can handle many types of data and provide clean, structured data about user activity and system metrics in real time.

> Data really powers everything that we do.
>
> —Jeff Weiner, *CEO of LinkedIn*

LinkedIn's Problem

Similar to the example described at the beginning of this chapter, LinkedIn had a system for collecting system and application metrics that used custom collectors and open source tools for storing and presenting data internally. In addition to traditional metrics, such as CPU usage and application performance, there was a sophisticated request-tracing feature that used the monitoring system and could provide introspection into how a single user request propagated through internal applications. The monitoring system had many faults, however. This included metrics collection based on polling, large intervals between metrics, and no ability for application owners to manage their own metrics. The system was high-touch, requiring human intervention for most simple tasks, and inconsistent, with differing metric names for the same measurement across different systems.

At the same time, there was a system created for tracking user activity information. This was an HTTP service that frontend servers would connect to periodically and publish a batch of messages (in XML format) to the HTTP service. These batches were then moved to offline processing, which is where the files were parsed and collated. This system had many faults. The XML formatting was inconsistent, and parsing it was computationally expensive. Changing the type of user activity that was tracked required a significant amount of coordinated work between frontends and offline processing. Even then, the system would break constantly due to changing schemas. Tracking was built on hourly batching, so it could not be used in real-time.

Monitoring and user-activity tracking could not use the same backend service. The monitoring service was too clunky, the data format was not oriented for activity tracking, and the polling model for monitoring was not compatible with the push model for tracking. At the same time, the tracking service was too fragile to use for metrics, and the batch-oriented processing was not the right model for real-time monitoring and alerting. However, the monitoring and tracking data shared many traits, and correlation of the information (such as how specific types of user activity affected application performance) was highly desirable. A drop in specific types of user activity could indicate problems with the application that serviced it, but hours of delay in processing activity batches meant a slow response to these types of issues.

At first, existing off-the-shelf open source solutions were thoroughly investigated to find a new system that would provide real-time access to the data and scale out to handle the amount of message traffic needed. Prototype systems were set up using ActiveMQ, but at the time it could not handle the scale. It was also a fragile solution for the way LinkedIn needed to use it, discovering many flaws in ActiveMQ that would cause the brokers to pause. This would back up connections to clients and interfere with the ability of the applications to serve requests to users. The decision was made to move forward with a custom infrastructure for the data pipeline.

The Birth of Kafka

The development team at LinkedIn was led by Jay Kreps, a principal software engineer who was previously responsible for the development and open source release of Voldemort, a distributed key-value storage system. The initial team also included Neha Narkhede and, later, Jun Rao. Together, they set out to create a messaging system that could meet the needs of both the monitoring and tracking systems, and scale for the future. The primary goals were to:

- Decouple producers and consumers by using a push-pull model
- Provide persistence for message data within the messaging system to allow multiple consumers
- Optimize for high throughput of messages
- Allow for horizontal scaling of the system to grow as the data streams grew

The result was a publish/subscribe messaging system that had an interface typical of messaging systems but a storage layer more like a log-aggregation system. Combined with the adoption of Apache Avro for message serialization, Kafka was effective for handling both metrics and user-activity tracking at a scale of billions of messages per day. The scalability of Kafka has helped LinkedIn's usage grow in excess of one trillion messages produced (as of August 2015) and over a petabyte of data consumed daily.

Open Source

Kafka was released as an open source project on GitHub in late 2010. As it started to gain attention in the open source community, it was proposed and accepted as an Apache Software Foundation incubator project in July of 2011. Apache Kafka graduated from the incubator in October of 2012. Since then, it has continuously been worked on and has found a robust community of contributors and committers outside of LinkedIn. Kafka is now used in some of the largest data pipelines in the world. In the fall of 2014, Jay Kreps, Neha Narkhede, and Jun Rao left LinkedIn to found Confluent, a company centered around providing development, enterprise support, and training for Apache Kafka. The two companies, along with ever-growing contributions from others in the open source community, continue to develop and maintain Kafka, making it the first choice for big data pipelines.

The Name

People often ask how Kafka got its name and if it has anything to do with the application itself. Jay Kreps offered the following insight:

> I thought that since Kafka was a system optimized for writing, using a writer's name would make sense. I had taken a lot of lit classes in college and liked Franz Kafka. Plus the name sounded cool for an open source project.

> So basically there is not much of a relationship.

Getting Started with Kafka

Now that we know all about Kafka and its history, we can set it up and build our own data pipeline. In the next chapter, we will explore installing and configuring Kafka. We will also cover selecting the right hardware to run Kafka on, and some things to keep in mind when moving to production operations.

## CHAPTER 2

Installing Kafka

This chapter describes how to get started with the Apache Kafka broker, including how to set up Apache Zookeeper, which is used by Kafka for storing metadata for the brokers. The chapter will also cover the basic configuration options for a Kafka deployment, as well as criteria for selecting the correct hardware to run the brokers on. Finally, we cover how to install multiple Kafka brokers as part of a single cluster and some specific concerns when using Kafka in a production environment.

First Things First

There are a few things that need to happen before using Apache Kafka. The following sections tell you what those things are.

Choosing an Operating System

Apache Kafka is a Java application, and can run on many operating systems. This includes Windows, MacOS, Linux, and others. The installation steps in this chapter will be focused on setting up and using Kafka in a Linux environment, as this is the most common OS on which it is installed. This is also the recommended OS for deploying Kafka for general use. For information on installing Kafka on Windows and MacOS, see Appendix A.

Installing Java

Prior to installing either Zookeeper or Kafka, you will need a Java environment set up and functioning. This should be a Java 8 version, and can be the version provided by your OS or one directly downloaded from java.com (*https://www.java.com/en/*). Though Zookeeper and Kafka will work with a runtime edition of Java, it may be more convenient when developing tools and applications to have the full Java Development Kit (JDK). The installation steps will assume you have installed JDK version 8 update 51 in /usr/java/jdk1.8.0_51.

Installing Zookeeper

Apache Kafka uses Zookeeper to store metadata about the Kafka cluster, as well as consumer client details, as shown in Figure 2-1. While it is possible to run a Zookeeper server using scripts contained in the Kafka distribution, it is trivial to install a full version of Zookeeper from the distribution.

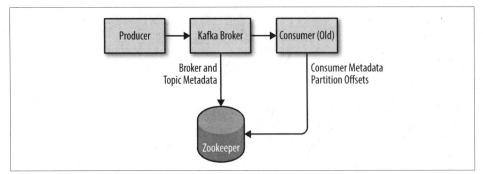

Figure 2-1. Kafka and Zookeeper

Kafka has been tested extensively with the stable 3.4.6 release of Zookeeper, which can be downloaded from apache.org at *http://bit.ly/2sDWSgJ*.

Standalone Server

The following example installs Zookeeper with a basic configuration in /usr/local/zookeeper, storing its data in /var/lib/zookeeper:

```
# tar -zxf zookeeper-3.4.6.tar.gz
# mv zookeeper-3.4.6 /usr/local/zookeeper
# mkdir -p /var/lib/zookeeper
# cat > /usr/local/zookeeper/conf/zoo.cfg << EOF
> tickTime=2000
> dataDir=/var/lib/zookeeper
> clientPort=2181
> EOF
# export JAVA_HOME=/usr/java/jdk1.8.0_51
# /usr/local/zookeeper/bin/zkServer.sh start
JMX enabled by default
Using config: /usr/local/zookeeper/bin/../conf/zoo.cfg
Starting zookeeper ... STARTED
#
```

You can now validate that Zookeeper is running correctly in standalone mode by connecting to the client port and sending the four-letter command srvr:

```
# telnet localhost 2181
Trying ::1...
Connected to localhost.
Escape character is '^]'.
srvr
Zookeeper version: 3.4.6-1569965, built on 02/20/2014 09:09 GMT
Latency min/avg/max: 0/0/0
Received: 1
Sent: 0
Connections: 1
Outstanding: 0
Zxid: 0x0
Mode: standalone
Node count: 4
Connection closed by foreign host.
#
```

Zookeeper ensemble

A Zookeeper cluster is called an *ensemble*. Due to the algorithm used, it is recommended that ensembles contain an odd number of servers (e.g., 3, 5, etc.) as a majority of ensemble members (a quorum) must be working in order for Zookeeper to respond to requests. This means that in a three-node ensemble, you can run with one node missing. With a five-node ensemble, you can run with two nodes missing.

Sizing Your Zookeeper Ensemble

Consider running Zookeeper in a five-node ensemble. In order to make configuration changes to the ensemble, including swapping a node, you will need to reload nodes one at a time. If your ensemble cannot tolerate more than one node being down, doing maintenance work introduces additional risk. It is also not recommended to run more than seven nodes, as performance can start to degrade due to the nature of the consensus protocol.

To configure Zookeeper servers in an ensemble, they must have a common configuration that lists all servers, and each server needs a myid file in the data directory that specifies the ID number of the server. If the hostnames of the servers in the ensemble are zoo1.example.com, zoo2.example.com, and zoo3.example.com, the configuration file might look like this:

```
tickTime=2000
dataDir=/var/lib/zookeeper
clientPort=2181
initLimit=20
syncLimit=5
server.1=zoo1.example.com:2888:3888
server.2=zoo2.example.com:2888:3888
server.3=zoo3.example.com:2888:3888
```

In this configuration, the `initLimit` is the amount of time to allow followers to connect with a leader. The `syncLimit` value limits how out-of-sync followers can be with the leader. Both values are a number of `tickTime` units, which makes the `initLimit` 20 * 2000 ms, or 40 seconds. The configuration also lists each server in the ensemble. The servers are specified in the format *server.X=hostname:peerPort:leaderPort*, with the following parameters:

X
> The ID number of the server. This must be an integer, but it does not need to be zero-based or sequential.

hostname
> The hostname or IP address of the server.

peerPort
> The TCP port over which servers in the ensemble communicate with each other.

leaderPort
> The TCP port over which leader election is performed.

Clients only need to be able to connect to the ensemble over the clientPort, but the members of the ensemble must be able to communicate with each other over all three ports.

In addition to the shared configuration file, each server must have a file in the `data Dir` directory with the name `myid`. This file must contain the ID number of the server, which must match the configuration file. Once these steps are complete, the servers will start up and communicate with each other in an ensemble.

Installing a Kafka Broker

Once Java and Zookeeper are configured, you are ready to install Apache Kafka. The current release of Kafka can be downloaded at *http://kafka.apache.org/down loads.html*. At press time, that version is 0.9.0.1 running under Scala version 2.11.0.

The following example installs Kafka in `/usr/local/kafka`, configured to use the Zookeeper server started previously and to store the message log segments stored in `/tmp/kafka-logs`:

```
# tar -zxf kafka_2.11-0.9.0.1.tgz
# mv kafka_2.11-0.9.0.1 /usr/local/kafka
# mkdir /tmp/kafka-logs
# export JAVA_HOME=/usr/java/jdk1.8.0_51
# /usr/local/kafka/bin/kafka-server-start.sh -daemon
/usr/local/kafka/config/server.properties
#
```

Once the Kafka broker is started, we can verify that it is working by performing some simple operations against the cluster creating a test topic, producing some messages, and consuming the same messages.

Create and verify a topic:

```
# /usr/local/kafka/bin/kafka-topics.sh --create --zookeeper localhost:2181
--replication-factor 1 --partitions 1 --topic test
Created topic "test".
# /usr/local/kafka/bin/kafka-topics.sh --zookeeper localhost:2181
--describe --topic test
Topic:test     PartitionCount:1     ReplicationFactor:1     Configs:
    Topic: test     Partition: 0     Leader: 0     Replicas: 0     Isr: 0
#
```

Produce messages to a test topic:

```
# /usr/local/kafka/bin/kafka-console-producer.sh --broker-list
localhost:9092 --topic test
Test Message 1
Test Message 2
^D
#
```

Consume messages from a test topic:

```
# /usr/local/kafka/bin/kafka-console-consumer.sh --zookeeper
localhost:2181 --topic test --from-beginning
Test Message 1
Test Message 2
^C
Consumed 2 messages
#
```

Broker Configuration

The example configuration provided with the Kafka distribution is sufficient to run a standalone server as a proof of concept, but it will not be sufficient for most installations. There are numerous configuration options for Kafka that control all aspects of setup and tuning. Many options can be left to the default settings, as they deal with tuning aspects of the Kafka broker that will not be applicable until you have a specific use case to work with and a specific use case that requires adjusting these settings.

General Broker

There are several broker configurations that should be reviewed when deploying Kafka for any environment other than a standalone broker on a single server. These parameters deal with the basic configuration of the broker, and most of them must be changed to run properly in a cluster with other brokers.

broker.id

Every Kafka broker must have an integer identifier, which is set using the `broker.id` configuration. By default, this integer is set to 0, but it can be any value. The most important thing is that the integer must be unique within a single Kafka cluster. The selection of this number is arbitrary, and it can be moved between brokers if necessary for maintenance tasks. A good guideline is to set this value to something intrinsic to the host so that when performing maintenance it is not onerous to map broker ID numbers to hosts. For example, if your hostnames contain a unique number (such as `host1.example.com`, `host2.example.com`, etc.), that is a good choice for the `broker.id` value.

port

The example configuration file starts Kafka with a listener on TCP port 9092. This can be set to any available port by changing the `port` configuration parameter. Keep in mind that if a port lower than 1024 is chosen, Kafka must be started as root. Running Kafka as root is not a recommended configuration.

zookeeper.connect

The location of the Zookeeper used for storing the broker metadata is set using the `zookeeper.connect` configuration parameter. The example configuration uses a Zookeeper running on port 2181 on the local host, which is specified as `localhost:2181`. The format for this parameter is a semicolon-separated list of `hostname:port/path` strings, which include:

- `hostname`, the hostname or IP address of the Zookeeper server.
- `port`, the client port number for the server.
- `/path`, an optional Zookeeper path to use as a chroot environment for the Kafka cluster. If it is omitted, the root path is used.

If a chroot path is specified and does not exist, it will be created by the broker when it starts up.

Why Use a Chroot Path

It is generally considered to be good practice to use a chroot path for the Kafka cluster. This allows the Zookeeper ensemble to be shared with other applications, including other Kafka clusters, without a conflict. It is also best to specify multiple Zookeeper servers (which are all part of the same ensemble) in this configuration. This allows the Kafka broker to connect to another member of the Zookeeper ensemble in the event of server failure.

log.dirs

Kafka persists all messages to disk, and these log segments are stored in the directories specified in the *log.dirs* configuration. This is a comma-separated list of paths on the local system. If more than one path is specified, the broker will store partitions on them in a "least-used" fashion with one partition's log segments stored within the same path. Note that the broker will place a new partition in the path that has the least number of partitions currently stored in it, not the least amount of disk space used in the following situations:

num.recovery.threads.per.data.dir

Kafka uses a configurable pool of threads for handling log segments. Currently, this thread pool is used:

- When starting normally, to open each partition's log segments
- When starting after a failure, to check and truncate each partition's log segments
- When shutting down, to cleanly close log segments

By default, only one thread per log directory is used. As these threads are only used during startup and shutdown, it is reasonable to set a larger number of threads in order to parallelize operations. Specifically, when recovering from an unclean shutdown, this can mean the difference of several hours when restarting a broker with a large number of partitions! When setting this parameter, remember that the number configured is per log directory specified with *log.dirs*. This means that if `num.recovery.threads.per.data.dir` is set to 8, and there are 3 paths specified in `log.dirs`, this is a total of 24 threads.

auto.create.topics.enable

The default Kafka configuration specifies that the broker should automatically create a topic under the following circumstances:

- When a producer starts writing messages to the topic
- When a consumer starts reading messages from the topic
- When any client requests metadata for the topic

In many situations, this can be undesirable behavior, especially as there is no way to validate the existence of a topic through the Kafka protocol without causing it to be created. If you are managing topic creation explicitly, whether manually or through a provisioning system, you can set the `auto.create.topics.enable` configuration to `false`.

Topic Defaults

The Kafka server configuration specifies many default configurations for topics that are created. Several of these parameters, including partition counts and message retention, can be set per-topic using the administrative tools (covered in Chapter 9). The defaults in the server configuration should be set to baseline values that are appropriate for the majority of the topics in the cluster.

Using Per-Topic Overrides

In previous versions of Kafka, it was possible to specify per-topic overrides for these configurations in the broker configuration using the parameters `log.retention.hours.per.topic`, `log.retention.bytes.per.topic`, and `log.segment.bytes.per.topic`. These parameters are no longer supported, and overrides must be specified using the administrative tools.

num.partitions

The `num.partitions` parameter determines how many partitions a new topic is created with, primarily when automatic topic creation is enabled (which is the default setting). This parameter defaults to one partition. Keep in mind that the number of partitions for a topic can only be increased, never decreased. This means that if a topic needs to have fewer partitions than `num.partitions`, care will need to be taken to manually create the topic (discussed in Chapter 9).

As described in Chapter 1, partitions are the way a topic is scaled within a Kafka cluster, which makes it important to use partition counts that will balance the message load across the entire cluster as brokers are added. Many users will have the partition count for a topic be equal to, or a multiple of, the number of brokers in the cluster. This allows the partitions to be evenly distributed to the brokers, which will evenly distribute the message load. This is not a requirement, however, as you can also balance message load by having multiple topics.

How to Choose the Number of Partitions

There are several factors to consider when choosing the number of partitions:

- What is the throughput you expect to achieve for the topic? For example, do you expect to write 100 KB per second or 1 GB per second?

- What is the maximum throughput you expect to achieve when consuming from a single partition? You will always have, at most, one consumer reading from a partition, so if you know that your slower consumer writes the data to a database and this database never handles more than 50 MB per second from each thread writing to it, then you know you are limited to 60MB throughput when consuming from a partition.

- You can go through the same exercise to estimate the maximum throughput per producer for a single partition, but since producers are typically much faster than consumers, it is usually safe to skip this.

- If you are sending messages to partitions based on keys, adding partitions later can be very challenging, so calculate throughput based on your expected future usage, not the current usage.

- Consider the number of partitions you will place on each broker and available diskspace and network bandwidth per broker.

- Avoid overestimating, as each partition uses memory and other resources on the broker and will increase the time for leader elections.

With all this in mind, it's clear that you want many partitions but not too many. If you have some estimate regarding the target throughput of the topic and the expected throughput of the consumers, you can divide the target throughput by the expected consumer throughput and derive the number of partitions this way. So if I want to be able to write and read 1 GB/sec from a topic, and I know each consumer can only process 50 MB/s, then I know I need at least 20 partitions. This way, I can have 20 consumers reading from the topic and achieve 1 GB/sec.

If you don't have this detailed information, our experience suggests that limiting the size of the partition on the disk to less than 6 GB per day of retention often gives satisfactory results.

log.retention.ms

The most common configuration for how long Kafka will retain messages is by time. The default is specified in the configuration file using the `log.retention.hours` parameter, and it is set to 168 hours, or one week. However, there are two other parameters allowed, `log.retention.minutes` and `log.retention.ms`. All three of these specify the same configuration—the amount of time after which messages may be deleted—but the recommended parameter to use is `log.retention.ms`, as the smaller unit size will take precedence if more than one is specified. This will make sure that the value set for `log.retention.ms` is always the one used. If more than one is specified, the smaller unit size will take precedence.

Retention By Time and Last Modified Times

Retention by time is performed by examining the last modified time (mtime) on each log segment file on disk. Under normal cluster operations, this is the time that the log segment was closed, and represents the timestamp of the last message in the file. However, when using administrative tools to move partitions between brokers, this time is not accurate and will result in excess retention for these partitions. More information on this is provided in Chapter 9 when discussing partition moves.

log.retention.bytes

Another way to expire messages is based on the total number of bytes of messages retained. This value is set using the `log.retention.bytes` parameter, and it is applied per-partition. This means that if you have a topic with 8 partitions, and `log.retention.bytes` is set to 1 GB, the amount of data retained for the topic will be 8 GB at most. Note that all retention is performed for individual partitions, not the topic. This means that should the number of partitions for a topic be expanded, the retention will also increase if `log.retention.bytes` is used.

Configuring Retention by Size and Time

If you have specified a value for both `log.retention.bytes` and `log.retention.ms` (or another parameter for retention by time), messages may be removed when either criteria is met. For example, if `log.retention.ms` is set to 86400000 (1 day) and `log.retention.bytes` is set to 1000000000 (1 GB), it is possible for messages that are less than 1 day old to get deleted if the total volume of messages over the course of the day is greater than 1 GB. Conversely, if the volume is less than 1 GB, messages can be deleted after 1 day even if the total size of the partition is less than 1 GB.

log.segment.bytes

The log-retention settings previously mentioned operate on log segments, not individual messages. As messages are produced to the Kafka broker, they are appended to the current log segment for the partition. Once the log segment has reached the size specified by the log.segment.bytes parameter, which defaults to 1 GB, the log segment is closed and a new one is opened. Once a log segment has been closed, it can be considered for expiration. A smaller log-segment size means that files must be closed and allocated more often, which reduces the overall efficiency of disk writes.

Adjusting the size of the log segments can be important if topics have a low produce rate. For example, if a topic receives only 100 megabytes per day of messages, and log.segment.bytes is set to the default, it will take 10 days to fill one segment. As messages cannot be expired until the log segment is closed, if log.retention.ms is set to 604800000 (1 week), there will actually be up to 17 days of messages retained until the closed log segment expires. This is because once the log segment is closed with the current 10 days of messages, that log segment must be retained for 7 days before it expires based on the time policy (as the segment cannot be removed until the last message in the segment can be expired).

Retrieving Offsets by Timestamp

The size of the log segment also affects the behavior of fetching offsets by timestamp. When requesting offsets for a partition at a specific timestamp, Kafka finds the log segment file that was being written at that time. It does this by using the creation and last modified time of the file, and looking for a file that was created before the timestamp specified and last modified after the timestamp. The offset at the beginning of that log segment (which is also the filename) is returned in the response.

log.segment.ms

Another way to control when log segments are closed is by using the log.segment.ms parameter, which specifies the amount of time after which a log segment should be closed. As with the log.retention.bytes and log.retention.ms parameters, log.segment.bytes and log.segment.ms are not mutually exclusive properties. Kafka will close a log segment either when the size limit is reached or when the time limit is reached, whichever comes first. By default, there is no setting for log.segment.ms, which results in only closing log segments by size.

Disk Performance When Using Time-Based Segments

When using a time-based log segment limit, it is important to consider the impact on disk performance when multiple log segments are closed simultaneously. This can happen when there are many partitions that never reach the size limit for log segments, as the clock for the time limit will start when the broker starts and will always execute at the same time for these low-volume partitions.

message.max.bytes

The Kafka broker limits the maximum size of a message that can be produced, configured by the `message.max.bytes` parameter, which defaults to 1000000, or 1 MB. A producer that tries to send a message larger than this will receive an error back from the broker, and the message will not be accepted. As with all byte sizes specified on the broker, this configuration deals with compressed message size, which means that producers can send messages that are much larger than this value uncompressed, provided they compress to under the configured `message.max.bytes` size.

There are noticeable performance impacts from increasing the allowable message size. Larger messages will mean that the broker threads that deal with processing network connections and requests will be working longer on each request. Larger messages also increase the size of disk writes, which will impact I/O throughput.

Coordinating Message Size Configurations

The message size configured on the Kafka broker must be coordinated with the `fetch.message.max.bytes` configuration on consumer clients. If this value is smaller than `message.max.bytes`, then consumers that encounter larger messages will fail to fetch those messages, resulting in a situation where the consumer gets stuck and cannot proceed. The same rule applies to the `rep lica.fetch.max.bytes` configuration on the brokers when configured in a cluster.

Hardware Selection

Selecting an appropriate hardware configuration for a Kafka broker can be more art than science. Kafka itself has no strict requirement on a specific hardware configuration, and will run without issue on any system. Once performance becomes a concern, however, there are several factors that will contribute to the overall performance: disk throughput and capacity, memory, networking, and CPU. Once you have determined which types of performance are the most critical for your environment, you will be able to select an optimized hardware configuration that fits within your budget.

Disk Throughput

The performance of producer clients will be most directly influenced by the throughput of the broker disk that is used for storing log segments. Kafka messages must be committed to local storage when they are produced, and most clients will wait until at least one broker has confirmed that messages have been committed before considering the send successful. This means that faster disk writes will equal lower produce latency.

The obvious decision when it comes to disk throughput is whether to use traditional spinning hard drives (HDD) or solid-state disks (SSD). SSDs have drastically lower seek and access times and will provide the best performance. HDDs, on the other hand, are more economical and provide more capacity per unit. You can also improve the performance of HDDs by using more of them in a broker, whether by having multiple data directories or by setting up the drives in a redundant array of independent disks (RAID) configuration. Other factors, such as the specific drive technology (e.g., serial attached storage or serial ATA), as well as the quality of the drive controller, will affect throughput.

Disk Capacity

Capacity is the other side of the storage discussion. The amount of disk capacity that is needed is determined by how many messages need to be retained at any time. If the broker is expected to receive 1 TB of traffic each day, with 7 days of retention, then the broker will need a minimum of 7 TB of useable storage for log segments. You should also factor in at least 10% overhead for other files, in addition to any buffer that you wish to maintain for fluctuations in traffic or growth over time.

Storage capacity is one of the factors to consider when sizing a Kafka cluster and determining when to expand it. The total traffic for a cluster can be balanced across it by having multiple partitions per topic, which will allow additional brokers to augment the available capacity if the density on a single broker will not suffice. The decision on how much disk capacity is needed will also be informed by the replication strategy chosen for the cluster (which is discussed in more detail in Chapter 6).

Memory

The normal mode of operation for a Kafka consumer is reading from the end of the partitions, where the consumer is caught up and lagging behind the producers very little, if at all. In this situation, the messages the consumer is reading are optimally stored in the system's page cache, resulting in faster reads than if the broker has to reread the messages from disk. Therefore, having more memory available to the system for page cache will improve the performance of consumer clients.

Kafka itself does not need much heap memory configured for the Java Virtual Machine (JVM). Even a broker that is handling X messages per second and a data rate of X megabits per second can run with a 5 GB heap. The rest of the system memory will be used by the page cache and will benefit Kafka by allowing the system to cache log segments in use. This is the main reason it is not recommended to have Kafka collocated on a system with any other significant application, as they will have to share the use of the page cache. This will decrease the consumer performance for Kafka.

Networking

The available network throughput will specify the maximum amount of traffic that Kafka can handle. This is often the governing factor, combined with disk storage, for cluster sizing. This is complicated by the inherent imbalance between inbound and outbound network usage that is created by Kafka's support for multiple consumers. A producer may write 1 MB per second for a given topic, but there could be any number of consumers that create a multiplier on the outbound network usage. Other operations such as cluster replication (covered in Chapter 6) and mirroring (discussed in Chapter 8) will also increase requirements. Should the network interface become saturated, it is not uncommon for cluster replication to fall behind, which can leave the cluster in a vulnerable state.

CPU

Processing power is not as important as disk and memory, but it will affect overall performance of the broker to some extent. Ideally, clients should compress messages to optimize network and disk usage. The Kafka broker must decompress all message batches, however, in order to validate the checksum of the individual messages and assign offsets. It then needs to recompress the message batch in order to store it on disk. This is where the majority of Kafka's requirement for processing power comes from. This should not be the primary factor in selecting hardware, however.

Kafka in the Cloud

A common installation for Kafka is within cloud computing environments, such as Amazon Web Services (AWS). AWS provides many compute instances, each with a different combination of CPU, memory, and disk, and so the various performance characteristics of Kafka must be prioritized in order to select the correct instance configuration to use. A good place to start is with the amount of data retention required, followed by the performance needed from the producers. If very low latency is necessary, I/O optimized instances that have local SSD storage might be required. Otherwise, ephemeral storage (such as the AWS Elastic Block Store) might be sufficient. Once these decisions are made, the CPU and memory options available will be appropriate for the performance.

In real terms, this will mean that for AWS either the m4 or r3 instance types are a common choice. The m4 instance will allow for greater retention periods, but the throughput to the disk will be less because it is on elastic block storage. The r3 instance will have much better throughput with local SSD drives, but those drives will limit the amount of data that can be retained. For the best of both worlds, it is necessary to move up to either the i2 or d2 instance types, which are significantly more expensive.

Kafka Clusters

A single Kafka server works well for local development work, or for a proof-of-concept system, but there are significant benefits to having multiple brokers configured as a cluster, as shown in Figure 2-2. The biggest benefit is the ability to scale the load across multiple servers. A close second is using replication to guard against data loss due to single system failures. Replication will also allow for performing maintenance work on Kafka or the underlying systems while still maintaining availability for clients. This section focuses on configuring only a Kafka cluster. Chapter 6 contains more more information on replication of data.

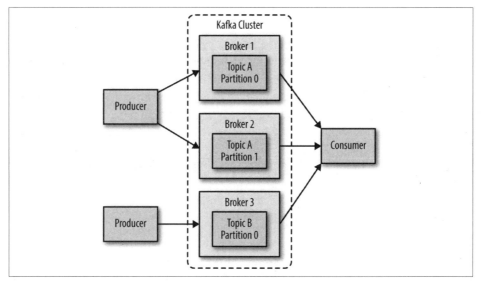

Figure 2-2. A simple Kafka cluster

How Many Brokers?

The appropriate size for a Kafka cluster is determined by several factors. The first factor to consider is how much disk capacity is required for retaining messages and how much storage is available on a single broker. If the cluster is required to retain 10 TB of data and a single broker can store 2 TB, then the minimum cluster size is five brokers. In addition, using replication will increase the storage requirements by at least 100%, depending on the replication factor chosen (see Chapter 6). This means that this same cluster, configured with replication, now needs to contain at least 10 brokers.

The other factor to consider is the capacity of the cluster to handle requests. For example, what is the capacity of the network interfaces, and can they handle the client traffic if there are multiple consumers of the data or if the traffic is not consistent over the retention period of the data (e.g., bursts of traffic during peak times). If the network interface on a single broker is used to 80% capacity at peak, and there are two consumers of that data, the consumers will not be able to keep up with peak traffic unless there are two brokers. If replication is being used in the cluster, this is an additional consumer of the data that must be taken into account. It may also be desirable to scale out to more brokers in a cluster in order to handle performance concerns caused by lesser disk throughput or system memory available.

Broker Configuration

There are only two requirements in the broker configuration to allow multiple Kafka brokers to join a single cluster. The first is that all brokers must have the same configuration for the zookeeper.connect parameter. This specifies the Zookeeper ensemble and path where the cluster stores metadata. The second requirement is that all brokers in the cluster must have a unique value for the broker.id parameter. If two brokers attempt to join the same cluster with the same broker.id, the second broker will log an error and fail to start. There are other configuration parameters used when running a cluster—specifically, parameters that control replication, which are covered in later chapters.

OS Tuning

While most Linux distributions have an out-of-the-box configuration for the kernel-tuning parameters that will work fairly well for most applications, there are a few changes that can be made for a Kafka broker that will improve performance. These primarily revolve around the virtual memory and networking subsystems, as well as specific concerns for the disk mount point that is used for storing log segments. These parameters are typically configured in the */etc/sysctl.conf* file, but you should refer to your Linux distribution's documentation for specific details regarding how to adjust the kernel configuration.

Virtual Memory

In general, the Linux virtual memory system will automatically adjust itself for the workload of the system. We can make some adjustments to both how swap space is handled, as well as to dirty memory pages, to tune it for Kafka's workload.

As with most applications—specifically ones where throughput is a concern—it is best to avoid swapping at (almost) all costs. The cost incurred by having pages of memory swapped to disk will show up as a noticeable impact on all aspects of performance in Kafka. In addition, Kafka makes heavy use of the system page cache, and if the VM system is swapping to disk, there is not enough memory being allocated to page cache.

One way to avoid swapping is just to not configure any swap space at all. Having swap is not a requirement, but it does provide a safety net if something catastrophic happens on the system. Having swap can prevent the OS from abruptly killing a process due to an out-of-memory condition. For this reason, the recommendation is to set the vm.swappiness parameter to a very low value, such as 1. The parameter is a percentage of how likely the VM subsystem is to use swap space rather than dropping pages from the page cache. It is preferable to reduce the size of the page cache rather than swap.

Why Not Set Swappiness to Zero?

Previously, the recommendation for vm.swappiness was always to set it to 0. This value used to have the meaning "do not swap unless there is an out-of-memory condition." However, the meaning of this value changed as of Linux kernel version 3.5-rc1, and that change was backported into many distributions, including Red Hat Enterprise Linux kernels as of version 2.6.32-303. This changed the meaning of the value 0 to "never swap under any circumstances." It is for this reason that a value of 1 is now recommended.

There is also a benefit to adjusting how the kernel handles dirty pages that must be flushed to disk. Kafka relies on disk I/O performance to provide good response times to producers. This is also the reason that the log segments are usually put on a fast disk, whether that is an individual disk with a fast response time (e.g., SSD) or a disk subsystem with significant NVRAM for caching (e.g., RAID). The result is that the number of dirty pages that are allowed, before the flush background process starts writing them to disk, can be reduced. This is accomplished by setting the =vm.dirty_background_ratio value lower than the default of 10. The value is a percentage of the total amount of system memory, and setting this value to 5 is appropriate in many situations. This setting should not be set to zero, however, as that would cause the kernel to continually flush pages, which would then eliminate the ability of the kernel to buffer disk writes against temporary spikes in the underlying device performance.

The total number of dirty pages that are allowed before the kernel forces synchronous operations to flush them to disk can also be increased by changing the value of vm.dirty_ratio, increasing it to above the default of 20 (also a percentage of total system memory). There is a wide range of possible values for this setting, but between 60 and 80 is a reasonable number. This setting does introduce a small amount of risk, both in regards to the amount of unflushed disk activity as well as the potential for long I/O pauses if synchronous flushes are forced. If a higher setting for vm.dirty_ratio is chosen, it is highly recommended that replication be used in the Kafka cluster to guard against system failures.

When choosing values for these parameters, it is wise to review the number of dirty pages over time while the Kafka cluster is running under load, whether in production or simulated. The current number of dirty pages can be determined by checking the */proc/vmstat* file:

```
# cat /proc/vmstat | egrep "dirty|writeback"
nr_dirty 3875
nr_writeback 29
nr_writeback_temp 0
#
```

Disk

Outside of selecting the disk device hardware, as well as the configuration of RAID if it is used, the choice of filesystem used for this disk can have the next largest impact on performance. There are many different filesystems available, but the most common choices for local filesystems are either EXT4 (fourth extended file system) or Extents File System (XFS). Recently, XFS has become the default filesystem for many Linux distributions, and this is for good reason—it outperforms EXT4 for most workloads with minimal tuning required. EXT4 can perform well, but it requires using tuning parameters that are considered less safe. This includes setting the commit interval to a longer time than the default of five to force less frequent flushes. EXT4 also introduced delayed allocation of blocks, which brings with it a greater chance of data loss and filesystem corruption in the case of a system failure. The XFS filesystem also uses a delayed allocation algorithm, but it is generally safer than the one used by EXT4. XFS also has better performance for Kafka's workload without requiring tuning beyond the automatic tuning performed by the filesystem. It is also more efficient when batching disk writes, all of which combine to give better overall I/O throughput.

Regardless of which filesystem is chosen for the mount that holds the log segments, it is advisable to set the noatime mount option for the mount point. File metadata contains three timestamps: creation time (ctime), last modified time (mtime), and last access time (`atime`). By default, the `atime` is updated every time a file is read. This generates a large number of disk writes. The `atime` attribute is generally considered to be of little use, unless an application needs to know if a file has been accessed since it was last modified (in which case the `realtime` option can be used). The `atime` is not used by Kafka at all, so disabling it is safe to do. Setting `noatime` on the mount will prevent these timestamp updates from happening, but will not affect the proper handling of the `ctime` and `mtime` attributes.

Networking

Adjusting the default tuning of the Linux networking stack is common for any application that generates a high amount of network traffic, as the kernel is not tuned by default for large, high-speed data transfers. In fact, the recommended changes for Kafka are the same as those suggested for most web servers and other networking applications. The first adjustment is to change the default and maximum amount of memory allocated for the send and receive buffers for each socket. This will significantly increase performance for large transfers. The relevant parameters for the send and receive buffer default size per socket are `net.core.wmem_default` and `net.core.rmem_default`, and a reasonable setting for these parameters is 131072, or 128 KiB. The parameters for the send and receive buffer maximum sizes are `net.core.wmem_max` and `net.core.rmem_max`, and a reasonable setting is 2097152, or 2 MiB. Keep in mind that the maximum size does not indicate that every socket will have this much buffer space allocated; it only allows up to that much if needed.

In addition to the socket settings, the send and receive buffer sizes for TCP sockets must be set separately using the `net.ipv4.tcp_wmem` and `net.ipv4.tcp_rmem` parameters. These are set using three space-separated integers that specify the minimum, default, and maximum sizes, respectively. The maximum size cannot be larger than the values specified for all sockets using `net.core.wmem_max` and `net.core.rmem_max`. An example setting for each of these parameters is "4096 65536 2048000," which is a 4 KiB minimum, 64 KiB default, and 2 MiB maximum buffer. Based on the actual workload of your Kafka brokers, you may want to increase the maximum sizes to allow for greater buffering of the network connections.

There are several other network tuning parameters that are useful to set. Enabling TCP window scaling by setting `net.ipv4.tcp_window_scaling` to 1 will allow clients to transfer data more efficiently, and allow that data to be buffered on the broker side. Increasing the value of `net.ipv4.tcp_max_syn_backlog` above the default of 1024 will allow a greater number of simultaneous connections to be accepted. Increasing the value of `net.core.netdev_max_backlog` to greater than the default of 1000 can assist with bursts of network traffic, specifically when using multigigabit network connection speeds, by allowing more packets to be queued for the kernel to process them.

Production Concerns

Once you are ready to move your Kafka environment out of testing and into your production operations, there are a few more things to think about that will assist with setting up a reliable messaging service.

Garbage Collector Options

Tuning the Java garbage-collection options for an application has always been something of an art, requiring detailed information about how the application uses memory and a significant amount of observation and trial and error. Thankfully, this has changed with Java 7 and the introduction of the Garbage First (or G1) garbage collector. G1 is designed to automatically adjust to different workloads and provide consistent pause times for garbage collection over the lifetime of the application. It also handles large heap sizes with ease by segmenting the heap into smaller zones and not collecting over the entire heap in each pause.

G1 does all of this with a minimal amount of configuration in normal operation. There are two configuration options for G1 used to adjust its performance:

MaxGCPauseMillis
> This option specifies the preferred pause time for each garbage-collection cycle. It is not a fixed maximum—G1 can and will exceed this time if it is required. This value defaults to 200 milliseconds. This means that G1 will attempt to schedule the frequency of GC cycles, as well as the number of zones that are collected in each cycle, such that each cycle will take approximately 200ms.

InitiatingHeapOccupancyPercent
> This option specifies the percentage of the total heap that may be in use before G1 will start a collection cycle. The default value is 45. This means that G1 will not start a collection cycle until after 45% of the heap is in use. This includes both the new (Eden) and old zone usage in total.

The Kafka broker is fairly efficient with the way it utilizes heap memory and creates garbage objects, so it is possible to set these options lower. The GC tuning options provided in this section have been found to be appropriate for a server with 64 GB of memory, running Kafka in a 5GB heap. For MaxGCPauseMillis, this broker can be configured with a value of 20 ms. The value for InitiatingHeapOccupancyPercent is set to 35, which causes garbage collection to run slightly earlier than with the default value.

The start script for Kafka does not use the G1 collector, instead defaulting to using parallel new and concurrent mark and sweep garbage collection. The change is easy to make via environment variables. Using the start command from earlier in the chapter, modify it as follows:

```
# export JAVA_HOME=/usr/java/jdk1.8.0_51
# export KAFKA_JVM_PERFORMANCE_OPTS="-server -XX:+UseG1GC
-XX:MaxGCPauseMillis=20 -XX:InitiatingHeapOccupancyPercent=35
-XX:+DisableExplicitGC -Djava.awt.headless=true"
# /usr/local/kafka/bin/kafka-server-start.sh -daemon
/usr/local/kafka/config/server.properties
#
```

Datacenter Layout

For development systems, the physical location of the Kafka brokers within a data-center is not as much of a concern, as there is not as severe an impact if the cluster is partially or completely unavailable for short periods of time. When serving production traffic, however, downtime means dollars lost, whether through loss of services to users or loss of telemetry on what the users are doing. This is when it becomes critical to configure replication within the Kafka cluster (see Chapter 6), which is also when it is important to consider the physical location of brokers in their racks in the datacenter. If not addressed prior to deploying Kafka, expensive maintenance to move servers around may be needed.

The Kafka broker has no rack-awareness when assigning new partitions to brokers. This means that it cannot take into account that two brokers may be located in the same physical rack, or in the same availability zone (if running in a cloud service like AWS), and therefore can easily assign all replicas for a partition to brokers that share the same power and network connections in the same rack. Should that rack have a failure, these partitions would be offline and inaccessible to clients. In addition, it can result in additional lost data on recovery due to an unclean leader election (more about this in Chapter 6).

The best practice is to have each Kafka broker in a cluster installed in a different rack, or at the very least not share single points of failure for infrastructure services such as power and network. This typically means at least deploying the servers that will run brokers with dual power connections (to two different circuits) and dual network switches (with a bonded interface on the servers themselves to failover seamlessly). Even with dual connections, there is a benefit to having brokers in completely separate racks. From time to time, it may be neccessary to perform physical maintenance on a rack or cabinet that requires it to be offline (such as moving servers around, or rewiring power connections).

Colocating Applications on Zookeeper

Kafka utilizes Zookeeper for storing metadata information about the brokers, topics, and partitions. Writes to Zookeeper are only performed on changes to the membership of consumer groups or on changes to the Kafka cluster itself. This amount of traffic is minimal, and it does not justify the use of a dedicated Zookeeper ensemble for a single Kafka cluster. In fact, many deployments will use a single Zookeeper ensemble for multiple Kafka clusters (using a chroot Zookeeper path for each cluster, as described earlier in this chapter).

Kafka Consumers and Zookeeper

Prior to Apache Kafka 0.9.0.0, consumers, in addition to the brokers, utilized Zookeeper to directly store information about the composition of the consumer group, what topics it was consuming, and to periodically commit offsets for each partition being consumed (to enable failover between consumers in the group). With version 0.9.0.0, a new consumer interface was introduced which allows this to be managed directly with the Kafka brokers. This is the consumer discussed in Chapter 4.

However, there is a concern with consumers and Zookeeper under certain configurations. Consumers have a configurable choice to use either Zookeeper or Kafka for committing offsets, and they can also configure the interval between commits. If the consumer uses Zookeeper for offsets, each consumer will perform a Zookeeper write at every interval for every partition it consumes. A reasonable interval for offset commits is 1 minute, as this is the period of time over which a consumer group will read duplicate messages in the case of a consumer failure. These commits can be a significant amount of Zookeeper traffic, especially in a cluster with many consumers, and will need to be taken into account. It may be neccessary to use a longer commit interval if the Zookeeper ensemble is not able to handle the traffic. However, it is recommended that consumers using the latest Kafka libraries use Kafka for committing offsets, removing the dependency on Zookeeper.

Outside of using a single ensemble for multiple Kafka clusters, it is not recommended to share the ensemble with other applications, if it can be avoided. Kafka is sensitive to Zookeeper latency and timeouts, and an interruption in communications with the ensemble will cause the brokers to behave unpredictably. This can easily cause multiple brokers to go offline at the same time, should they lose Zookeeper connections, which will result in offline partitions. It also puts stress on the cluster controller, which can show up as subtle errors long after the interruption has passed, such as when trying to perform a controlled shutdown of a broker. Other applications that can put stress on the Zookeeper ensemble, either through heavy usage or improper operations, should be segregated to their own ensemble.

Summary

In this chapter we learned how to get Apache Kafka up and running. We also covered picking the right hardware for your brokers, and specific concerns around getting set up in a production environment. Now that you have a Kafka cluster, we will walk through the basics of Kafka client applications. The next two chapters will cover how to create clients for both producing messages to Kafka (Chapter 3), as well as consuming those messages out again (Chapter 4).

Kafka Producers: Writing Messages to Kafka

Whether you use Kafka as a queue, message bus, or data storage platform, you will always use Kafka by writing a producer that writes data to Kafka, a consumer that reads data from Kafka, or an application that serves both roles.

For example, in a credit card transaction processing system, there will be a client application, perhaps an online store, responsible for sending each transaction to Kafka immediately when a payment is made. Another application is responsible for immediately checking this transaction against a rules engine and determining whether the transaction is approved or denied. The approve/deny response can then be written back to Kafka and the response can propagate back to the online store where the transaction was initiated. A third application can read both transactions and the approval status from Kafka and store them in a database where analysts can later review the decisions and perhaps improve the rules engine.

Apache Kafka ships with built-in client APIs that developers can use when developing applications that interact with Kafka.

In this chapter we will learn how to use the Kafka producer, starting with an overview of its design and components. We will show how to create `KafkaProducer` and `ProducerRecord` objects, how to send records to Kafka, and how to handle the errors that Kafka may return. We'll then review the most important configuration options used to control the producer behavior. We'll conclude with a deeper look at how to use different partitioning methods and serializers, and how to write your own serializers and partitioners.

In Chapter 4 we will look at Kafka's consumer client and reading data from Kafka.

Third-Party Clients

In addition to the built-in clients, Kafka has a binary wire protocol. This means that it is possible for applications to read messages from Kafka or write messages to Kafka simply by sending the correct byte sequences to Kafka's network port. There are multiple clients that implement Kafka's wire protocol in different programming languages, giving simple ways to use Kafka not just in Java applications but also in languages like C++, Python, Go, and many more. Those clients are not part of Apache Kafka project, but a list of non-Java clients is maintained in the project wiki (*https://cwiki.apache.org/confluence/display/KAFKA/Clients*). The wire protocol and the external clients are outside the scope of the chapter.

Producer Overview

There are many reasons an application might need to write messages to Kafka: recording user activities for auditing or analysis, recording metrics, storing log messages, recording information from smart appliances, communicating asynchronously with other applications, buffering information before writing to a database, and much more.

Those diverse use cases also imply diverse requirements: is every message critical, or can we tolerate loss of messages? Are we OK with accidentally duplicating messages? Are there any strict latency or throughput requirements we need to support?

In the credit card transaction processing example we introduced earlier, we can see that it is critical to never lose a single message nor duplicate any messages. Latency should be low but latencies up to 500ms can be tolerated, and throughput should be very high—we expect to process up to a million messages a second.

A different use case might be to store click information from a website. In that case, some message loss or a few duplicates can be tolerated; latency can be high as long as there is no impact on the user experience. In other words, we don't mind if it takes a few seconds for the message to arrive at Kafka, as long as the next page loads immediately after the user clicked on a link. Throughput will depend on the level of activity we anticipate on our website.

The different requirements will influence the way you use the producer API to write messages to Kafka and the configuration you use.

While the producer APIs are very simple, there is a bit more that goes on under the hood of the producer when we send data. Figure 3-1 shows the main steps involved in sending data to Kafka.

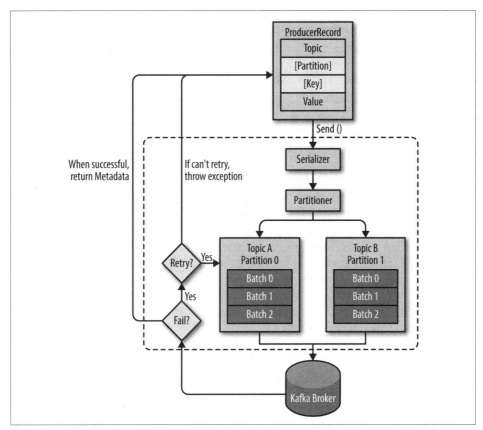

Figure 3-1. High-level overview of Kafka producer components

We start producing messages to Kafka by creating a `ProducerRecord`, which must include the topic we want to send the record to and a value. Optionally, we can also specify a key and/or a partition. Once we send the `ProducerRecord`, the first thing the producer will do is serialize the key and value objects to ByteArrays so they can be sent over the network.

Next, the data is sent to a partitioner. If we specified a partition in the `ProducerRecord`, the partitioner doesn't do anything and simply returns the partition we specified. If we didn't, the partitioner will choose a partition for us, usually based on the `ProducerRecord` key. Once a partition is selected, the producer knows which topic and partition the record will go to. It then adds the record to a batch of records that will also be sent to the same topic and partition. A separate thread is responsible for sending those batches of records to the appropriate Kafka brokers.

When the broker receives the messages, it sends back a response. If the messages were successfully written to Kafka, it will return a `RecordMetadata` object with the topic, partition, and the offset of the record within the partition. If the broker failed to write the messages, it will return an error. When the producer receives an error, it may retry sending the message a few more times before giving up and returning an error.

Constructing a Kafka Producer

The first step in writing messages to Kafka is to create a producer object with the properties you want to pass to the producer. A Kafka producer has three mandatory properties:

`bootstrap.servers`
> List of `host:port` pairs of brokers that the producer will use to establish initial connection to the Kafka cluster. This list doesn't need to include all brokers, since the producer will get more information after the initial connection. But it is recommended to include at least two, so in case one broker goes down, the producer will still be able to connect to the cluster.

`key.serializer`
> Name of a class that will be used to serialize the keys of the records we will produce to Kafka. Kafka brokers expect byte arrays as keys and values of messages. However, the producer interface allows, using parameterized types, any Java object to be sent as a key and value. This makes for very readable code, but it also means that the producer has to know how to convert these objects to byte arrays. `key.serializer` should be set to a name of a class that implements the `org.apache.kafka.common.serialization.Serializer` interface. The producer will use this class to serialize the key object to a byte array. The Kafka client package includes `ByteArraySerializer` (which doesn't do much), `StringSerializer`, and `IntegerSerializer`, so if you use common types, there is no need to implement your own serializers. Setting `key.serializer` is required even if you intend to send only values.

`value.serializer`
> Name of a class that will be used to serialize the values of the records we will produce to Kafka. The same way you set `key.serializer` to a name of a class that will serialize the message key object to a byte array, you set `value.serializer` to a class that will serialize the message value object.

The following code snippet shows how to create a new producer by setting just the mandatory parameters and using defaults for everything else:

```
private Properties kafkaProps = new Properties();  ❶
kafkaProps.put("bootstrap.servers", "broker1:9092,broker2:9092");

kafkaProps.put("key.serializer",
```

```
    "org.apache.kafka.common.serialization.StringSerializer"); ❷
kafkaProps.put("value.serializer",
    "org.apache.kafka.common.serialization.StringSerializer");

producer = new KafkaProducer<String, String>(kafkaProps); ❸
```

❶ We start with a `Properties` object.

❷ Since we plan on using strings for message key and value, we use the built-in
    `StringSerializer`.

❸ Here we create a new producer by setting the appropriate key and value types
    and passing the `Properties` object.

With such a simple interface, it is clear that most of the control over producer behavior is done by setting the correct configuration properties. Apache Kafka documentation covers all the configuration options (*http://bit.ly/2sMu1c8*), and we will go over the important ones later in this chapter.

Once we instantiate a producer, it is time to start sending messages. There are three primary methods of sending messages:

Fire-and-forget
> We send a message to the server and don't really care if it arrives succesfully or not. Most of the time, it will arrive successfully, since Kafka is highly available and the producer will retry sending messages automatically. However, some messages will get lost using this method.

Synchronous send
> We send a message, the `send()` method returns a Future object, and we use `get()` to wait on the future and see if the `send()` was successful or not.

Asynchronous send
> We call the `send()` method with a callback function, which gets triggered when it receives a response from the Kafka broker.

In the examples that follow, we will see how to send messages using these methods and how to handle the different types of errors that might occur.

While all the examples in this chapter are single threaded, a producer object can be used by multiple threads to send messages. You will probably want to start with one producer and one thread. If you need better throughput, you can add more threads that use the same producer. Once this ceases to increase throughput, you can add more producers to the application to achieve even higher throughput.

Sending a Message to Kafka

The simplest way to send a message is as follows:

```
ProducerRecord<String, String> record =
        new ProducerRecord<>("CustomerCountry", "Precision Products",
            "France"); ❶
try {
  producer.send(record); ❷
} catch (Exception e) {
        e.printStackTrace(); ❸
}
```

❶ The producer accepts `ProducerRecord` objects, so we start by creating one. `ProducerRecord` has multiple constructors, which we will discuss later. Here we use one that requires the name of the topic we are sending data to, which is always a string, and the key and value we are sending to Kafka, which in this case are also strings. The types of the key and value must match our `serializer` and `producer` objects.

❷ We use the producer object `send()` method to send the `ProducerRecord`. As we've seen in the producer architecture diagram in Figure 3-1, the message will be placed in a buffer and will be sent to the broker in a separate thread. The `send()` method returns a Java Future object (*http://bit.ly/2rG7Cg6*) with `Record Metadata`, but since we simply ignore the returned value, we have no way of knowing whether the message was sent successfully or not. This method of sending messages can be used when dropping a message silently is acceptable. This is not typically the case in production applications.

❸ While we ignore errors that may occur while sending messages to Kafka brokers or in the brokers themselves, we may still get an exception if the producer encountered errors before sending the message to Kafka. Those can be a `SerializationException` when it fails to serialize the message, a `BufferExhaustedException` or `TimeoutException` if the buffer is full, or an InterruptException if the sending thread was interrupted.

Sending a Message Synchronously

The simplest way to send a message synchronously is as follows:

```
ProducerRecord<String, String> record =
        new ProducerRecord<>("CustomerCountry", "Precision Products", "France");
try {
        producer.send(record).get(); ❶
} catch (Exception e) {
```

```
        e.printStackTrace(); ❷
}
```

❶ Here, we are using `Future.get()` to wait for a reply from Kafka. This method will throw an exception if the record is not sent successfully to Kafka. If there were no errors, we will get a `RecordMetadata` object that we can use to retrieve the offset the message was written to.

❷ If there were any errors before sending data to Kafka, while sending, if the Kafka brokers returned a nonretriable exceptions or if we exhausted the available retries, we will encounter an exception. In this case, we just print any exception we ran into.

`KafkaProducer` has two types of errors. *Retriable* errors are those that can be resolved by sending the message again. For example, a connection error can be resolved because the connection may get reestablished. A "no leader" error can be resolved when a new leader is elected for the partition. `KafkaProducer` can be configured to retry those errors automatically, so the application code will get retriable exceptions only when the number of retries was exhausted and the error was not resolved. Some errors will not be resolved by retrying. For example, "message size too large." In those cases, `KafkaProducer` will not attempt a retry and will return the exception immediately.

Sending a Message Asynchronously

Suppose the network roundtrip time between our application and the Kafka cluster is 10ms. If we wait for a reply after sending each message, sending 100 messages will take around 1 second. On the other hand, if we just send all our messages and not wait for any replies, then sending 100 messages will barely take any time at all. In most cases, we really don't need a reply—Kafka sends back the topic, partition, and offset of the record after it was written, which is usually not required by the sending app. On the other hand, we do need to know when we failed to send a message completely so we can throw an exception, log an error, or perhaps write the message to an "errors" file for later analysis.

In order to send messages asynchronously and still handle error scenarios, the producer supports adding a callback when sending a record. Here is an example of how we use a callback:

```
private class DemoProducerCallback implements Callback { ❶
       @Override
    public void onCompletion(RecordMetadata recordMetadata, Exception e) {
     if (e != null) {
        e.printStackTrace(); ❷
        }
    }
}

ProducerRecord<String, String> record =
       new ProducerRecord<>("CustomerCountry", "Biomedical Materials", "USA");
❸
producer.send(record, new DemoProducerCallback()); ❹
```

❶ To use callbacks, you need a class that implements the `org.apache.kafka.`
`clients.producer.Callback` interface, which has a single function—`onComple`
`tion()`.

❷ If Kafka returned an error, `onCompletion()` will have a nonnull exception. Here
we "handle" it by printing, but production code will probably have more robust
error handling functions.

❸ The records are the same as before.

❹ And we pass a `Callback` object along when sending the record.

Configuring Producers

So far we've seen very few configuration parameters for the producers—just the
mandatory `bootstrap.servers` URI and serializers.

The producer has a large number of configuration parameters; most are documented
in Apache Kafka documentation (*http://kafka.apache.org/documentation.html#produ*
cerconfigs) and many have reasonable defaults so there is no reason to tinker with
every single parameter. However, some of the parameters have a significant impact on
memory use, performance, and reliability of the producers. We will review those here.

acks

The `acks` parameter controls how many partition replicas must receive the record
before the producer can consider the write successful. This option has a significant
impact on how likely messages are to be lost. There are three allowed values for the
`acks` parameter:

- If `acks=0`, the producer will not wait for a reply from the broker before assuming
  the message was sent successfully. This means that if something went wrong and

the broker did not receive the message, the producer will not know about it and the message will be lost. However, because the producer is not waiting for any response from the server, it can send messages as fast as the network will support, so this setting can be used to achieve very high throughput.

- If `acks=1`, the producer will receive a success response from the broker the moment the leader replica received the message. If the message can't be written to the leader (e.g., if the leader crashed and a new leader was not elected yet), the producer will receive an error response and can retry sending the message, avoiding potential loss of data. The message can still get lost if the leader crashes and a replica without this message gets elected as the new leader (via unclean leader election). In this case, throughput depends on whether we send messages synchronously or asynchronously. If our client code waits for a reply from the server (by calling the `get()` method of the `Future` object returned when sending a message) it will obviously increase latency significantly (at least by a network roundtrip). If the client uses callbacks, latency will be hidden, but throughput will be limited by the number of in-flight messages (i.e., how many messages the producer will send before receiving replies from the server).

- If `acks=all`, the producer will receive a success response from the broker once all in-sync replicas received the message. This is the safest mode since you can make sure more than one broker has the message and that the message will survive even in the case of crash (more information on this in Chapter 5). However, the latency we discussed in the `acks=1` case will be even higher, since we will be waiting for more than just one broker to receive the message.

buffer.memory

This sets the amount of memory the producer will use to buffer messages waiting to be sent to brokers. If messages are sent by the application faster than they can be delivered to the server, the producer may run out of space and additional `send()` calls will either block or throw an exception, based on the `block.on.buffer.full` parameter (replaced with `max.block.ms` in release 0.9.0.0, which allows blocking for a certain time and then throwing an exception).

compression.type

By default, messages are sent uncompressed. This parameter can be set to `snappy`, `gzip`, or `lz4`, in which case the corresponding compression algorithms will be used to compress the data before sending it to the brokers. Snappy compression was invented by Google to provide decent compression ratios with low CPU overhead and good performance, so it is recommended in cases where both performance and bandwidth are a concern. Gzip compression will typically use more CPU and time but result in better compression ratios, so it recommended in cases where network bandwidth is more restricted. By enabling compression, you reduce network utilization and storage, which is often a bottleneck when sending messages to Kafka.

retries

When the producer receives an error message from the server, the error could be transient (e.g., a lack of leader for a partition). In this case, the value of the `retries` parameter will control how many times the producer will retry sending the message before giving up and notifying the client of an issue. By default, the producer will wait 100ms between retries, but you can control this using the `retry.backoff.ms` parameter. We recommend testing how long it takes to recover from a crashed broker (i.e., how long until all partitions get new leaders) and setting the number of retries and delay between them such that the total amount of time spent retrying will be longer than the time it takes the Kafka cluster to recover from the crash—otherwise, the producer will give up too soon. Not all errors will be retried by the producer. Some errors are not transient and will not cause retries (e.g., "message too large" error). In general, because the producer handles retries for you, there is no point in handling retries within your own application logic. You will want to focus your efforts on handling nonretriable errors or cases where retry attempts were exhausted.

batch.size

When multiple records are sent to the same partition, the producer will batch them together. This parameter controls the amount of memory in bytes (not messages!) that will be used for each batch. When the batch is full, all the messages in the batch will be sent. However, this does not mean that the producer will wait for the batch to become full. The producer will send half-full batches and even batches with just a single message in them. Therefore, setting the batch size too large will not cause delays in sending messages; it will just use more memory for the batches. Setting the batch size too small will add some overhead because the producer will need to send messages more frequently.

linger.ms

`linger.ms` controls the amount of time to wait for additional messages before sending the current batch. `KafkaProducer` sends a batch of messages either when the current batch is full or when the `linger.ms` limit is reached. By default, the producer will send messages as soon as there is a sender thread available to send them, even if there's just one message in the batch. By setting `linger.ms` higher than 0, we instruct the producer to wait a few milliseconds to add additional messages to the batch before sending it to the brokers. This increases latency but also increases throughput (because we send more messages at once, there is less overhead per message).

client.id

This can be any string, and will be used by the brokers to identify messages sent from the client. It is used in logging and metrics, and for quotas.

max.in.flight.requests.per.connection

This controls how many messages the producer will send to the server without receiving responses. Setting this high can increase memory usage while improving throughput, but setting it too high can reduce throughput as batching becomes less efficient. Setting this to 1 will guarantee that messages will be written to the broker in the order in which they were sent, even when retries occur.

timeout.ms, request.timeout.ms, and metadata.fetch.timeout.ms

These parameters control how long the producer will wait for a reply from the server when sending data (`request.timeout.ms`) and when requesting metadata such as the current leaders for the partitions we are writing to (`metadata.fetch.timeout.ms`). If the timeout is reached without reply, the producer will either retry sending or respond with an error (either through exception or the send callback). `timeout.ms` controls the time the broker will wait for in-sync replicas to acknowledge the message in order to meet the `acks` configuration—the broker will return an error if the time elapses without the necessary acknowledgments.

max.block.ms

This parameter controls how long the producer will block when calling `send()` and when explicitly requesting metadata via `partitionsFor()`. Those methods block when the producer's send buffer is full or when metadata is not available. When `max.block.ms` is reached, a timeout exception is thrown.

max.request.size

This setting controls the size of a produce request sent by the producer. It caps both the size of the largest message that can be sent and the number of messages that the producer can send in one request. For example, with a default maximum request size of 1 MB, the largest message you can send is 1 MB or the producer can batch 1,000 messages of size 1 K each into one request. In addition, the broker has its own limit on the size of the largest message it will accept (`message.max.bytes`). It is usually a good idea to have these configurations match, so the producer will not attempt to send messages of a size that will be rejected by the broker.

receive.buffer.bytes and send.buffer.bytes

These are the sizes of the TCP send and receive buffers used by the sockets when writing and reading data. If these are set to -1, the OS defaults will be used. It is a good idea to increase those when producers or consumers communicate with brokers in a different datacenter because those network links typically have higher latency and lower bandwidth.

Ordering Guarantees

Apache Kafka preserves the order of messages within a partition. This means that if messages were sent from the producer in a specific order, the broker will write them to a partition in that order and all consumers will read them in that order. For some use cases, order is very important. There is a big difference between depositing $100 in an account and later withdrawing it, and the other way around! However, some use cases are less sensitive.

Setting the `retries` parameter to nonzero and the `max.in.flights.requests.per.session` to more than one means that it is possible that the broker will fail to write the first batch of messages, succeed to write the second (which was already in-flight), and then retry the first batch and succeed, thereby reversing the order.

Usually, setting the number of retries to zero is not an option in a reliable system, so if guaranteeing order is critical, we recommend setting `in.flight.requests.per.session=1` to make sure that while a batch of messages is retrying, additional messages will not be sent (because this has the potential to reverse the correct order). This will severely limit the throughput of the producer, so only use this when order is important.

Serializers

As seen in previous examples, producer configuration includes mandatory serializers. We've seen how to use the default String serializer. Kafka also includes serializers for integers and `ByteArrays`, but this does not cover most use cases. Eventually, you will want to be able to serialize more generic records.

We will start by showing how to write your own serializer and then introduce the Avro serializer as a recommended alternative.

Custom Serializers

When the object you need to send to Kafka is not a simple string or integer, you have a choice of either using a generic serialization library like Avro, Thrift, or Protobuf to create records, or creating a custom serialization for objects you are already using. We highly recommend using a generic serialization library. In order to understand how the serializers work and why it is a good idea to use a serialization library, let's see what it takes to write your own custom serializer.

Suppose that instead of recording just the customer name, you create a simple class to represent customers:

```
public class Customer {
        private int customerID;
        private String customerName;

        public Customer(int ID, String name) {
                this.customerID = ID;
                this.customerName = name;
        }

    public int getID() {
      return customerID;
    }

    public String getName() {
     return customerName;
    }
}
```

Now suppose we want to create a custom serializer for this class. It will look something like this:

```
import org.apache.kafka.common.errors.SerializationException;

import java.nio.ByteBuffer;
import java.util.Map;

public class CustomerSerializer implements Serializer<Customer> {

        @Override
    public void configure(Map configs, boolean isKey) {
     // nothing to configure
    }

    @Override
    /**
    We are serializing Customer as:
    4 byte int representing customerId
    4 byte int representing length of customerName in UTF-8 bytes (0 if name is
    Null)
     N bytes representing customerName in UTF-8
    */
    public byte[] serialize(String topic, Customer data) {
     try {
                    byte[] serializedName;
                    int stringSize;
        if (data == null)
          return null;
```

```
            else {
                                   if (data.getName() != null) {
            serializeName = data.getName().getBytes("UTF-8");
            stringSize = serializedName.length;
                                   } else {
                                          serializedName = new byte[0];
                                          stringSize = 0;
                                   }
                    }

        ByteBuffer buffer = ByteBuffer.allocate(4 + 4 + stringSize);
        buffer.putInt(data.getID());
        buffer.putInt(stringSize);
        buffer.put(serializedName);

        return buffer.array();
            } catch (Exception e) {
        throw new SerializationException("Error when serializing Customer to
    byte[] " + e);
        }
    }

    @Override
    public void close() {
            // nothing to close
    }
}
```

Configuring a producer with this `CustomerSerializer` will allow you to define `ProducerRecord<String, Customer>`, and send `Customer` data and pass `Customer` objects directly to the producer. This example is pretty simple, but you can see how fragile the code is. If we ever have too many customers, for example, and need to change customerID to `Long`, or if we ever decide to add a `startDate` field to `Customer`, we will have a serious issue in maintaining compatibility between old and new messages. Debugging compatibility issues between different versions of serializers and deserializers is fairly challenging—you need to compare arrays of raw bytes. To make matters even worse, if multiple teams in the same company end up writing `Customer` data to Kafka, they will all need to use the same serializers and modify the code at the exact same time.

For these reasons, we recommend using existing serializers and deserializers such as JSON, Apache Avro, Thrift, or Protobuf. In the following section we will describe Apache Avro and then show how to serialize Avro records and send them to Kafka.

Serializing Using Apache Avro

Apache Avro is a language-neutral data serialization format. The project was created by Doug Cutting to provide a way to share data files with a large audience.

Avro data is described in a language-independent schema. The schema is usually described in JSON and the serialization is usually to binary files, although serializing to JSON is also supported. Avro assumes that the schema is present when reading and writing files, usually by embedding the schema in the files themselves.

One of the most interesting features of Avro, and what makes it a good fit for use in a messaging system like Kafka, is that when the application that is writing messages switches to a new schema, the applications reading the data can continue processing messages without requiring any change or update.

Suppose the original schema was:

```
{"namespace": "customerManagement.avro",
 "type": "record",
 "name": "Customer",
 "fields": [
     {"name": "id", "type": "int"},
     {"name": "name",  "type": "string""},
     {"name": "faxNumber", "type": ["null", "string"], "default": "null"} ❶
 ]
}
```

❶ id and name fields are mandatory, while fax number is optional and defaults to null.

We used this schema for a few months and generated a few terabytes of data in this format. Now suppose that we decide that in the new version, we will upgrade to the twenty-first century and will no longer include a fax number field and will instead use an email field.

The new schema would be:

```
{"namespace": "customerManagement.avro",
 "type": "record",
 "name": "Customer",
 "fields": [
     {"name": "id", "type": "int"},
     {"name": "name",  "type": "string"},
     {"name": "email", "type": ["null", "string"], "default": "null"}
 ]
}
```

Now, after upgrading to the new version, old records will contain "faxNumber" and new records will contain "email." In many organizations, upgrades are done slowly and over many months. So we need to consider how preupgrade applications that still use the fax numbers and postupgrade applications that use email will be able to handle all the events in Kafka.

The reading application will contain calls to methods similar to getName(), getId(), and getFaxNumber. If it encounters a message written with the new schema, get

Name() and getId() will continue working with no modification, but getFax
Number() will return null because the message will not contain a fax number.

Now suppose we upgrade our reading application and it no longer has the getFax
Number() method but rather getEmail(). If it encounters a message written with the
old schema, getEmail() will return null because the older messages do not contain
an email address.

This example illustrates the benefit of using Avro: even though we changed the
schema in the messages without changing all the applications reading the data, there
will be no exceptions or breaking errors and no need for expensive updates of exist‐
ing data.

However, there are two caveats to this scenario:

- The schema used for writing the data and the schema expected by the reading
  application must be compatible. The Avro documentation includes compatibility
  rules. (*http://bit.ly/2t9FmEb*)
- The deserializer will need access to the schema that was used when writing the
  data, even when it is different than the schema expected by the application that
  accesses the data. In Avro files, the writing schema is included in the file itself,
  but there is a better way to handle this for Kafka messages. We will look at that
  next.

Using Avro Records with Kafka

Unlike Avro files, where storing the entire schema in the data file is associated with a
fairly reasonable overhead, storing the entire schema in each record will usually more
than double the record size. However, Avro still requires the entire schema to be
present when reading the record, so we need to locate the schema elsewhere. To ach‐
ieve this, we follow a common architecture pattern and use a *Schema Registry*. The
Schema Registry is not part of Apache Kafka but there are several open source
options to choose from. We'll use the Confluent Schema Registry for this example.
You can find the Schema Registry code on GitHub (*https://github.com/confluentinc/
schema-registry*), or you can install it as part of the Confluent Platform (*http://
docs.confluent.io/current/installation.html*). If you decide to use the Schema Registry,
then we recommend checking the documentation (*http://docs.confluent.io/current/
schema-registry/docs/index.html*).

The idea is to store all the schemas used to write data to Kafka in the registry. Then
we simply store the identifier for the schema in the record we produce to Kafka. The
consumers can then use the identifier to pull the record out of the schema registry
and deserialize the data. The key is that all this work—storing the schema in the reg‐
istry and pulling it up when required—is done in the serializers and deserializers. The

code that produces data to Kafka simply uses the Avro serializer just like it would any other serializer. Figure 3-2 demonstrates this process.

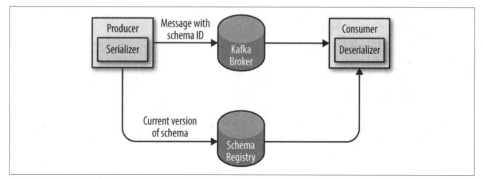

Figure 3-2. Flow diagram of serialization and deserialization of Avro records

Here is an example of how to produce generated Avro objects to Kafka (see the Avro Documentation (*http://avro.apache.org/docs/current/*) for how to use code generation with Avro):

```
Properties props = new Properties();

props.put("bootstrap.servers", "localhost:9092");
props.put("key.serializer",
    "io.confluent.kafka.serializers.KafkaAvroSerializer");
props.put("value.serializer",
    "io.confluent.kafka.serializers.KafkaAvroSerializer"); ❶
props.put("schema.registry.url", schemaUrl); ❷

String topic = "customerContacts";
int wait = 500;

Producer<String, Customer> producer = new KafkaProducer<String,
    Customer>(props); ❸

// We keep producing new events until someone ctrl-c
while (true) {
    Customer customer = CustomerGenerator.getNext();
    System.out.println("Generated customer " +
        customer.toString());
    ProducerRecord<String, Customer> record =
                    new ProducerRecord<>(topic, customer.getId(), cus-
tomer); ❹
    producer.send(record); ❺
}
```

❶ We use the `KafkaAvroSerializer` to serialize our objects with Avro. Note that the `AvroSerializer` can also handle primitives, which is why we can later use `String` as the record key and our `Customer` object as the value.

`schema.registry.url` is a new parameter. This simply points to where we store the schemas.

❸ `Customer` is our generated object. We tell the producer that our records will contain `Customer` as the value.

❹ We also instantiate `ProducerRecord` with `Customer` as the value type, and pass a `Customer` object when creating the new record.

❺ That's it. We send the record with our `Customer` object and `KafkaAvroSerializer` will handle the rest.

What if you prefer to use generic Avro objects rather than the generated Avro objects? No worries. In this case, you just need to provide the schema:

```
Properties props = new Properties();
props.put("bootstrap.servers", "localhost:9092");
props.put("key.serializer",
    "io.confluent.kafka.serializers.KafkaAvroSerializer"); ❶
props.put("value.serializer",
    "io.confluent.kafka.serializers.KafkaAvroSerializer");
props.put("schema.registry.url", url); ❷

    String schemaString = "{\"namespace\": \"customerManagement.avro\",

\"type\": \"record\", " + ❸
                        "\"name\": \"Customer\"," +
                        "\"fields\": [" +
                        "{\"name\": \"id\", \"type\": \"int\"}," +
                        "{\"name\": \"name\", \"type\": \"string\"}," +
                        "{\"name\": \"email\", \"type\": [\"null\",\"string
\"], \"default\":\"null\" }" +
                        "]}";
    Producer<String, GenericRecord> producer =
        new KafkaProducer<String, GenericRecord>(props); ❹

    Schema.Parser parser = new Schema.Parser();
    Schema schema = parser.parse(schemaString);

    for (int nCustomers = 0; nCustomers < customers; nCustomers++) {
      String name = "exampleCustomer" + nCustomers;
      String email = "example " + nCustomers + "@example.com"

      GenericRecord customer = new GenericData.Record(schema); ❺
      customer.put("id", nCustomer);
      customer.put("name", name);
      customer.put("email", email);

      ProducerRecord<String, GenericRecord> data =
                            new ProducerRecord<String,
```

```
                                          GenericRecord>("customerContacts",
name, customer);
      producer.send(data);
    }
  }
```

❶ We still use the same `KafkaAvroSerializer`.

❷ And we provide the URI of the same schema registry.

❸ But now we also need to provide the Avro schema, since it is not provided by the Avro-generated object.

❹ Our object type is an Avro `GenericRecord`, which we initialize with our schema and the data we want to write.

❺ Then the value of the `ProducerRecord` is simply a `GenericRecord` that countains our schema and data. The serializer will know how to get the schema from this record, store it in the schema registry, and serialize the object data.

Partitions

In previous examples, the `ProducerRecord` objects we created included a topic name, key, and value. Kafka messages are key-value pairs and while it is possible to create a `ProducerRecord` with just a topic and a value, with the key set to `null` by default, most applications produce records with keys. Keys serve two goals: they are additional information that gets stored with the message, and they are also used to decide which one of the topic partitions the message will be written to. All messages with the same key will go to the same partition. This means that if a process is reading only a subset of the partitions in a topic (more on that in Chapter 4), all the records for a single key will be read by the same process. To create a key-value record, you simply create a `ProducerRecord` as follows:

```
ProducerRecord<Integer, String> record =
        new ProducerRecord<>("CustomerCountry", "Laboratory Equipment", "USA");
```

When creating messages with a null key, you can simply leave the key out:

```
ProducerRecord<Integer, String> record =
        new ProducerRecord<>("CustomerCountry", "USA"); ❶
```

❶ Here, the key will simply be set to `null`, which may indicate that a customer name was missing on a form.

When the key is `null` and the default partitioner is used, the record will be sent to one of the available partitions of the topic at random. A round-robin algorithm will be used to balance the messages among the partitions.

If a key exists and the default partitioner is used, Kafka will hash the key (using its own hash algorithm, so hash values will not change when Java is upgraded), and use the result to map the message to a specific partition. Since it is important that a key is always mapped to the same partition, we use all the partitions in the topic to calculate the mapping—not just the available partitions. This means that if a specific partition is unavailable when you write data to it, you might get an error. This is fairly rare, as you will see in Chapter 6 when we discuss Kafka's replication and availability.

The mapping of keys to partitions is consistent only as long as the number of partitions in a topic does not change. So as long as the number of partitions is constant, you can be sure that, for example, records regarding user 045189 will always get written to partition 34. This allows all kinds of optimization when reading data from partitions. However, the moment you add new partitions to the topic, this is no longer guaranteed—the old records will stay in partition 34 while new records will get written to a different partition. When partitioning keys is important, the easiest solution is to create topics with sufficient partitions (Chapter 2 includes suggestions for how to determine a good number of partitions) and never add partitions.

Implementing a custom partitioning strategy

So far, we have discussed the traits of the default partitioner, which is the one most commonly used. However, Kafka does not limit you to just hash partitions, and sometimes there are good reasons to partition data differently. For example, suppose that you are a B2B vendor and your biggest customer is a company that manufactures handheld devices called Bananas. Suppose that you do so much business with customer "Banana" that over 10% of your daily transactions are with this customer. If you use default hash partitioning, the Banana records will get allocated to the same partition as other accounts, resulting in one partition being about twice as large as the rest. This can cause servers to run out of space, processing to slow down, etc. What we really want is to give Banana its own partition and then use hash partitioning to map the rest of the accounts to partitions.

Here is an example of a custom partitioner:

```
import org.apache.kafka.clients.producer.Partitioner;
import org.apache.kafka.common.Cluster;
import org.apache.kafka.common.PartitionInfo;
import org.apache.kafka.common.record.InvalidRecordException;
import org.apache.kafka.common.utils.Utils;

public class BananaPartitioner implements Partitioner {

    public void configure(Map<String, ?> configs) {} ❶

    public int partition(String topic, Object key, byte[] keyBytes,
                         Object value, byte[] valueBytes,
                         Cluster cluster) {
        List<PartitionInfo> partitions =
            cluster.partitionsForTopic(topic);
        int numPartitions = partitions.size();

        if ((keyBytes == null) || (!(key instanceOf String))) ❷
          throw new InvalidRecordException("We expect all messages
            to have customer name as key")

        if (((String) key).equals("Banana"))
          return numPartitions; // Banana will always go to last
                                      partition

        // Other records will get hashed to the rest of the
            partitions
        return (Math.abs(Utils.murmur2(keyBytes)) % (numPartitions - 1))
        }

    public void close() {}
}
```

❶ Partitioner interface includes `configure`, `partition`, and `close` methods. Here we only implement `partition`, although we really should have passed the special customer name through `configure` instead of hard-coding it in `partition`.

❷ We only expect String keys, so we throw an exception if that is not the case.

Old Producer APIs

In this chapter we've discussed the Java producer client that is part of the `org.apache.kafka.clients` package. However, Apache Kafka still has two older clients written in Scala that are part of the `kafka.producer` package and the core Kafka module. These producers are called `SyncProducers` (which, depending on the value of the `acks` parameter, may wait for the server to `ack` each message or batch of messages before sending additional messages) and `AsyncProducer` (which batches messages in the background, sends them in a separate thread, and does not provide feedback regarding success to the client).

Because the current producer supports both behaviors and provides much more reliability and control to the developer, we will not discuss the older APIs. If you are interested in using them, think twice and then refer to Apache Kafka documentation to learn more.

Summary

We began this chapter with a simple example of a producer—just 10 lines of code that send events to Kafka. We added to the simple example by adding error handling and experimenting with synchronous and asynchronous producing. We then explored the most important producer configuration parameters and saw how they modify the behavior of the producers. We discussed serializers, which let us control the format of the events we write to Kafka. We looked in-depth at Avro, one of many ways to serialize events, but one that is very commonly used with Kafka. We concluded the chapter with a discussion of partitioning in Kafka and an example of an advanced custom partitioning technique.

Now that we know how to write events to Kafka, in Chapter 4 we'll learn all about consuming events from Kafka.

Kafka Consumers: Reading Data from Kafka

Applications that need to read data from Kafka use a `KafkaConsumer` to subscribe to Kafka topics and receive messages from these topics. Reading data from Kafka is a bit different than reading data from other messaging systems, and there are few unique concepts and ideas involved. It is difficult to understand how to use the consumer API without understanding these concepts first. We'll start by explaining some of the important concepts, and then we'll go through some examples that show the different ways consumer APIs can be used to implement applications with varying requirements.

Kafka Consumer Concepts

In order to understand how to read data from Kafka, you first need to understand its consumers and consumer groups. The following sections cover those concepts.

Consumers and Consumer Groups

Suppose you have an application that needs to read messages from a Kafka topic, run some validations against them, and write the results to another data store. In this case your application will create a consumer object, subscribe to the appropriate topic, and start receiving messages, validating them and writing the results. This may work well for a while, but what if the rate at which producers write messages to the topic exceeds the rate at which your application can validate them? If you are limited to a single consumer reading and processing the data, your application may fall farther and farther behind, unable to keep up with the rate of incoming messages. Obviously there is a need to scale consumption from topics. Just like multiple producers can write to the same topic, we need to allow multiple consumers to read from the same topic, splitting the data between them.

Kafka consumers are typically part of a `consumer group`. When multiple consumers are subscribed to a topic and belong to the same consumer group, each consumer in the group will receive messages from a different subset of the partitions in the topic.

Let's take topic T1 with four partitions. Now suppose we created a new consumer, C1, which is the only consumer in group G1, and use it to subscribe to topic T1. Consumer C1 will get all messages from all four t1 partitions. See Figure 4-1.

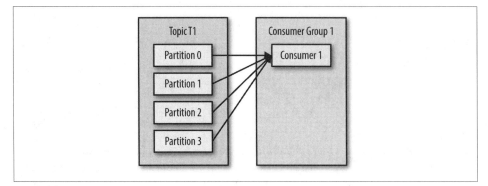

Figure 4-1. One Consumer group with four partitions

If we add another consumer, C2, to group G1, each consumer will only get messages from two partitions. Perhaps messages from partition 0 and 2 go to C1 and messages from partitions 1 and 3 go to consumer C2. See Figure 4-2.

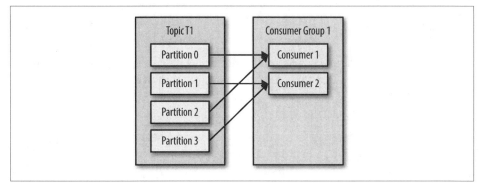

Figure 4-2. Four partitions split to two consumer groups

If G1 has four consumers, then each will read messages from a single partition. See Figure 4-3.

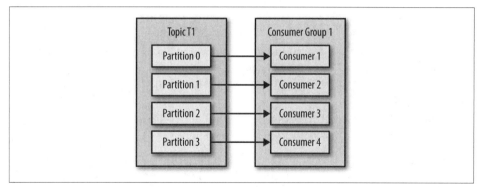

Figure 4-3. Four consumer groups to one partition each

If we add more consumers to a single group with a single topic than we have partitions, some of the consumers will be idle and get no messages at all. See Figure 4-4.

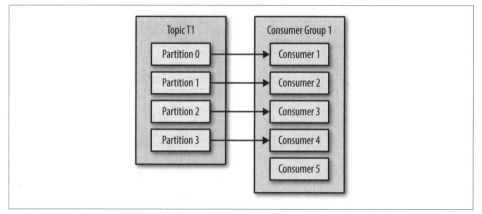

Figure 4-4. More consumer groups than partitions means missed messages

The main way we scale data consumption from a Kafka topic is by adding more consumers to a consumer group. It is common for Kafka consumers to do high-latency operations such as write to a database or a time-consuming computation on the data. In these cases, a single consumer can't possibly keep up with the rate data flows into a topic, and adding more consumers that share the load by having each consumer own just a subset of the partitions and messages is our main method of scaling. This is a good reason to create topics with a large number of partitions—it allows adding more consumers when the load increases. Keep in mind that there is no point in adding more consumers than you have partitions in a topic—some of the consumers will just be idle. Chapter 2 includes some suggestions on how to choose the number of partitions in a topic.

In addition to adding consumers in order to scale a single application, it is very common to have multiple applications that need to read data from the same topic. In fact, one of the main design goals in Kafka was to make the data produced to Kafka topics available for many use cases throughout the organization. In those cases, we want each application to get all of the messages, rather than just a subset. To make sure an application gets all the messages in a topic, ensure the application has its own consumer group. Unlike many traditional messaging systems, Kafka scales to a large number of consumers and consumer groups without reducing performance.

In the previous example, if we add a new consumer group G2 with a single consumer, this consumer will get all the messages in topic T1 independent of what G1 is doing. G2 can have more than a single consumer, in which case they will each get a subset of partitions, just like we showed for G1, but G2 as a whole will still get all the messages regardless of other consumer groups. See Figure 4-5.

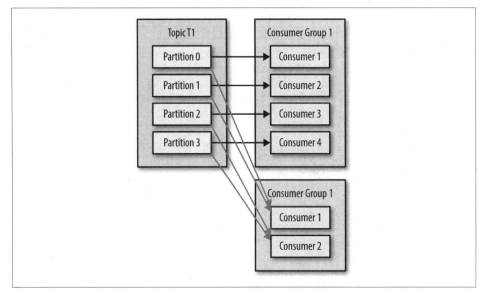

Figure 4-5. Adding a new consumer group ensures no messages are missed

To summarize, you create a new consumer group for each application that needs all the messages from one or more topics. You add consumers to an existing consumer group to scale the reading and processing of messages from the topics, so each additional consumer in a group will only get a subset of the messages.

Consumer Groups and Partition Rebalance

As we saw in the previous section, consumers in a consumer group share ownership of the partitions in the topics they subscribe to. When we add a new consumer to the group, it starts consuming messages from partitions previously consumed by another consumer. The same thing happens when a consumer shuts down or crashes; it leaves the group, and the partitions it used to consume will be consumed by one of the remaining consumers. Reassignment of partitions to consumers also happen when the topics the consumer group is consuming are modified (e.g., if an administrator adds new partitions).

Moving partition ownership from one consumer to another is called a *rebalance*. Rebalances are important because they provide the consumer group with high availability and scalability (allowing us to easily and safely add and remove consumers), but in the normal course of events they are fairly undesirable. During a rebalance, consumers can't consume messages, so a rebalance is basically a short window of unavailability of the entire consumer group. In addition, when partitions are moved from one consumer to another, the consumer loses its current state; if it was caching any data, it will need to refresh its caches—slowing down the application until the consumer sets up its state again. Throughout this chapter we will discuss how to safely handle rebalances and how to avoid unnecessary ones.

The way consumers maintain membership in a consumer group and ownership of the partitions assigned to them is by sending *heartbeats* to a Kafka broker designated as the *group coordinator* (this broker can be different for different consumer groups). As long as the consumer is sending heartbeats at regular intervals, it is assumed to be alive, well, and processing messages from its partitions. Heartbeats are sent when the consumer polls (i.e., retrieves records) and when it commits records it has consumed.

If the consumer stops sending heartbeats for long enough, its session will time out and the group coordinator will consider it dead and trigger a rebalance. If a consumer crashed and stopped processing messages, it will take the group coordinator a few seconds without heartbeats to decide it is dead and trigger the rebalance. During those seconds, no messages will be processed from the partitions owned by the dead consumer. When closing a consumer cleanly, the consumer will notify the group coordinator that it is leaving, and the group coordinator will trigger a rebalance immediately, reducing the gap in processing. Later in this chapter we will discuss configuration options that control heartbeat frequency and session timeouts and how to set those to match your requirements.

Changes to Heartbeat Behavior in Recent Kafka Versions

In release 0.10.1, the Kafka community introduced a separate heartbeat thread that will send heartbeats in between polls as well. This allows you to separate the heartbeat frequency (and therefore how long it takes for the consumer group to detect that a consumer crashed and is no longer sending heartbeats) from the frequency of polling (which is determined by the time it takes to process the data returned from the brokers). With newer versions of Kafka, you can configure how long the application can go without polling before it will leave the group and trigger a rebalance. This configuration is used to prevent a *livelock*, where the application did not crash but fails to make progress for some reason. This configuration is separate from `session.time out.ms`, which controls the time it takes to detect a consumer crash and stop sending heartbeats.

The rest of the chapter will discuss some of the challenges with older behaviors and how the programmer can handle them. This chapter includes discussion about how to handle applications that take longer to process records. This is less relevant to readers running Apache Kafka 0.10.1 or later. If you are using a new version and need to handle records that take longer to process, you simply need to tune `max.poll.interval.ms` so it will handle longer delays between polling for new records.

How Does the Process of Assigning Partitions to Brokers Work?

When a consumer wants to join a group, it sends a `JoinGroup` request to the group coordinator. The first consumer to join the group becomes the group *leader*. The leader receives a list of all consumers in the group from the group coordinator (this will include all consumers that sent a heartbeat recently and which are therefore considered alive) and is responsible for assigning a subset of partitions to each consumer. It uses an implementation of `Parti tionAssignor` to decide which partitions should be handled by which consumer.

Kafka has two built-in partition assignment policies, which we will discuss in more depth in the configuration section. After deciding on the partition assignment, the consumer leader sends the list of assignments to the `GroupCoordinator`, which sends this information to all the consumers. Each consumer only sees his own assignment—the leader is the only client process that has the full list of consumers in the group and their assignments. This process repeats every time a rebalance happens.

Creating a Kafka Consumer

The first step to start consuming records is to create a `KafkaConsumer` instance. Creating a `KafkaConsumer` is very similar to creating a `KafkaProducer`—you create a Java `Properties` instance with the properties you want to pass to the consumer. We will discuss all the properties in depth later in the chapter. To start we just need to use the three mandatory properties: `bootstrap.servers`, `key.deserializer`, and `value.deserializer`.

The first property, `bootstrap.servers`, is the connection string to a Kafka cluster. It is used the exact same way as in `KafkaProducer` (you can refer to Chapter 3 for details on how this is defined). The other two properties, `key.deserializer` and `value.deserializer`, are similar to the `serializers` defined for the producer, but rather than specifying classes that turn Java objects to byte arrays, you need to specify classes that can take a byte array and turn it into a Java object.

There is a fourth property, which is not strictly mandatory, but for now we will pretend it is. The property is `group.id` and it specifies the consumer group the `KafkaConsumer` instance belongs to. While it is possible to create consumers that do not belong to any consumer group, this is uncommon, so for most of the chapter we will assume the consumer is part of a group.

The following code snippet shows how to create a `KafkaConsumer`:

```
Properties props = new Properties();
props.put("bootstrap.servers", "broker1:9092,broker2:9092");
props.put("group.id", "CountryCounter");
props.put("key.deserializer",
  "org.apache.kafka.common.serialization.StringDeserializer");
props.put("value.deserializer",
  "org.apache.kafka.common.serialization.StringDeserializer");

KafkaConsumer<String, String> consumer = new KafkaConsumer<String,
String>(props);
```

Most of what you see here should be familiar if you've read Chapter 3 on creating producers. We assume that the records we consume will have `String` objects as both the key and the value of the record. The only new property here is `group.id`, which is the name of the consumer group this consumer belong to.

Subscribing to Topics

Once we create a consumer, the next step is to subscribe to one or more topics. The `subcribe()` method takes a list of topics as a parameter, so it's pretty simple to use:

```
consumer.subscribe(Collections.singletonList("customerCountries")); ❶
```

 Here we simply create a list with a single element: the topic name `customerCountries`.

It is also possible to call `subscribe` with a regular expression. The expression can match multiple topic names, and if someone creates a new topic with a name that matches, a rebalance will happen almost immediately and the consumers will start consuming from the new topic. This is useful for applications that need to consume from multiple topics and can handle the different types of data the topics will contain. Subscribing to multiple topics using a regular expression is most commonly used in applications that replicate data between Kafka and another system.

To subscribe to all test topics, we can call:

```
consumer.subscribe("test.*");
```

The Poll Loop

At the heart of the consumer API is a simple loop for polling the server for more data. Once the consumer subscribes to topics, the poll loop handles all details of coordination, partition rebalances, heartbeats, and data fetching, leaving the developer with a clean API that simply returns available data from the assigned partitions. The main body of a consumer will look as follows:

```
try {
    while (true) { ❶
        ConsumerRecords<String, String> records = consumer.poll(100); ❷
        for (ConsumerRecord<String, String> record : records) ❸
        {
            log.debug("topic = %s, partition = %s, offset = %d,
                customer = %s, country = %s\n",
                record.topic(), record.partition(), record.offset(),
                record.key(), record.value());

            int updatedCount = 1;
            if (custCountryMap.countainsValue(record.value())) {
                updatedCount = custCountryMap.get(record.value()) + 1;
            }
            custCountryMap.put(record.value(), updatedCount)

            JSONObject json = new JSONObject(custCountryMap);
            System.out.println(json.toString(4)) ❹
        }
    }
} finally {
    consumer.close(); ❺
}
```

❶ This is indeed an infinite loop. Consumers are usually long-running applications that continuously poll Kafka for more data. We will show later in the chapter how to cleanly exit the loop and close the consumer.

❷ This is the most important line in the chapter. The same way that sharks must keep moving or they die, consumers must keep polling Kafka or they will be considered dead and the partitions they are consuming will be handed to another consumer in the group to continue consuming. The parameter we pass, poll(), is a timeout interval and controls how long poll() will block if data is not available in the consumer buffer. If this is set to 0, poll() will return immediately; otherwise, it will wait for the specified number of milliseconds for data to arrive from the broker.

❸   `poll()` returns a list of records. Each record contains the topic and partition the record came from, the offset of the record within the partition, and of course the key and the value of the record. Typically we want to iterate over the list and process the records individually. The `poll()` method takes a timeout parameter. This specifies how long it will take `poll` to return, with or without data. The value is typically driven by application needs for quick responses—how fast do you want to return control to the thread that does the polling?

❹   Processing usually ends in writing a result in a data store or updating a stored record. Here, the goal is to keep a running count of customers from each county, so we update a hashtable and print the result as JSON. A more realistic example would store the updates result in a data store.

❺   Always `close()` the consumer before exiting. This will close the network connections and sockets. It will also trigger a rebalance immediately rather than wait for the group coordinator to discover that the consumer stopped sending heartbeats and is likely dead, which will take longer and therefore result in a longer period of time in which consumers can't consume messages from a subset of the partitions.

The `poll` loop does a lot more than just get data. The first time you call `poll()` with a new consumer, it is responsible for finding the `GroupCoordinator`, joining the consumer group, and receiving a partition assignment. If a rebalance is triggered, it will be handled inside the poll loop as well. And of course the heartbeats that keep consumers alive are sent from within the poll loop. For this reason, we try to make sure that whatever processing we do between iterations is fast and efficient.

Thread Safety

You can't have multiple consumers that belong to the same group in one thread and you can't have multiple threads safely use the same consumer. One consumer per thread is the rule. To run multiple consumers in the same group in one application, you will need to run each in its own thread. It is useful to wrap the consumer logic in its own object and then use Java's `ExecutorService` to start multiple threads each with its own consumer. The Confluent blog has a tutorial (*http://bit.ly/2tfVu6O*) that shows how to do just that.

Configuring Consumers

So far we have focused on learning the consumer API, but we've only looked at a few of the configuration properties—just the mandatory `bootstrap.servers`, `group.id`, `key.deserializer`, and `value.deserializer`. All the consumer configuration is documented in Apache Kafka documentation (*http://kafka.apache.org/documenta tion.html#newconsumerconfigs*). Most of the parameters have reasonable defaults and do not require modification, but some have implications on the performance and availability of the consumers. Let's take a look at some of the more important properties.

fetch.min.bytes

This property allows a consumer to specify the minimum amount of data that it wants to receive from the broker when fetching records. If a broker receives a request for records from a consumer but the new records amount to fewer bytes than `min.fetch.bytes`, the broker will wait until more messages are available before sending the records back to the consumer. This reduces the load on both the consumer and the broker as they have to handle fewer back-and-forth messages in cases where the topics don't have much new activity (or for lower activity hours of the day). You will want to set this parameter higher than the default if the consumer is using too much CPU when there isn't much data available, or reduce load on the brokers when you have large number of consumers.

fetch.max.wait.ms

By setting `fetch.min.bytes`, you tell Kafka to wait until it has enough data to send before responding to the consumer. `fetch.max.wait.ms` lets you control how long to wait. By default, Kafka will wait up to 500 ms. This results in up to 500 ms of extra latency in case there is not enough data flowing to the Kafka topic to satisfy the minimum amount of data to return. If you want to limit the potential latency (usually due to SLAs controlling the maximum latency of the application), you can set `fetch.max.wait.ms` to a lower value. If you set `fetch.max.wait.ms` to 100 ms and `fetch.min.bytes` to 1 MB, Kafka will recieve a fetch request from the consumer and will respond with data either when it has 1 MB of data to return or after 100 ms, whichever happens first.

max.partition.fetch.bytes

This property controls the maximum number of bytes the server will return per partition. The default is 1 MB, which means that when `KafkaConsumer.poll()` returns `ConsumerRecords`, the record object will use at most `max.partition.fetch.bytes` per partition assigned to the consumer. So if a topic has 20 partitions, and you have 5 consumers, each consumer will need to have 4 MB of memory available for `Consumer` `Records`. In practice, you will want to allocate more memory as each consumer will need to handle more partitions if other consumers in the group fail. `max.` `partition.fetch.bytes` must be larger than the largest message a broker will accept (determined by the `max.message.size` property in the broker configuration), or the broker may have messages that the consumer will be unable to consume, in which case the consumer will hang trying to read them. Another important consideration when setting `max.partition.fetch.bytes` is the amount of time it takes the consumer to process data. As you recall, the consumer must call `poll()` frequently enough to avoid session timeout and subsequent rebalance. If the amount of data a single `poll()` returns is very large, it may take the consumer longer to process, which means it will not get to the next iteration of the poll loop in time to avoid a session timeout. If this occurs, the two options are either to lower `max.` `partition.fetch.bytes` or to increase the session timeout.

session.timeout.ms

The amount of time a consumer can be out of contact with the brokers while still considered alive defaults to 3 seconds. If more than `session.timeout.ms` passes without the consumer sending a heartbeat to the group coordinator, it is considered dead and the group coordinator will trigger a rebalance of the consumer group to allocate partitions from the dead consumer to the other consumers in the group. This property is closely related to `heartbeat.interval.ms`. `heartbeat.interval.ms` controls how frequently the `KafkaConsumer poll()` method will send a heartbeat to the group coordinator, whereas `session.timeout.ms` controls how long a consumer can go without sending a heartbeat. Therefore, those two properties are typically modified together—`heatbeat.interval.ms` must be lower than `session.timeout.ms`, and is usually set to one-third of the timeout value. So if `session.timeout.ms` is 3 seconds, `heartbeat.interval.ms` should be 1 second. Setting `session.timeout.ms` lower than the default will allow consumer groups to detect and recover from failure sooner, but may also cause unwanted rebalances as a result of consumers taking longer to complete the poll loop or garbage collection. Setting `session.timeout.ms` higher will reduce the chance of accidental rebalance, but also means it will take longer to detect a real failure.

auto.offset.reset

This property controls the behavior of the consumer when it starts reading a partition for which it doesn't have a committed offset or if the committed offset it has is invalid (usually because the consumer was down for so long that the record with that offset was already aged out of the broker). The default is "latest," which means that lacking a valid offset, the consumer will start reading from the newest records (records that were written after the consumer started running). The alternative is "earliest," which means that lacking a valid offset, the consumer will read all the data in the partition, starting from the very beginning.

enable.auto.commit

We discussed the different options for committing offsets earlier in this chapter. This parameter controls whether the consumer will commit offsets automatically, and defaults to true. Set it to false if you prefer to control when offsets are committed, which is necessary to minimize duplicates and avoid missing data. If you set enable.auto.commit to true, then you might also want to control how frequently offsets will be committed using auto.commit.interval.ms.

partition.assignment.strategy

We learned that partitions are assigned to consumers in a consumer group. A PartitionAssignor is a class that, given consumers and topics they subscribed to, decides which partitions will be assigned to which consumer. By default, Kafka has two assignment strategies:

Range

Assigns to each consumer a consecutive subset of partitions from each topic it subscribes to. So if consumers C1 and C2 are subscribed to two topics, T1 and T2, and each of the topics has three partitions, then C1 will be assigned partitions 0 and 1 from topics T1 and T2, while C2 will be assigned partition 2 from those topics. Because each topic has an uneven number of partitions and the assignment is done for each topic independently, the first consumer ends up with more partitions than the second. This happens whenever Range assignment is used and the number of consumers does not divide the number of partitions in each topic neatly.

RoundRobin

Takes all the partitions from all subscribed topics and assigns them to consumers sequentially, one by one. If C1 and C2 described previously used RoundRobin assignment, C1 would have partitions 0 and 2 from topic T1 and partition 1 from topic T2. C2 would have partition 1 from topic T1 and partitions 0 and 2 from topic T2. In general, if all consumers are subscribed to the same topics (a very common scenario), RoundRobin assignment will end up with all consumers having the same number of partitions (or at most 1 partition difference).

The partition.assignment.strategy allows you to choose a partition-assignment strategy. The default is org.apache.kafka.clients.consumer.RangeAssignor, which implements the Range strategy described above. You can replace it with org.apache.kafka.clients.consumer.RoundRobinAssignor. A more advanced option is to implement your own assignment strategy, in which case partition.assignment.strategy should point to the name of your class.

client.id

This can be any string, and will be used by the brokers to identify messages sent from the client. It is used in logging and metrics, and for quotas.

max.poll.records

This controls the maximum number of records that a single call to poll() will return. This is useful to help control the amount of data your application will need to process in the polling loop.

receive.buffer.bytes and send.buffer.bytes

These are the sizes of the TCP send and receive buffers used by the sockets when writing and reading data. If these are set to -1, the OS defaults will be used. It can be a good idea to increase those when producers or consumers communicate with brokers in a different datacenter, because those network links typically have higher latency and lower bandwidth.

Commits and Offsets

Whenever we call poll(), it returns records written to Kafka that consumers in our group have not read yet. This means that we have a way of tracking which records were read by a consumer of the group. As discussed before, one of Kafka's unique characteristics is that it does not track acknowledgments from consumers the way many JMS queues do. Instead, it allows consumers to use Kafka to track their position (offset) in each partition.

We call the action of updating the current position in the partition a commit.

How does a consumer commit an offset? It produces a message to Kafka, to a special __consumer_offsets topic, with the committed offset for each partition. As long as all your consumers are up, running, and churning away, this will have no impact. However, if a consumer crashes or a new consumer joins the consumer group, this will *trigger a rebalance*. After a rebalance, each consumer may be assigned a new set of partitions than the one it processed before. In order to know where to pick up the work, the consumer will read the latest committed offset of each partition and continue from there.

If the committed offset is smaller than the offset of the last message the client processed, the messages between the last processed offset and the committed offset will be processed twice. See Figure 4-6.

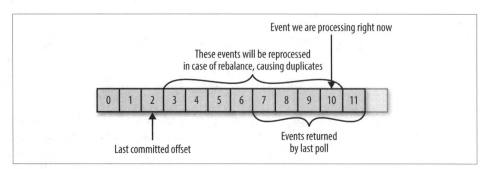

Figure 4-6. Re-processed messages

If the committed offset is larger than the offset of the last message the client actually processed, all messages between the last processed offset and the committed offset will be missed by the consumer group. See Figure 4-7.

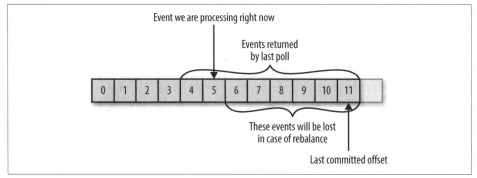

Figure 4-7. Missed messages between offsets

Clearly, managing offsets has a big impact on the client application. The KafkaConsumer API provides multiple ways of committing offsets:

Automatic Commit

The easiest way to commit offsets is to allow the consumer to do it for you. If you configure enable.auto.commit=true, then every five seconds the consumer will commit the largest offset your client received from poll(). The five-second interval is the default and is controlled by setting auto.commit.interval.ms. Just like everything else in the consumer, the automatic commits are driven by the poll loop. Whenever you poll, the consumer checks if it is time to commit, and if it is, it will commit the offsets it returned in the last poll.

Before using this convenient option, however, it is important to understand the consequences.

Consider that, by default, automatic commits occur every five seconds. Suppose that we are three seconds after the most recent commit and a rebalance is triggered. After the rebalancing, all consumers will start consuming from the last offset committed. In this case, the offset is three seconds old, so all the events that arrived in those three seconds will be processed twice. It is possible to configure the commit interval to commit more frequently and reduce the window in which records will be duplicated, but it is impossible to completely eliminate them.

With autocommit enabled, a call to poll will always commit the last offset returned by the previous poll. It doesn't know which events were actually processed, so it is critical to always process all the events returned by poll() before calling poll() again. (Just like poll(), close() also commits offsets automatically.) This is usually not an issue, but pay attention when you handle exceptions or exit the poll loop prematurely.

Automatic commits are convenient, but they don't give developers enough control to avoid duplicate messages.

Commit Current Offset

Most developers exercise more control over the time at which offsets are committed —both to eliminate the possibility of missing messages and to reduce the number of messages duplicated during rebalancing. The consumer API has the option of committing the current offset at a point that makes sense to the application developer rather than based on a timer.

By setting auto.commit.offset=false, offsets will only be committed when the application explicitly chooses to do so. The simplest and most reliable of the commit APIs is commitSync(). This API will commit the latest offset returned by poll() and return once the offset is committed, throwing an exception if commit fails for some reason.

It is important to remember that commitSync() will commit the latest offset returned by poll(), so make sure you call commitSync() after you are done processing all the records in the collection, or you risk missing messages as described previously. When rebalance is triggered, all the messages from the beginning of the most recent batch until the time of the rebalance will be processed twice.

Here is how we would use commitSync to commit offsets after we finished processing the latest batch of messages:

```
while (true) {
    ConsumerRecords<String, String> records = consumer.poll(100);
    for (ConsumerRecord<String, String> record : records)
    {
        System.out.printf("topic = %s, partition = %s, offset =
        %d, customer = %s, country = %s\n",
            record.topic(), record.partition(),
```

```
                record.offset(), record.key(), record.value()); ❶
      }
      try {
        consumer.commitSync(); ❷
      } catch (CommitFailedException e) {
          log.error("commit failed", e) ❸
      }
    }
```

❶ Let's assume that by printing the contents of a record, we are done processing it. Your application will likely do a lot more with the records—modify them, enrich them, aggregate them, display them on a dashboard, or notify users of important events. You should determine when you are "done" with a record according to your use case.

❷ Once we are done "processing" all the records in the current batch, we call com mitSync to commit the last offset in the batch, before polling for additional messages.

❸ commitSync retries committing as long as there is no error that can't be recovered. If this happens, there is not much we can do except log an error.

Asynchronous Commit

One drawback of manual commit is that the application is blocked until the broker responds to the commit request. This will limit the throughput of the application. Throughput can be improved by committing less frequently, but then we are increasing the number of potential duplicates that a rebalance will create.

Another option is the asynchronous commit API. Instead of waiting for the broker to respond to a commit, we just send the request and continue on:

```
while (true) {
    ConsumerRecords<String, String> records = consumer.poll(100);
    for (ConsumerRecord<String, String> record : records)
    {
        System.out.printf("topic = %s, partition = %s,
        offset = %d, customer = %s, country = %s\n",
        record.topic(), record.partition(), record.offset(),
        record.key(), record.value());
    }
    consumer.commitAsync(); ❶
}
```

❶ Commit the last offset and carry on.

The drawback is that while commitSync() will retry the commit until it either succeeds or encounters a nonretriable failure, commitAsync() will not retry. The reason it does not retry is that by the time `commitAsync()` receives a response from the server, there may have been a later commit that was already successful. Imagine that we sent a request to commit offset 2000. There is a temporary communication problem, so the broker never gets the request and therefore never responds. Meanwhile, we processed another batch and successfully committed offset 3000. If `commitA sync()` now retries the previously failed commit, it might succeed in committing offset 2000 *after* offset 3000 was already processed and committed. In the case of a rebalance, this will cause more duplicates.

We mention this complication and the importance of correct order of commits, because `commitAsync()` also gives you an option to pass in a callback that will be triggered when the broker responds. It is common to use the callback to log commit errors or to count them in a metric, but if you want to use the callback for retries, you need to be aware of the problem with commit order:

```
while (true) {
    ConsumerRecords<String, String> records = consumer.poll(100);
    for (ConsumerRecord<String, String> record : records) {
        System.out.printf("topic = %s, partition = %s,
        offset = %d, customer = %s, country = %s\n",
        record.topic(), record.partition(), record.offset(),
        record.key(), record.value());
    }
    consumer.commitAsync(new OffsetCommitCallback() {
        public void onComplete(Map<TopicPartition,
        OffsetAndMetadata> offsets, Exception exception) {
            if (e != null)
                log.error("Commit failed for offsets {}", offsets, e);
        }
    }); ❶
}
```

❶ We send the commit and carry on, but if the commit fails, the failure and the offsets will be logged.

Retrying Async Commits

A simple pattern to get commit order right for asynchronous retries is to use a monotonically increasing sequence number. Increase the sequence number every time you commit and add the sequence number at the time of the commit to the `commitAsync` callback. When you're getting ready to send a retry, check if the commit sequence number the callback got is equal to the instance variable; if it is, there was no newer commit and it is safe to retry. If the instance sequence number is higher, don't retry because a newer commit was already sent.

Combining Synchronous and Asynchronous Commits

Normally, occasional failures to commit without retrying are not a huge problem because if the problem is temporary, the following commit will be successful. But if we know that this is the last commit before we close the consumer, or before a rebalance, we want to make extra sure that the commit succeeds.

Therefore, a common pattern is to combine `commitAsync()` with `commitSync()` just before shutdown. Here is how it works (we will discuss how to commit just before rebalance when we get to the section about rebalance listeners):

```
try {
    while (true) {
        ConsumerRecords<String, String> records = consumer.poll(100);
        for (ConsumerRecord<String, String> record : records) {
            System.out.printf("topic = %s, partition = %s, offset = %d,
            customer = %s, country = %s\n",
            record.topic(), record.partition(),
            record.offset(), record.key(), record.value());
        }
        consumer.commitAsync(); ❶
    }
} catch (Exception e) {
    log.error("Unexpected error", e);
} finally {
    try {
        consumer.commitSync(); ❷
    } finally {
        consumer.close();
    }
}
```

❶ While everything is fine, we use `commitAsync`. It is faster, and if one commit fails, the next commit will serve as a retry.

❷ But if we are closing, there is no "next commit." We call `commitSync()`, because it will retry until it succeeds or suffers unrecoverable failure.

Commit Specified Offset

Committing the latest offset only allows you to commit as often as you finish processing batches. But what if you want to commit more frequently than that? What if `poll()` returns a huge batch and you want to commit offsets in the middle of the batch to avoid having to process all those rows again if a rebalance occurs? You can't just call `commitSync()` or `commitAsync()`—this will commit the last offset returned, which you didn't get to process yet.

Fortunately, the consumer API allows you to call `commitSync()` and `commitAsync()` and pass a map of partitions and offsets that you wish to commit. If you are in the middle of processing a batch of records, and the last message you got from partition 3 in topic "customers" has offset 5000, you can call `commitSync()` to commit offset 5000 for partition 3 in topic "customers." Since your consumer may be consuming more than a single partition, you will need to track offsets on all of them, which adds complexity to your code.

Here is what a commit of specific offsets looks like:

```
private Map<TopicPartition, OffsetAndMetadata> currentOffsets =
    new HashMap<>(); ❶
int count = 0;

....

while (true) {
    ConsumerRecords<String, String> records = consumer.poll(100);
    for (ConsumerRecord<String, String> record : records)
    {
        System.out.printf("topic = %s, partition = %s, offset = %d,
        customer = %s, country = %s\n",
        record.topic(), record.partition(), record.offset(),
        record.key(), record.value()); ❷
        currentOffsets.put(new TopicPartition(record.topic(),
        record.partition()), new
        OffsetAndMetadata(record.offset()+1, "no metadata")); ❸
        if (count % 1000 == 0)    ❹
            consumer.commitAsync(currentOffsets, null); ❺
        count++;
    }
}
```

❶ This is the map we will use to manually track offsets.

❷ Remember, `println` is a stand-in for whatever processing you do for the records you consume.

❸ After reading each record, we update the offsets map with the offset of the next message we expect to process. This is where we'll start reading next time we start.

❹ Here, we decide to commit current offsets every 1,000 records. In your application, you can commit based on time or perhaps content of the records.

❺ I chose to call `commitAsync()`, but `commitSync()` is also completely valid here. Of course, when committing specific offsets you still need to perform all the error handling we've seen in previous sections.

Rebalance Listeners

As we mentioned in the previous section about committing offsets, a consumer will want to do some cleanup work before exiting and also before partition rebalancing.

If you know your consumer is about to lose ownership of a partition, you will want to commit offsets of the last event you've processed. If your consumer maintained a buffer with events that it only processes occasionally (e.g., the currentRecords map we used when explaining pause() functionality), you will want to process the events you accumulated before losing ownership of the partition. Perhaps you also need to close file handles, database connections, and such.

The consumer API allows you to run your own code when partitions are added or removed from the consumer. You do this by passing a ConsumerRebalanceListener when calling the subscribe() method we discussed previously. ConsumerRebalance Listener has two methods you can implement:

public void onPartitionsRevoked(Collection<TopicPartition> partitions)
> Called before the rebalancing starts and after the consumer stopped consuming messages. This is where you want to commit offsets, so whoever gets this partition next will know where to start.

public void onPartitionsAssigned(Collection<TopicPartition> partitions)
> Called after partitions have been reassigned to the broker, but before the consumer starts consuming messages.

This example will show how to use onPartitionsRevoked() to commit offsets before losing ownership of a partition. In the next section we will show a more involved example that also demonstrates the use of onPartitionsAssigned():

```
private Map<TopicPartition, OffsetAndMetadata> currentOffsets =
    new HashMap<>();

private class HandleRebalance implements ConsumerRebalanceListener { ❶
    public void onPartitionsAssigned(Collection<TopicPartition>
      partitions) { ❷
    }

    public void onPartitionsRevoked(Collection<TopicPartition>
      partitions) {
        System.out.println("Lost partitions in rebalance.
          Committing current
        offsets:" + currentOffsets);
        consumer.commitSync(currentOffsets); ❸
    }
}

try {
```

```
        consumer.subscribe(topics, new HandleRebalance()); ❹

        while (true) {
            ConsumerRecords<String, String> records =
              consumer.poll(100);
            for (ConsumerRecord<String, String> record : records)
            {
                System.out.printf("topic = %s, partition = %s, offset = %d,
                  customer = %s, country = %s\n",
                  record.topic(), record.partition(), record.offset(),
                  record.key(), record.value());
                currentOffsets.put(new TopicPartition(record.topic(),
                  record.partition()), new
                  OffsetAndMetadata(record.offset()+1, "no metadata"));
            }
            consumer.commitAsync(currentOffsets, null);
        }
} catch (WakeupException e) {
    // ignore, we're closing
} catch (Exception e) {
    log.error("Unexpected error", e);
} finally {
    try {
        consumer.commitSync(currentOffsets);
    } finally {
        consumer.close();
        System.out.println("Closed consumer and we are done");
    }
}
```

❶ We start by implementing a `ConsumerRebalanceListener`.

❷ In this example we don't need to do anything when we get a new partition; we'll just start consuming messages.

❸ However, when we are about to lose a partition due to rebalancing, we need to commit offsets. Note that we are committing the latest offsets we've processed, not the latest offsets in the batch we are still processing. This is because a partition could get revoked while we are still in the middle of a batch. We are committing offsets for all partitions, not just the partitions we are about to lose—because the offsets are for events that were already processed, there is no harm in that. And we are using `commitSync()` to make sure the offsets are committed before the rebalance proceeds.

❹ The most important part: pass the `ConsumerRebalanceListener` to the sub scribe() method so it will get invoked by the consumer.

Consuming Records with Specific Offsets

So far we've seen how to use `poll()` to start consuming messages from the last committed offset in each partition and to proceed in processing all messages in sequence.
However, sometimes you want to start reading at a different offset.

If you want to start reading all messages from the beginning of the partition, or you
want to skip all the way to the end of the partition and start consuming only new
messages, there are APIs specifically for that: `seekToBeginning(TopicPartition tp)`
and `seekToEnd(TopicPartition tp)`.

However, the Kafka API also lets you seek a specific offset. This ability can be used in
a variety of ways; for example, to go back a few messages or skip ahead a few messages (perhaps a time-sensitive application that is falling behind will want to skip
ahead to more relevant messages). The most exciting use case for this ability is when
offsets are stored in a system other than Kafka.

Think about this common scenario: Your application is reading events from Kafka
(perhaps a clickstream of users in a website), processes the data (perhaps remove
records that indicate clicks from automated programs rather than users), and then
stores the results in a database, NoSQL store, or Hadoop. Suppose that we really don't
want to lose any data, nor do we want to store the same results in the database twice.

In these cases, the consumer loop may look a bit like this:

```
while (true) {
    ConsumerRecords<String, String> records = consumer.poll(100);
    for (ConsumerRecord<String, String> record : records)
    {
        currentOffsets.put(new TopicPartition(record.topic(),
        record.partition()),
        record.offset());
        processRecord(record);
        storeRecordInDB(record);
        consumer.commitAsync(currentOffsets);
    }
}
```

In this example, we are very paranoid, so we commit offsets after processing each
record. However, there is still a chance that our application will crash after the record
was stored in the database but before we committed offsets, causing the record to be
processed again and the database to contain duplicates.

This could be avoided if there was a way to store both the record and the offset in one
atomic action. Either both the record and the offset are committed, or neither of
them are committed. As long as the records are written to a database and the offsets
to Kafka, this is impossible.

But what if we wrote both the record and the offset to the database, in one transaction? Then we'll know that either we are done with the record and the offset is committed or we are not and the record will be reprocessed.

Now the only problem is if the record is stored in a database and not in Kafka, how will our consumer know where to start reading when it is assigned a partition? This is exactly what seek() can be used for. When the consumer starts or when new partitions are assigned, it can look up the offset in the database and seek() to that location.

Here is a skeleton example of how this may work. We use ConsumerRebalanceLister and seek() to make sure we start processing at the offsets stored in the database:

```
public class SaveOffsetsOnRebalance implements
  ConsumerRebalanceListener {

    public void onPartitionsRevoked(Collection<TopicPartition>
      partitions) {
              commitDBTransaction();  ❶
        }

    public void onPartitionsAssigned(Collection<TopicPartition>
      partitions) {
        for(TopicPartition partition: partitions)
            consumer.seek(partition, getOffsetFromDB(partition));  ❷
      }
  }
}


consumer.subscribe(topics, new SaveOffsetOnRebalance(consumer));
consumer.poll(0);

for (TopicPartition partition: consumer.assignment())
  consumer.seek(partition, getOffsetFromDB(partition));     ❸

while (true) {
    ConsumerRecords<String, String> records =
      consumer.poll(100);
    for (ConsumerRecord<String, String> record : records)
    {
        processRecord(record);
        storeRecordInDB(record);
        storeOffsetInDB(record.topic(), record.partition(),
          record.offset());  ❹
    }
    commitDBTransaction();
}
```

We use an imaginary method here to commit the transaction in the database. The idea here is that the database records and offsets will be inserted to the database as we process the records, and we just need to commit the transactions when we are about to lose the partition to make sure this information is persisted.

❷ We also have an imaginary method to fetch the offsets from the database, and then we seek() to those records when we get ownership of new partitions.

❸ When the consumer first starts, after we subscribe to topics, we call poll() once to make sure we join a consumer group and get assigned partitions, and then we immediately seek() to the correct offset in the partitions we are assigned to. Keep in mind that seek() only updates the position we are consuming from, so the next poll() will fetch the right messages. If there was an error in seek() (e.g., the offset does not exist), the exception will be thrown by poll().

❹ Another imaginary method: this time we update a table storing the offsets in our database. Here we assume that updating records is fast, so we do an update on every record, but commits are slow, so we only commit at the end of the batch. However, this can be optimized in different ways.

There are many different ways to implement exactly-once semantics by storing offsets and data in an external store, but all of them will need to use the ConsumerRebalance Listener and seek() to make sure offsets are stored in time and that the consumer starts reading messages from the correct location.

But How Do We Exit?

Earlier in this chapter, when we discussed the poll loop, I told you not to worry about the fact that the consumer polls in an infinite loop and that we would discuss how to exit the loop cleanly. So, let's discuss how to exit cleanly.

When you decide to exit the poll loop, you will need another thread to call con sumer.wakeup(). If you are running the consumer loop in the main thread, this can be done from ShutdownHook. Note that consumer.wakeup() is the only consumer method that is safe to call from a different thread. Calling wakeup will cause poll() to exit with WakeupException, or if consumer.wakeup() was called while the thread was not waiting on poll, the exception will be thrown on the next iteration when poll() is called. The WakeupException doesn't need to be handled, but before exiting the thread, you must call consumer.close(). Closing the consumer will commit offsets if needed and will send the group coordinator a message that the consumer is leaving the group. The consumer coordinator will trigger rebalancing immediately and you won't need to wait for the session to time out before partitions from the consumer you are closing will be assigned to another consumer in the group.

Here is what the exit code will look like if the consumer is running in the main application thread. This example is a bit truncated, but you can view the full example at *http://bit.ly/2u47e9A*.

```
Runtime.getRuntime().addShutdownHook(new Thread() {
        public void run() {
            System.out.println("Starting exit...");
            consumer.wakeup(); ❶
            try {
                mainThread.join();
            } catch (InterruptedException e) {
                e.printStackTrace();
            }
        }
    });


...


try {
        // looping until ctrl-c, the shutdown hook will
           cleanup on exit
        while (true) {
            ConsumerRecords<String, String> records =
              movingAvg.consumer.poll(1000);
            System.out.println(System.currentTimeMillis() + "
               --  waiting for data...");
            for (ConsumerRecord<String, String> record :
              records) {
                System.out.printf("offset = %d, key = %s,
                  value = %s\n",
                  record.offset(), record.key(),
                  record.value());
            }
            for (TopicPartition tp: consumer.assignment())
                System.out.println("Committing offset at
                  position:" +
                  consumer.position(tp));
            movingAvg.consumer.commitSync();
        }
    } catch (WakeupException e) {
        // ignore for shutdown ❷
    } finally {
        consumer.close(); ❸
        System.out.println("Closed consumer and we are done");
    }
}
```

❶ ShutdownHook runs in a seperate thread, so the only safe action we can take is to call wakeup to break out of the poll loop.

❷ Another thread calling wakeup will cause poll to throw a WakeupException. You'll want to catch the exception to make sure your application doesn't exit unexpectedly, but there is no need to do anything with it.

❸ Before exiting the consumer, make sure you close it cleanly.

Deserializers

As discussed in the previous chapter, Kafka producers require *serializers* to convert objects into byte arrays that are then sent to Kafka. Similarly, Kafka consumers require *deserializers* to convert byte arrays recieved from Kafka into Java objects. In previous examples, we just assumed that both the key and the value of each message are strings and we used the default StringDeserializer in the consumer configuration.

In Chapter 3 about the Kafka producer, we saw how to serialize custom types and how to use Avro and AvroSerializers to generate Avro objects from schema definitions and then serialize them when producing messages to Kafka. We will now look at how to create custom deserializers for your own objects and how to use Avro and its deserializers.

It should be obvious that the serializer used to produce events to Kafka must match the deserializer that will be used when consuming events. Serializing with IntSerializer and then deserializing with StringDeserializer will not end well. This means that as a developer you need to keep track of which serializers were used to write into each topic, and make sure each topic only contains data that the deserializers you use can interpret. This is one of the benefits of using Avro and the Schema Repository for serializing and deserializing—the AvroSerializer can make sure that all the data written to a specific topic is compatible with the schema of the topic, which means it can be deserialized with the matching deserializer and schema. Any errors in compatibility—on the producer or the consumer side—will be caught easily with an appropriate error message, which means you will not need to try to debug byte arrays for serialization errors.

We will start by quickly showing how to write a custom deserializer, even though this is the less common method, and then we will move on to an example of how to use Avro to deserialize message keys and values.

Custom deserializers

Let's take the same custom object we serialized in Chapter 3, and write a deserializer for it:

```java
public class Customer {
        private int customerID;
        private String customerName;

        public Customer(int ID, String name) {
                this.customerID = ID;
                this.customerName = name;
        }

    public int getID() {
      return customerID;
    }

    public String getName() {
      return customerName;
    }
}
```

The custom deserializer will look as follows:

```java
import org.apache.kafka.common.errors.SerializationException;

import java.nio.ByteBuffer;
import java.util.Map;

public class CustomerDeserializer implements
    Deserializer<Customer> { ❶

        @Override
    public void configure(Map configs, boolean isKey) {
     // nothing to configure
    }

    @Override
    public Customer deserialize(String topic, byte[] data) {

      int id;
      int nameSize;
      String name;

      try {
        if (data == null)
          return null;
        if (data.length < 8)
          throw new SerializationException("Size of data received by
            IntegerDeserializer is shorter than expected");

        ByteBuffer buffer = ByteBuffer.wrap(data);
```

```
        id = buffer.getInt();
        String nameSize = buffer.getInt();

        byte[] nameBytes = new Array[Byte](nameSize);
        buffer.get(nameBytes);
        name = new String(nameBytes, 'UTF-8');

        return new Customer(id, name); ❷

    } catch (Exception e) {
     throw new SerializationException("Error when serializing
        Customer
        to byte[] " + e);
    }
   }

   @Override
   public void close() {
          // nothing to close
   }
  }
```

❶ The consumer also needs the implementation of the Customer class, and both the class and the serializer need to match on the producing and consuming applications. In a large organization with many consumers and producers sharing access to the data, this can become challenging.

❷ We are just reversing the logic of the serializer here—we get the customer ID and name out of the byte array and use them to construct the object we need.

The consumer code that uses this serializer will look similar to this example:

```
Properties props = new Properties();
props.put("bootstrap.servers", "broker1:9092,broker2:9092");
props.put("group.id", "CountryCounter");
props.put("key.deserializer",
    "org.apache.kafka.common.serialization.StringDeserializer");
props.put("value.deserializer",
    "org.apache.kafka.common.serialization.CustomerDeserializer");

KafkaConsumer<String, Customer> consumer =
  new KafkaConsumer<>(props);

consumer.subscribe("customerCountries")

while (true) {
    ConsumerRecords<String, Customer> records =
      consumer.poll(100);
    for (ConsumerRecord<String, Customer> record : records)
    {
    System.out.println("current customer Id: " +
```

```
    record.value().getId() + " and
      current customer name: " + record.value().getName());
    }
  }
```

Again, it is important to note that implementing a custom serializer and deserializer is not recommended. It tightly couples producers and consumers and is fragile and error-prone. A better solution would be to use a standard message format such as JSON, Thrift, Protobuf, or Avro. We'll now see how to use Avro deserializers with the Kafka consumer. For background on Apache Avro, its schemas, and schema-compatibility capabilities, refer back to Chapter 3.

Using Avro deserialization with Kafka consumer

Let's assume we are using the implementation of the Customer class in Avro that was shown in Chapter 3. In order to consume those objects from Kafka, you want to implement a consuming application similar to this:

```
Properties props = new Properties();
props.put("bootstrap.servers", "broker1:9092,broker2:9092");
props.put("group.id", "CountryCounter");
props.put("key.serializer",
    "org.apache.kafka.common.serialization.StringDeserializer");
props.put("value.serializer",
    "io.confluent.kafka.serializers.KafkaAvroDeserializer"); ❶
props.put("schema.registry.url", schemaUrl); ❷
String topic = "customerContacts"

KafkaConsumer consumer = new
    KafkaConsumer(createConsumerConfig(brokers, groupId, url));
consumer.subscribe(Collections.singletonList(topic));

System.out.println("Reading topic:" + topic);

while (true) {
    ConsumerRecords<String, Customer> records =
      consumer.poll(1000); ❸

    for (ConsumerRecord<String, Customer> record: records) {
        System.out.println("Current customer name is: " +
          record.value().getName()); ❹
    }
    consumer.commitSync();
}
```

❶ We use KafkaAvroDeserializer to deserialize the Avro messages.

❷ schema.registry.url is a new parameter. This simply points to where we store the schemas. This way the consumer can use the schema that was registered by the producer to deserialize the message.

❸ We specify the generated class, `Customer`, as the type for the record value.

❹ `record.value()` is a `Customer` instance and we can use it accordingly.

Standalone Consumer: Why and How to Use a Consumer Without a Group

So far, we have discussed consumer groups, which are where partitions are assigned automatically to consumers and are rebalanced automatically when consumers are added or removed from the group. Typically, this behavior is just what you want, but in some cases you want something much simpler. Sometimes you know you have a single consumer that always needs to read data from all the partitions in a topic, or from a specific partition in a topic. In this case, there is no reason for groups or rebalances—just assign the consumer-specific topic and/or partitions, consume messages, and commit offsets on occasion.

When you know exactly which partitions the consumer should read, you don't *subscribe* to a topic—instead, you *assign* yourself a few partitions. A consumer can either subscribe to topics (and be part of a consumer group), or assign itself partitions, but not both at the same time.

Here is an example of how a consumer can assign itself all partitions of a specific topic and consume from them:

```
List<PartitionInfo> partitionInfos = null;
partitionInfos = consumer.partitionsFor("topic"); ❶

if (partitionInfos != null) {
    for (PartitionInfo partition : partitionInfos)
        partitions.add(new TopicPartition(partition.topic(),
            partition.partition()));
    consumer.assign(partitions); ❷

    while (true) {
        ConsumerRecords<String, String> records =
          consumer.poll(1000);

        for (ConsumerRecord<String, String> record: records) {
            System.out.printf("topic = %s, partition = %s, offset = %d,
                customer = %s, country = %s\n",
                record.topic(), record.partition(), record.offset(),
                record.key(), record.value());
        }
        consumer.commitSync();
    }
}
```

❶ We start by asking the cluster for the partitions available in the topic. If you only plan on consuming a specific partition, you can skip this part.

❷ Once we know which partitions we want, we call `assign()` with the list.

Other than the lack of rebalances and the need to manually find the partitions, everything else is business as usual. Keep in mind that if someone adds new partitions to the topic, the consumer will not be notified. You will need to handle this by checking `consumer.partitionsFor()` periodically or simply by bouncing the application whenever partitions are added.

Older Consumer APIs

In this chapter we discussed the Java `KafkaConsumer` client that is part of the `org.apache.kafka.clients` package. At the time of writing, Apache Kafka still has two older clients written in Scala that are part of the `kafka.consumer` package, which is part of the core Kafka module. These consumers are called `SimpleConsumer` (which is not very simple). `SimpleConsumer` is a thin wrapper around the Kafka APIs that allows you to consume from specific partitions and offsets. The other old API is called high-level consumer or `ZookeeperConsumerConnector`. The high-level consumer is somewhat similar to the current consumer in that it has consumer groups and it rebalances partitions, but it uses Zookeeper to manage consumer groups and does not give you the same control over commits and rebalances as we have now.

Because the current consumer supports both behaviors and provides much more reliability and control to the developer, we will not discuss the older APIs. If you are interested in using them, please think twice and then refer to Apache Kafka documentation to learn more.

Summary

We started this chapter with an in-depth explanation of Kafka's consumer groups and the way they allow multiple consumers to share the work of reading events from topics. We followed the theoretical discussion with a practical example of a consumer subscribing to a topic and continuously reading events. We then looked into the most important consumer configuration parameters and how they affect consumer behavior. We dedicated a large part of the chapter to discussing offsets and how consumers keep track of them. Understanding how consumers commit offsets is critical when writing reliable consumers, so we took time to explain the different ways this can be done. We then discussed additional parts of the consumer APIs, handling rebalances and closing the consumer.

We concluded by discussing the deserializers used by consumers to turn bytes stored in Kafka into Java objects that the applications can process. We discussed Avro deserializers in some detail, even though they are just one type of deserializer you can use, because these are most commonly used with Kafka.

Now that you know how to produce and consume events with Kafka, the next chapter explains some of the internals of a Kafka implementation.

## CHAPTER 5

Kafka Internals

It is not strictly necessary to understand Kafka's internals in order to run Kafka in production or write applications that use it. However, knowing how Kafka works does provide context when troubleshooting or trying to understand why Kafka behaves the way it does. Since covering every single implementation detail and design decision is beyond the scope of this book, in this chapter we focus on three topics that are especially relevant to Kafka practitioners:

- How Kafka replication works
- How Kafka handles requests from producers and consumers
- How Kafka handles storage such as file format and indexes

Understanding these topics in-depth will be especially useful when tuning Kafka—understanding the mechanisms that the tuning knobs control goes a long way toward using them with precise intent rather than fiddling with them randomly.

Cluster Membership

Kafka uses Apache Zookeeper to maintain the list of brokers that are currently members of a cluster. Every broker has a unique identifier that is either set in the broker configuration file or automatically generated. Every time a broker process starts, it registers itself with its ID in Zookeeper by creating an *ephemeral node* (*http://bit.ly/ 2s3MYHh*). Different Kafka components subscribe to the /brokers/ids path in Zookeeper where brokers are registered so they get notified when brokers are added or removed.

If you try to start another broker with the same ID, you will get an error—the new broker will try to register, but fail because we already have a Zookeeper node for the same broker ID.

When a broker loses connectivity to Zookeeper (usually as a result of the broker stopping, but this can also happen as a result of network partition or a long garbage-collection pause), the ephemeral node that the broker created when starting will be automatically removed from Zookeeper. Kafka components that are watching the list of brokers will be notified that the broker is gone.

Even though the node representing the broker is gone when the broker is stopped, the broker ID still exists in other data structures. For example, the list of replicas of each topic (see "Replication" on page 97) contains the broker IDs for the replica. This way, if you completely lose a broker and start a brand new broker with the ID of the old one, it will immediately join the cluster in place of the missing broker with the same partitions and topics assigned to it.

The Controller

The controller is one of the Kafka brokers that, in addition to the usual broker functionality, is responsible for electing partition leaders (we'll discuss partition leaders and what they do in the next section). The first broker that starts in the cluster becomes the controller by creating an ephemeral node in ZooKeeper called /control ler. When other brokers start, they also try to create this node, but receive a "node already exists" exception, which causes them to "realize" that the controller node already exists and that the cluster already has a controller. The brokers create a *Zookeeper watch* (*http://bit.ly/2sKoTTN*) on the controller node so they get notified of changes to this node. This way, we guarantee that the cluster will only have one controller at a time.

When the controller broker is stopped or loses connectivity to Zookeeper, the ephemeral node will disappear. Other brokers in the cluster will be notified through the Zookeeper watch that the controller is gone and will attempt to create the controller node in Zookeeper themselves. The first node to create the new controller in Zookeeper is the new controller, while the other nodes will receive a "node already exists" exception and re-create the watch on the new controller node. Each time a controller is elected, it receives a new, higher *controller epoch* number through a Zookeeper conditional increment operation. The brokers know the current controller epoch and if they receive a message from a controller with an older number, they know to ignore it.

When the controller notices that a broker left the cluster (by watching the relevant Zookeeper path), it knows that all the partitions that had a leader on that broker will need a new leader. It goes over all the partitions that need a new leader, determines who the new leader should be (simply the next replica in the replica list of that partition), and sends a request to all the brokers that contain either the new leaders or the existing followers for those partitions. The request contains information on the new leader and the followers for the partitions. Each new leader knows that it needs to start serving producer and consumer requests from clients while the followers know that they need to start replicating messages from the new leader.

When the controller notices that a broker joined the cluster, it uses the broker ID to check if there are replicas that exist on this broker. If there are, the controller notifies both new and existing brokers of the change, and the replicas on the new broker start replicating messages from the existing leaders.

To summarize, Kafka uses Zookeeper's ephemeral node feature to elect a controller and to notify the controller when nodes join and leave the cluster. The controller is responsible for electing leaders among the partitions and replicas whenever it notices nodes join and leave the cluster. The controller uses the epoch number to prevent a "split brain" scenario where two nodes believe each is the current controller.

Replication

Replication is at the heart of Kafka's architecture. The very first sentence in Kafka's documentation describes it as "a distributed, partitioned, replicated commit log service." Replication is critical because it is the way Kafka guarantees availability and durability when individual nodes inevitably fail.

As we've already discussed, data in Kafka is organized by topics. Each topic is partitioned, and each partition can have multiple replicas. Those replicas are stored on brokers, and each broker typically stores hundreds or even thousands of replicas belonging to different topics and partitions.

There are two types of replicas:

Leader replica

Each partition has a single replica designated as the leader. All produce and consume requests go through the leader, in order to guarantee consistency.

Follower replica

All replicas for a partition that are not leaders are called followers. Followers don't serve client requests; their only job is to replicate messages from the leader and stay up-to-date with the most recent messages the leader has. In the event that a leader replica for a partition crashes, one of the follower replicas will be promoted to become the new leader for the partition.

Another task the leader is responsible for is knowing which of the follower replicas is up-to-date with the leader. Followers attempt to stay up-to-date by replicating all the messages from the leader as the messages arrive, but they can fail to stay in sync for various reasons, such as when network congestion slows down replication or when a broker crashes and all replicas on that broker start falling behind until we start the broker and they can start replicating again.

In order to stay in sync with the leader, the replicas send the leader `Fetch` requests, the exact same type of requests that consumers send in order to consume messages. In response to those requests, the leader sends the messages to the replicas. Those `Fetch` requests contain the offset of the message that the replica wants to receive next, and will always be in order.

A replica will request message 1, then message 2, and then message 3, and it will not request message 4 before it gets all the previous messages. This means that the leader can know that a replica got all messages up to message 3 when the replica requests message 4. By looking at the last offset requested by each replica, the leader can tell how far behind each replica is. If a replica hasn't requested a message in more than 10 seconds or if it has requested messages but hasn't caught up to the most recent message in more than 10 seconds, the replica is considered *out of sync*. If a replica fails to keep up with the leader, it can no longer become the new leader in the event of failure —after all, it does not contain all the messages.

The inverse of this, replicas that are consistently asking for the latest messages, is called *in-sync replicas*. Only in-sync replicas are eligible to be elected as partition leaders in case the existing leader fails.

The amount of time a follower can be inactive or behind before it is considered out of sync is controlled by the `replica.lag.time.max.ms` configuration parameter. This allowed lag has implications on client behavior and data retention during leader election. We will discuss this in depth in Chapter 6, when we discuss reliability guarantees.

In addition to the current leader, each partition has a *preferred leader*—the replica that was the leader when the topic was originally created. It is preferred because when partitions are first created, the leaders are balanced between brokers (we explain the algorithm for distributing replicas and leaders among brokers later in the chapter). As a result, we expect that when the preferred leader is indeed the leader for all partitions in the cluster, load will be evenly balanced between brokers. By default, Kafka is configured with `auto.leader.rebalance.enable=true`, which will check if the preferred leader replica is not the current leader but is in-sync and trigger leader election to make the preferred leader the current leader.

Finding the Preferred Leaders

The best way to identify the current preferred leader is by looking at the list of replicas for a partition (You can see details of partitions and replicas in the output of the `kafka-topics.sh` tool. We'll discuss this and other admin tools in Chapter 10.) The first replica in the list is always the preferred leader. This is true no matter who is the current leader and even if the replicas were reassigned to different brokers using the replica reassignment tool. In fact, if you manually reassign replicas, it is important to remember that the replica you specify first will be the preferred replica, so make sure you spread those around different brokers to avoid overloading some brokers with leaders while other brokers are not handling their fair share of the work.

Request Processing

Most of what a Kafka broker does is process requests sent to the partition leaders from clients, partition replicas, and the controller. Kafka has a binary protocol (over TCP) that specifies the format of the requests and how brokers respond to them—both when the request is processed successfully or when the broker encounters errors while processing the request. Clients always initiate connections and send requests, and the broker processes the requests and responds to them. All requests sent to the broker from a specific client will be processed in the order in which they were received—this guarantee is what allows Kafka to behave as a message queue and provide ordering guarantees on the messages it stores.

All requests have a standard header that includes:

- Request type (also called API key)
- Request version (so the brokers can handle clients of different versions and respond accordingly)
- Correlation ID: a number that uniquely identifies the request and also appears in the response and in the error logs (the ID is used for troubleshooting)
- Client ID: used to identify the application that sent the request

We will not describe the protocol here because it is described in significant detail in the Kafka documentation (*http://kafka.apache.org/protocol.html*). However, it is helpful to take a look at how requests are processed by the broker—later, when we discuss how to monitor Kafka and the various configuration options, you will have context about which queues and threads the metrics and configuration parameters refer to.

For each port the broker listens on, the broker runs an *acceptor* thread that creates a connection and hands it over to a *processor* thread for handling. The number of processor threads (also called *network threads*) is configurable. The network threads are responsible for taking requests from client connections, placing them in a *request queue*, and picking up responses from a *response queue* and sending them back to clients. See Figure 5-1 for a visual of this process.

Once requests are placed on the request queue, *IO threads* are responsible for picking them up and processing them. The most common types of requests are:

Produce requests
    Sent by producers and contain messages the clients write to Kafka brokers.

Fetch requests
    Sent by consumers and follower replicas when they read messages from Kafka brokers.

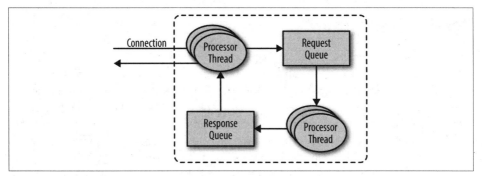

Figure 5-1. Request processing inside Apache Kafka

Both produce requests and fetch requests have to be sent to the leader replica of a partition. If a broker receives a produce request for a specific partition and the leader for this partition is on a different broker, the client that sent the produce request will get an error response of "Not a Leader for Partition." The same error will occur if a fetch request for a specific partition arrives at a broker that does not have the leader for that partition. Kafka's clients are responsible for sending produce and fetch requests to the broker that contains the leader for the relevant partition for the request.

How do the clients know where to send the requests? Kafka clients use another request type called a *metadata request*, which includes a list of topics the client is interested in. The server response specifies which partitions exist in the topics, the replicas for each partition, and which replica is the leader. Metadata requests can be sent to any broker because all brokers have a metadata cache that contains this information.

Clients typically cache this information and use it to direct produce and fetch requests to the correct broker for each partition. They also need to occasionally refresh this information (refresh intervals are controlled by the `meta data.max.age.ms` configuration parameter) by sending another metadata request so they know if the topic metadata changed—for example, if a new broker was added or some replicas were moved to a new broker (Figure 5-2). In addition, if a client receives the "Not a Leader" error to one of its requests, it will refresh its metadata before trying to send the request again, since the error indicates that the client is using outdated information and is sending requests to the wrong broker.

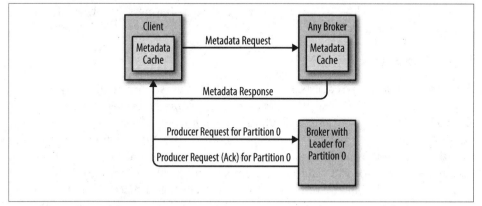

Figure 5-2. Client routing requests

Produce Requests

As we saw in Chapter 3, a configuration parameter called `acks` is the number of brokers who need to acknowledge receiving the message before it is considered a successful write. Producers can be configured to consider messages as "written successfully" when the message was accepted by just the leader (`acks=1`), all in-sync replicas (`acks=all`), or the moment the message was sent without waiting for the broker to accept it at all (`acks=0`).

When the broker that contains the lead replica for a partition receives a produce request for this partition, it will start by running a few validations:

- Does the user sending the data have write privileges on the topic?
- Is the number of `acks` specified in the request valid (only 0, 1, and "all" are allowed)?
- If `acks` is set to `all`, are there enough in-sync replicas for safely writing the message? (Brokers can be configured to refuse new messages if the number of in-sync replicas falls below a configurable number; we will discuss this in more detail in Chapter 6, when we discuss Kafka's durability and reliability guarantees.)

Then it will write the new messages to local disk. On Linux, the messages are written to the filesystem cache and there is no guarantee about when they will be written to disk. Kafka does not wait for the data to get persisted to disk—it relies on replication for message durability.

Once the message is written to the leader of the partition, the broker examines the `acks` configuration—if `acks` is set to 0 or 1, the broker will respond immediately; if `acks` is set to `all`, the request will be stored in a buffer called *purgatory* until the leader observes that the follower replicas replicated the message, at which point a response is sent to the client.

Fetch Requests

Brokers process fetch requests in a way that is very similar to the way produce requests are handled. The client sends a request, asking the broker to send messages from a list of topics, partitions, and offsets—something like "Please send me messages starting at offset 53 in partition 0 of topic Test and messages starting at offset 64 in partition 3 of topic Test." Clients also specify a limit to how much data the broker can return for each partition. The limit is important because clients need to allocate memory that will hold the response sent back from the broker. Without this limit, brokers could send back replies large enough to cause clients to run out of memory.

As we've discussed earlier, the request has to arrive to the leaders of the partitions specified in the request and the client will make the necessary metadata requests to make sure it is routing the fetch requests correctly. When the leader receives the request, it first checks if the request is valid—does this offset even exist for this particular partition? If the client is asking for a message that is so old that it got deleted from the partition or an offset that does not exist yet, the broker will respond with an error.

If the offset exists, the broker will read messages from the partition, up to the limit set by the client in the request, and send the messages to the client. Kafka famously uses a `zero-copy` method to send the messages to the clients—this means that Kafka sends messages from the file (or more likely, the Linux filesystem cache) directly to the network channel without any intermediate buffers. This is different than most databases where data is stored in a local cache before being sent to clients. This technique removes the overhead of copying bytes and managing buffers in memory, and results in much improved performance.

In addition to setting an upper boundary on the amount of data the broker can return, clients can also set a lower boundary on the amount of data returned. Setting the lower boundary to 10K, for example, is the client's way of telling the broker "Only return results once you have at least 10K bytes to send me." This is a great way to reduce CPU and network utilization when clients are reading from topics that are not seeing much traffic. Instead of the clients sending requests to the brokers every few milliseconds asking for data and getting very few or no messages in return, the clients send a request, the broker waits until there is a decent amount of data and returns the data, and only then will the client ask for more (Figure 5-3). The same amount of data is read overall but with much less back and forth and therefore less overhead.

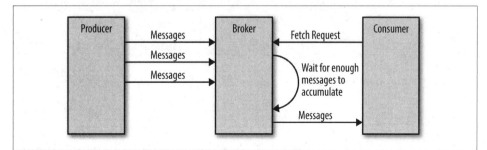

Figure 5-3. Broker delaying response until enough data accumulated

Of course, we wouldn't want clients to wait forever for the broker to have enough data. After a while, it makes sense to just take the data that exists and process that instead of waiting for more. Therefore, clients can also define a timeout to tell the broker "If you didn't satisfy the minimum amount of data to send within x milliseconds, just send what you got."

It is also interesting to note that not all the data that exists on the leader of the partition is available for clients to read. Most clients can only read messages that were written to all in-sync replicas (follower replicas, even though they are consumers, are exempt from this—otherwise replication would not work). We already discussed that the leader of the partition knows which messages were replicated to which replica, and until a message was written to all in-sync replicas, it will not be sent to consumers—attempts to fetch those messages will result in an empty response rather than an error.

The reason for this behavior is that messages not replicated to enough replicas yet are considered "unsafe"—if the leader crashes and another replica takes its place, these messages will no longer exist in Kafka. If we allowed clients to read messages that only exist on the leader, we could see inconsistent behavior. For example, if a consumer reads a message and the leader crashed and no other broker contained this message, the message is gone. No other consumer will be able to read this message, which can cause inconsistency with the consumer who did read it. Instead, we wait until all the in-sync replicas get the message and only then allow consumers to read it (Figure 5-4). This behavior also means that if replication between brokers is slow for some reason, it will take longer for new messages to arrive to consumers (since we wait for the messages to replicate first). This delay is limited to `replica.lag.time.max.ms`—the amount of time a replica can be delayed in replicating new messages while still being considered in-sync.

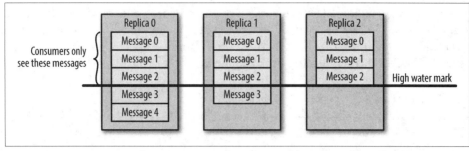

Figure 5-4. Consumers only see messages that were replicated to in-sync replicas

Other Requests

We just discussed the most common types of requests used by Kafka clients: `Meta data`, `Produce`, and `Fetch`. It is important to remember that we are talking about a generic binary protocol used by clients over the network. Whereas Kafka includes Java clients that were implemented and maintained by contributors to the Apache Kafka project, there are also clients in other languages such as C, Python, Go, and many others. You can see the full list on the Apache Kafka website (*http://bit.ly/ 2sKvTjx*) and they all communicate with Kafka brokers using this protocol.

In addition, the same protocol is used to communicate between the Kafka brokers themselves. Those requests are internal and should not be used by clients. For example, when the controller announces that a partition has a new leader, it sends a `Leader AndIsr` request to the new leader (so it will know to start accepting client requests) and to the followers (so they will know to follow the new leader).

The Kafka protocol currently handles 20 different request types, and more will be added. The protocol is ever-evolving—as we add more client capabilities, we need to grow the protocol to match. For example, in the past, Kafka Consumers used Apache Zookeeper to keep track of the offsets they receive from Kafka. So when a consumer is started, it can check Zookeeper for the last offset that was read from its partitions and know where to start processing. For various reasons, we decided to stop using Zookeeper for this, and instead store those offsets in a special Kafka topic. In order to do this, we had to add several requests to the protocol: `OffsetCommitRequest`, `Offset FetchRequest`, and `ListOffsetsRequest`. Now when an application calls the `commitOffset()` client API, the client no longer writes to Zookeeper; instead, it sends `OffsetCommitRequest` to Kafka.

Topic creation is still done by command-line tools that update the list of topics in Zookeeper directly, and brokers watch the topic list in Zookeeper to know when new topics are added. We are working on improving Kafka and adding a `Create TopicRequest` that will allow all clients (even in languages that don't have a Zookeeper library) to create topics by asking Kafka brokers directly.

In addition to evolving the protocol by adding new request types, we sometimes choose to modify existing requests to add some capabilities. For example, between Kafka 0.9.0 and Kafka 0.10.0, we decided to let clients know who the current controller is by adding the information to the `Metadata` response. As a result, we added a new version to the `Metadata` request and response. Now, 0.9.0 clients send `Metadata` requests of version 0 (because version 1 did not exist in 0.9.0 clients) and the brokers, whether they are 0.9.0 or 0.10.0 know to respond with a version 0 response, which does not have the controller information. This is fine, because 0.9.0 clients don't expect the controller information and wouldn't know how to parse it anyway. If you have the 0.10.0 client, it will send a version 1 `Metadata` request and 0.10.0 brokers will respond with a version 1 response that contains the controller information, which the 0.10.0 clients can use. If a 0.10.0 client sends a version 1 `Metadata` request to a 0.9.0 broker, the broker will not know how to handle the newer version of the request and will respond with an error. This is the reason we recommend upgrading the brokers before upgrading any of the clients—new brokers know how to handle old requests, but not vice versa.

In release 0.10.0 we added `ApiVersionRequest`, which allows clients to ask the broker which versions of each request is supported and to use the correct version accordingly. Clients that use this new capability correctly will be able to talk to older brokers by using a version of the protocol that is supported by the broker they are connecting to.

Physical Storage

The basic storage unit of Kafka is a partition replica. Partitions cannot be split between multiple brokers and not even between multiple disks on the same broker. So the size of a partition is limited by the space available on a single mount point. (A mount point will consist of either a single disk, if JBOD configuration is used, or multiple disks, if RAID is configured. See Chapter 2.)

When configuring Kafka, the administrator defines a list of directories in which the partitions will be stored—this is the `log.dirs` parameter (not to be confused with the location in which Kafka stores its error log, which is configured in the *log4j.properties* file). The usual configuration includes a directory for each mount point that Kafka will use.

Let's look at how Kafka uses the available directories to store data. First, we want to look at how data is allocated to the brokers in the cluster and the directories in the broker. Then we will look at how the broker manages the files—especially how the retention guarantees are handled. We will then dive inside the files and look at the file and index formats. Lastly we will look at Log Compaction, an advanced feature that allows turning Kafka into a long-term data store, and describe how it works.

Partition Allocation

When you create a topic, Kafka first decides how to allocate the partitions between brokers. Suppose you have 6 brokers and you decide to create a topic with 10 partitions and a replication factor of 3. Kafka now has 30 partition replicas to allocate to 6 brokers. When doing the allocations, the goals are:

- To spread replicas evenly among brokers—in our example, to make sure we allocate 5 replicas per broker.

- To make sure that for each partition, each replica is on a different broker. If partition 0 has the leader on broker 2, we can place the followers on brokers 3 and 4, but not on 2 and not both on 3.

- If the brokers have rack information (available in Kafka release 0.10.0 and higher), then assign the replicas for each partition to different racks if possible. This ensures that an event that causes downtime for an entire rack does not cause complete unavailability for partitions.

To do this, we start with a random broker (let's say, 4) and start assigning partitions to each broker in round-robin manner to determine the location for the leaders. So partition leader 0 will be on broker 4, partition 1 leader will be on broker 5, partition 2 will be on broker 0 (because we only have 6 brokers), and so on. Then, for each partition, we place the replicas at increasing offsets from the leader. If the leader for partition 0 is on broker 4, the first follower will be on broker 5 and the second on broker 0. The leader for partition 1 is on broker 5, so the first replica is on broker 0 and the second on broker 1.

When rack awareness is taken into account, instead of picking brokers in numerical order, we prepare a rack-alternating broker list. Suppose that we know that brokers 0, 1, and 2 are on the same rack, and brokers 3, 4, and 5 are on a separate rack. Instead of picking brokers in the order of 0 to 5, we order them as 0, 3, 1, 4, 2, 5—each broker is followed by a broker from a different rack (Figure 5-5). In this case, if the leader for partition 0 is on broker 4, the first replica will be on broker 2, which is on a completely different rack. This is great, because if the first rack goes offline, we know that we still have a surviving replica and therefore the partition is still available. This will be true for all our replicas, so we have guaranteed availability in the case of rack failure.

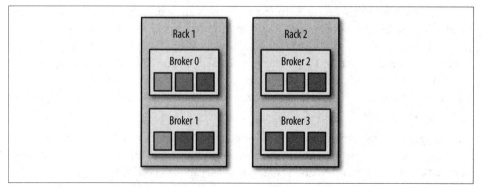

Figure 5-5. Partitions and replicas assigned to brokers on different racks

Once we choose the correct brokers for each partition and replica, it is time to decide which directory to use for the new partitions. We do this independently for each partition, and the rule is very simple: we count the number of partitions on each directory and add the new partition to the directory with the fewest partitions. This means that if you add a new disk, all the new partitions will be created on that disk. This is because, until things balance out, the new disk will always have the fewest partitions.

Mind the Disk Space

Note that the allocation of partitions to brokers does not take available space or existing load into account, and that allocation of partitions to disks takes the number of partitions into account, but not the size of the partitions. This means that if some brokers have more disk space than others (perhaps because the cluster is a mix of older and newer servers), some partitions are abnormally large, or you have disks of different sizes on the same broker, you need to be careful with the partition allocation.

File Management

Retention is an important concept in Kafka—Kafka does not keep data forever, nor does it wait for all consumers to read a message before deleting it. Instead, the Kafka administrator configures a retention period for each topic—either the amount of time to store messages before deleting them or how much data to store before older messages are purged.

Because finding the messages that need purging in a large file and then deleting a portion of the file is both time-consuming and error-prone, we instead split each partition into *segments*. By default, each segment contains either 1 GB of data or a week of data, whichever is smaller. As a Kafka broker is writing to a partition, if the segment limit is reached, we close the file and start a new one.

The segment we are currently writing to is called an *active segment*. The active segment is never deleted, so if you set log retention to only store a day of data but each segment contains five days of data, you will really keep data for five days because we can't delete the data before the segment is closed. If you choose to store data for a week and roll a new segment every day, you will see that every day we will roll a new segment while deleting the oldest segment—so most of the time the partition will have seven segments.

As you learned in Chapter 2, a Kafka broker will keep an open file handle to every segment in every partition—even inactive segments. This leads to an usually high number of open file handles, and the OS must be tuned accordingly.

File Format

Each segment is stored in a single data file. Inside the file, we store Kafka messages and their offsets. The format of the data on the disk is identical to the format of the messages that we send from the producer to the broker and later from the broker to the consumers. Using the same message format on disk and over the wire is what allows Kafka to use zero-copy optimization when sending messages to consumers and also avoid decompressing and recompressing messages that the producer already compressed.

Each message contains—in addition to its key, value, and offset—things like the message size, checksum code that allows us to detect corruption, magic byte that indicates the version of the message format, compression codec (Snappy, GZip, or LZ4), and a timestamp (added in release 0.10.0). The timestamp is given either by the producer when the message was sent or by the broker when the message arrived—depending on configuration.

If the producer is sending compressed messages, all the messages in a single producer batch are compressed together and sent as the "value" of a "wrapper message" (Figure 5-6). So the broker receives a single message, which it sends to the consumer. But when the consumer decompresses the message value, it will see all the messages that were contained in the batch, with their own timestamps and offsets.

This means that if you are using compression on the producer (recommended!), sending larger batches means better compression both over the network and on the broker disks. This also means that if we decide to change the message format that consumers use (e.g., add a timestamp to the message), both the wire protocol and the on-disk format need to change, and Kafka brokers need to know how to handle cases in which files contain messages of two formats due to upgrades.

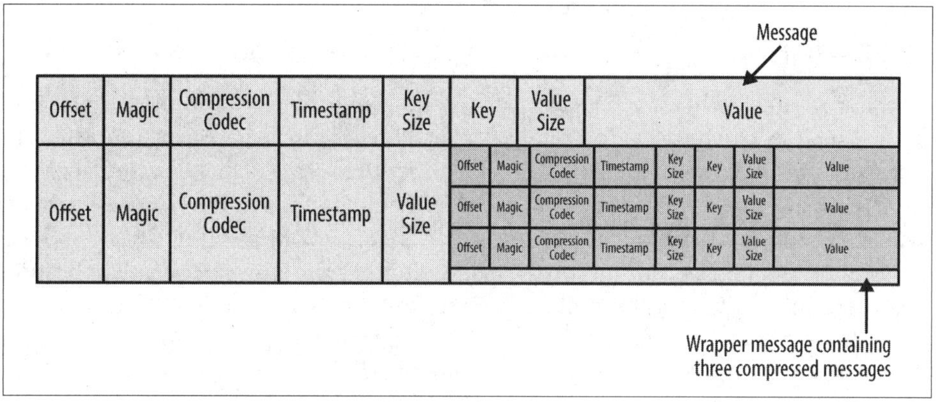

Message

Offset	Magic	Compression Codec	Timestamp	Key Size	Key	Value Size	Value

Offset	Magic	Compression Codec	Timestamp	Value Size	Offset	Magic	Compression Codec	Timestamp	Key Size	Key	Value Size	Value
					Offset	Magic	Compression Codec	Timestamp	Key Size	Key	Value Size	Value
					Offset	Magic	Compression Codec	Timestamp	Key Size	Key	Value Size	Value

Wrapper message containing three compressed messages

Figure 5-6. A normal message and a wrapper message

Kafka brokers ship with the DumpLogSegment tool, which allows you to look at a partition segment in the filesystem and examine its contents. It will show you the offset, checksum, magic byte, size, and compression codec for each message. You can run the tool using:

```
bin/kafka-run-class.sh kafka.tools.DumpLogSegments
```

If you choose the --deep-iteration parameter, it will show you information about messages compressed inside the wrapper messages.

Indexes

Kafka allows consumers to start fetching messages from any available offset. This means that if a consumer asks for 1 MB messages starting at offset 100, the broker must be able to quickly locate the message for offset 100 (which can be in any of the segments for the partition) and start reading the messages from that offset on. In order to help brokers quickly locate the message for a given offset, Kafka maintains an index for each partition. The index maps offsets to segment files and positions within the file.

Indexes are also broken into segments, so we can delete old index entries when the messages are purged. Kafka does not attempt to maintain checksums of the index. If the index becomes corrupted, it will get regenerated from the matching log segment simply by rereading the messages and recording the offsets and locations. It is also completely safe for an administrator to delete index segments if needed—they will be regenerated automatically.

Compaction

Normally, Kafka will store messages for a set amount of time and purge messages older than the retention period. However, imagine a case where you use Kafka to store shipping addresses for your customers. In that case, it makes more sense to store the last address for each customer rather than data for just the last week or year. This way, you don't have to worry about old addresses and you still retain the address for customers who haven't moved in a while. Another use case can be an application that uses Kafka to store its current state. Every time the state changes, the application writes the new state into Kafka. When recovering from a crash, the application reads those messages from Kafka to recover its latest state. In this case, it only cares about the latest state before the crash, not all the changes that occurred while it was running.

Kafka supports such use cases by allowing the retention policy on a topic to be *delete*, which deletes events older than retention time, to *compact*, which only stores the most recent value for each key in the topic. Obviously, setting the policy to compact only makes sense on topics for which applications produce events that contain both a key and a value. If the topic contains *null* keys, compaction will fail.

How Compaction Works

Each log is viewed as split into two portions (see Figure 5-7):

Clean
> Messages that have been compacted before. This section contains only one value for each key, which is the latest value at the time of the pervious compaction

Dirty
> Messages that were written after the last compaction.

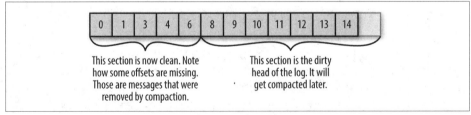

Figure 5-7. Partition with clean and dirty portions

If compaction is enabled when Kafka starts (using the awkwardly named `log.cleaner.enabled` configuration), each broker will start a compaction manager thread and a number of compaction threads. These are responsible for performing the compaction tasks. Each of these threads chooses the partition with the highest ratio of dirty messages to total partition size and cleans this partition.

To compact a partition, the cleaner thread reads the dirty section of the partition and creates an in-memory map. Each map entry is comprised of a 16-byte hash of a message key and the 8-byte offset of the previous message that had this same key. This means each map entry only uses 24 bytes. If we look at a 1 GB segment and assume that each message in the segment takes up 1 KB, the segment will contain 1 million such messages and we will only need a 24 MB map to compact the segment (we may need a lot less—if the keys repeat themselves, we will reuse the same hash entries often and use less memory). This is quite efficient!

When configuring Kafka, the administrator configures how much memory compaction threads can use for this offset map. Even though each thread has its own map, the configuration is for total memory across all threads. If you configured 1 GB for the compaction offset map and you have five cleaner threads, each thread will get 200 MB for its own offset map. Kafka doesn't require the entire dirty section of the partition to fit into the size allocated for this map, but at least one full segment has to fit. If it doesn't, Kafka will log an error and the administrator will need to either allocate more memory for the offset maps or use fewer cleaner threads. If only a few segments fit, Kafka will start by compacting the oldest segments that fit into the map. The rest will remain dirty and wait for the next compaction.

Once the cleaner thread builds the offset map, it will start reading off the clean segments, starting with the oldest, and check their contents against the offset map. For each message it checks, if the key of the message exists in the offset map. If the key does not exist in the map, the value of the message we've just read is still the latest and we copy over the message to a replacement segment. If the key does exist in the map, we omit the message because there is a message with an identical key but newer value later in the partition. Once we've copied over all the messages that still contain the latest value for their key, we swap the replacement segment for the original and move on to the next segment. At the end of the process, we are left with one message per key—the one with the latest value. See Figure 5-8.

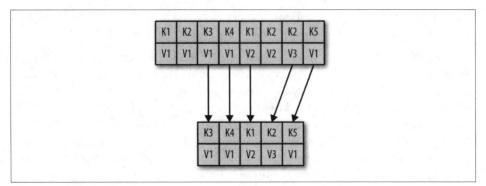

Figure 5-8. Partition segment before and after compaction

Deleted Events

If we always keep the latest message for each key, what do we do when we really want to delete all messages for a specific key, such as if a user left our service and we are legally obligated to remove all traces of that user from our system?

In order to delete a key from the system completely, not even saving the last message, the application must produce a message that contains that key and a null value. When the cleaner thread finds such a message, it will first do a normal compaction and retain only the message with the null value. It will keep this special message (known as a *tombstone*) around for a configurable amount of time. During this time, consumers will be able to see this message and know that the value is deleted. So if a consumer copies data from Kafka to a relational database, it will see the tombstone message and know to delete the user from the database. After this set amount of time, the cleaner thread will remove the tombstone message, and the key will be gone from the partition in Kafka. It is important to give consumers enough time to see the tombstone message, because if our consumer was down for a few hours and missed the tombstone message, it will simply not see the key when consuming and therefore not know that it was deleted from Kafka or to delete it from the database.

When Are Topics Compacted?

In the same way that the `delete` policy never deletes the current active segments, the `compact` policy never compacts the current segment. Messages are eligble for compaction only on inactive segments.

In version 0.10.0 and older, Kafka will start compacting when 50% of the topic contains dirty records. The goal is not to compact too often (since compaction can impact the read/write performance on a topic), but also not leave too many dirty records around (since they consume disk space). Wasting 50% of the disk space used by a topic on dirty records and then compacting them in one go seems like a reasonable trade-off, and it can be tuned by the administrator.

In future versions, we are planning to add a grace period during which we guarantee that messages will remain uncompacted. This will allow applications that need to see every message that was written to the topic enough time to be sure they indeed saw those messages even if they are lagging a bit.

Summary

There is obviously more to Kafka than we could cover in this chapter, but we hope this gave you a taste of the kind of design decisions and optimizations we've made when working on the project and perhaps explained some of the more obscure behaviors and configurations you've run into while using Kafka.

If you are really interested in Kafka internals, there is no substitute for reading the code. The Kafka developer mailing list (*dev@kafka.apache.org*) is a very friendly community and there is always someone willing to answer questions regarding how Kafka really works. And while you are reading the code, perhaps you can fix a bug or two—open source projects always welcome contributions.

## CHAPTER 6

Reliable Data Delivery

Reliable data delivery is one of the attributes of a system that cannot be left as an afterthought. Like performance, it has to be designed into a system from its very first whiteboard diagram. You cannot bolt on reliability after the fact. More so, reliability is a property of a system—not of a single component—so even when we are talking about the reliability guarantees of Apache Kafka, you will need to keep the entire system and its use cases in mind. When it comes to reliability, the systems that integrate with Kafka are as important as Kafka itself. And because reliability is a system concern, it cannot be the responsibility of just one person. Everyone—Kafka administrators, Linux administrators, network and storage administrators, and the application developers—must work together to build a reliable system.

Apache Kafka is very flexible about reliable data delivery. We understand that Kafka has many use cases, from tracking clicks in a website to credit card payments. Some of the use cases require utmost reliability while others prioritize speed and simplicity over reliability. Kafka was written to be configurable enough and its client API flexible enough to allow all kinds of reliability trade-offs.

Because of its flexibility, it is also easy to accidentally shoot yourself in the foot when using Kafka—believing that your system is reliable when in fact it is not. In this chapter, we will start by talking about different kinds of reliability and what they mean in the context of Apache Kafka. Then we will talk about Kafka's replication mechanism and how it contributes to the reliability of the system. We will then discuss Kafka's brokers and topics and how they should be configured for different use cases. Then we will discuss the clients, producer, and consumer, and how they should be used in different reliability scenarios. Last, we will discuss the topic of validating the system reliability, because it is not enough to believe a system is reliable—the assumption must be thoroughly tested.

Reliability Guarantees

When we talk about reliability, we usually talk in terms of *guarantees*, which are the behaviors a system is guaranteed to preserve under different circumstances.

Probably the best known reliability guarantee is ACID, which is the standard reliability guarantee that relational databases universally support. ACID stands for *atomicity*, *consistency*, *isolation*, and *durability*. When a vendor explains that their database is ACID-compliant, it means the database guarantees certain behaviors regarding transaction behavior.

Those guarantees are the reason people trust relational databases with their most critical applications—they know exactly what the system promises and how it will behave in different conditions. They understand the guarantees and can write safe applications by relying on those guarantees.

Understanding the guarantees Kafka provides is critical for those seeking to build reliable applications. This understanding allows the developers of the system to figure out how it will behave under different failure conditions. So, what does Apache Kafka guarantee?

- Kafka provides order guarantee of messages in a partition. If message B was written after message A, using the same producer in the same partition, then Kafka guarantees that the offset of message B will be higher than message A, and that consumers will read message B after message A.

- Produced messages are considered "committed" when they were written to the partition on all its in-sync replicas (but not necessarily flushed to disk). Producers can choose to receive acknowledgments of sent messages when the message was fully committed, when it was written to the leader, or when it was sent over the network.

- Messages that are committed will not be lost as long as at least one replica remains alive.

- Consumers can only read messages that are committed.

These basic guarantees can be used while building a reliable system, but in themselves, don't make the system fully reliable. There are trade-offs involved in building a reliable system, and Kafka was built to allow administrators and developers to decide how much reliability they need by providing configuration parameters that allow controlling these trade-offs. The trade-offs usually involve how important it is to reliably and consistently store messages versus other important considerations such as availability, high throughput, low latency, and hardware costs. We next review Kafka's replication mechanism, introduce terminology, and discuss how reliability is built into Kafka. After that, we go over the configuration parameters we just mentioned.

Replication

Kafka's replication mechanism, with its multiple replicas per partition, is at the core of all of Kafka's reliability guarantees. Having a message written in multiple replicas is how Kafka provides durability of messages in the event of a crash.

We explained Kafka's replication mechanism in depth in Chapter 5, but let's recap the highlights here.

Each Kafka topic is broken down into *partitions*, which are the basic data building blocks. A partition is stored on a single disk. Kafka guarantees order of events within a partition and a partition can be either online (available) or offline (unavailable). Each partition can have multiple replicas, one of which is a designated leader. All events are produced to and consumed from the leader replica. Other replicas just need to stay in sync with the leader and replicate all the recent events on time. If the leader becomes unavailable, one of the in-sync replicas becomes the new leader.

A replica is considered in-sync if it is the leader for a partition, or if it is a follower that:

- Has an active session with Zookeeper—meaning, it sent a heartbeat to Zookeeper in the last 6 seconds (configurable).
- Fetched messages from the leader in the last 10 seconds (configurable).
- Fetched the most recent messages from the leader in the last 10 seconds. That is, it isn't enough that the follower is still getting messages from the leader; it must have almost no lag.

If a replica loses connection to Zookeeper, stops fetching new messages, or falls behind and can't catch up within 10 seconds, the replica is considered out-of-sync. An out-of-sync replica gets back into sync when it connects to Zookeeper again and catches up to the most recent message written to the leader. This usually happens quickly after a temporary network glitch is healed but can take a while if the broker the replica is stored on was down for a longer period of time.

Out-of-Sync Replicas

Seeing one or more replicas rapidly flip between in-sync and out-of-sync status is a sure sign that something is wrong with the cluster. The cause is often a misconfiguration of Java's garbage collection on a broker. Misconfigured garbage collection can cause the broker to pause for a few seconds, during which it will lose connectivity to Zookeeper. When a broker loses connectivity to Zookeeper, it is considered out-of-sync with the cluster, which causes the flipping behavior.

An in-sync replica that is slightly behind can slow down producers and consumers—since they wait for all the in-sync replicas to get the message before it is *committed*. Once a replica falls out of sync, we no longer wait for it to get messages. It is still behind, but now there is no performance impact. The catch is that with fewer in-sync replicas, the effective replication factor of the partition is lower and therefore there is a higher risk for downtime or data loss.

In the next section, we will look at what this means in practice.

Broker Configuration

There are three configuration parameters in the broker that change Kafka's behavior regarding reliable message storage. Like many broker configuration variables, these can apply at the broker level, controlling configuration for all topics in the system, and at the topic level, controlling behavior for a specific topic.

Being able to control reliability trade-offs at the topic level means that the same Kafka cluster can be used to host reliable and nonreliable topics. For example, at a bank, the administrator will probably want to set very reliable defaults for the entire cluster but make an exception to the topic that stores customer complaints where some data loss is acceptable.

Let's look at these configuration parameters one by one and see how they affect reliability of message storage in Kafka and the trade-offs involved.

Replication Factor

The topic-level configuration is `replication.factor`. At the broker level, you control the `default.replication.factor` for automatically created topics.

Until this point, throughout the book, we always assumed that topics had a replication factor of three, meaning that each partition is replicated three times on three different brokers. This was a reasonable assumption, as this is Kafka's default, but this is also a configuration that users can modify. Even after a topic exists, you can choose to add or remove replicas and thereby modify the replication factor.

A replication factor of N allows you to lose N-1 brokers while still being able to read and write data to the topic reliably. So a higher replication factor leads to higher availability, higher reliability, and fewer disasters. On the flip side, for a replication factor of N, you will need at least N brokers and you will store N copies of the data, meaning you will need N times as much disk space. We are basically trading availability for hardware.

So how do you determine the right number of replicas for a topic? The answer is based on how critical a topic is and how much you are willing to pay for higher availability. It also depends a bit on how paranoid you are.

If you are totally OK with a specific topic being unavailable when a single broker is restarted (which is part of the normal operations of a cluster), then a replication factor of 1 may be enough. Don't forget to make sure your management and users are also OK with this trade-off—you are saving on disks or servers, but losing high availability. A replication factor of 2 means you can lose one broker and still be OK, which sounds like enough, but keep in mind that losing one broker can sometimes (mostly on older versions of Kafka) send the cluster into an unstable state, forcing you to restart another broker—the Kafka Controller. This means that with a replication factor of 2, you may be forced to go into unavailability in order to recover from an operational issue. This can be a tough choice.

For those reasons, we recommend a replication factor of 3 for any topic where availability is an issue. In rare cases, this is considered not safe enough—we've seen banks run critical topics with five replicas, just in case.

Placement of replicas is also very important. By default, Kafka will make sure each replica for a partition is on a separate broker. However, in some cases, this is not safe enough. If all replicas for a partition are placed on brokers that are on the same rack and the top-of-rack switch misbehaves, you will lose availability of the partition regardless of the replication factor. To protect against rack-level misfortune, we recommend placing brokers in multiple racks and using the broker.rack broker configuration parameter to configure the rack name for each broker. If rack names are configured, Kafka will make sure replicas for a partition are spread across multiple racks in order to guarantee even higher availability. In Chapter 5 we provided details on how Kafka places replicas on brokers and racks, if you are interested in understanding more.

Unclean Leader Election

This configuration is only available at the broker (and in practice, cluster-wide) level. The parameter name is unclean.leader.election.enable and by default it is set to true.

As explained earlier, when the leader for a partition is no longer available, one of the in-sync replicas will be chosen as the new leader. This leader election is "clean" in the sense that it guarantees no loss of committed data—by definition, committed data exists on all in-sync replicas.

But what do we do when no in-sync replica exists except for the leader that just became unavailable?

This situation can happen in one of two scenarios:

- The partition had three replicas, and the two followers became unavailable (let's say two brokers crashed). In this situation, as producers continue writing to the leader, all the messages are acknowledged and committed (since the leader is the one and only in-sync replica). Now let's say that the leader becomes unavailable (oops, another broker crash). In this scenario, if one of the out-of-sync followers starts first, we have an out-of-sync replica as the only available replica for the partition.

- The partition had three replicas and, due to network issues, the two followers fell behind so that even though they are up and replicating, they are no longer in sync. The leader keeps accepting messages as the only in-sync replica. Now if the leader becomes unavailable, the two available replicas are no longer in-sync.

In both these scenarios, we need to make a difficult decision:

- If we don't allow the out-of-sync replica to become the new leader, the partition will remain offline until we bring the old leader (and the last in-sync replica) back online. In some cases (e.g., memory chip needs replacement), this can take many hours.

- If we do allow the out-of-sync replica to become the new leader, we are going to lose all messages that were written to the old leader while that replica was out of sync and also cause some inconsistencies in consumers. Why? Imagine that while replicas 0 and 1 were not available, we wrote messages with offsets 100-200 to replica 2 (then the leader). Now replica 3 is unavailable and replica 0 is back online. Replica 0 only has messages 0-100 but not 100-200. If we allow replica 0 to become the new leader, it will allow producers to write new messages and allow consumers to read them. So, now the new leader has completely new messages 100-200. First, let's note that some consumers may have read the old messages 100-200, some consumers got the new 100-200, and some got a mix of both. This can lead to pretty bad consequences when looking at things like downstream reports. In addition, replica 2 will come back online and become a follower of the new leader. At that point, it will delete any messages it got that are ahead of the current leader. Those messages will not be available to any consumer in the future.

In summary, if we allow out-of-sync replicas to become leaders, we risk data loss and data inconsistencies. If we don't allow them to become leaders, we face lower availability as we must wait for the original leader to become available before the partition is back online.

Setting unclean.leader.election.enable to true means we allow out-of-sync replicas to become leaders (knowns as *unclean election*), knowing that we will lose messages when this occurs. If we set it to false, we choose to wait for the original leader to come back online, resulting in lower availability. We typically see unclean leader election disabled (configuration set to false) in systems where data quality and consistency are critical—banking systems are a good example (most banks would rather be unable to process credit card payments for few minutes or even hours than risk processing a payment incorrectly). In systems where availability is more important, such as real-time clickstream analysis, unclean leader election is often enabled.

Minimum In-Sync Replicas

Both the topic and the broker-level configuration are called `min.insync.replicas`.

As we've seen, there are cases where even though we configured a topic to have three replicas, we may be left with a single in-sync replica. If this replica becomes unavailable, we may have to choose between availability and consistency. This is never an easy choice. Note that part of the problem is that, per Kafka reliability guarantees, data is considered committed when it is written to all in-sync replicas, even when `all` means just one replica and the data could be lost if that replica is unavailable.

If you would like to be sure that committed data is written to more than one replica, you need to set the minimum number of in-sync replicas to a higher value. If a topic has three replicas and you set `min.insync.replicas` to 2, then you can only write to a partition in the topic if at least two out of the three replicas are in-sync.

When all three replicas are in-sync, everything proceeds normally. This is also true if one of the replicas becomes unavailable. However, if two out of three replicas are not available, the brokers will no longer accept produce requests. Instead, producers that attempt to send data will receive `NotEnoughReplicasException`. Consumers can continue reading existing data. In effect, with this configuration, a single in-sync replica becomes read-only. This prevents the undesirable situation where data is produced and consumed, only to disappear when unclean election occurs. In order to recover from this read-only situation, we must make one of the two unavailable partitions available again (maybe restart the broker) and wait for it to catch up and get in-sync.

Using Producers in a Reliable System

Even if we configure the brokers in the most reliable configuration possible, the system as a whole can still accidentally lose data if we don't configure the producers to be reliable as well.

Here are two example scenarios to demonstrate this:

- We configured the brokers with three replicas, and unclean leader election is disabled. So we should never lose a single message that was committed to the Kafka cluster. However, we configured the producer to send messages with `acks=1`. We send a message from the producer and it was written to the leader, but not yet to the in-sync replicas. The leader sent back a response to the producer saying "Message was written successfully" and immediately crashes before the data was replicated to the other replicas. The other replicas are still considered in-sync (remember that it takes a while before we declare a replica out of sync) and one of them will become the leader. Since the message was not written to the replicas, it will be lost. But the producing application thinks it was written successfully. The system is consistent because no consumer saw the message (it was never committed because the replicas never got it), but from the producer perspective, a message was lost.

- We configured the brokers with three replicas, and unclean leader election is disabled. We learned from our mistakes and started producing messages with `acks=all`. Suppose that we are attempting to write a message to Kafka, but the leader for the partition we are writing to just crashed and a new one is still getting elected. Kafka will respond with "Leader not Available." At this point, if the producer doesn't handle the error correctly and doesn't retry until the write is successful, the message may be lost. Once again, this is not a broker reliability issue because the broker never got the message; and it is not a consistency issue because the consumers never got the message either. But if producers don't handle errors correctly, they may cause message loss.

So how do we avoid these tragic results? As the examples show, there are two important things that everyone who writes applications that produce to Kafka must pay attention to:

- Use the correct `acks` configuration to match reliability requirements
- Handle errors correctly both in configuration and in code

We discussed producer modes in depth in Chapter 3, but let's go over the important points again.

Send Acknowledgments

Producers can choose between three different acknowledgment modes:

- `acks=0` means that a message is considered to be written successfully to Kafka if the producer managed to send it over the network. You will still get errors if the object you are sending cannot be serialized or if the network card failed, but you won't get any error if the partition is offline or if the entire Kafka cluster decided to take a long vacation. This means that even in the expected case of a clean leader election, your producer will lose messages because it won't know that the leader is unavailable while a new leader is being elected. Running with `acks=0` is very fast (which is why you see a lot of benchmarks with this configuration). You can get amazing throughput and utilize most of your bandwidth, but you are guaranteed to lose some messages if you choose this route.

- `acks=1` means that the leader will send either an acknowledgment or an error the moment it got the message and wrote it to the partition data file (but not necessarily synced to disk). This means that under normal circumstances of leader election, your producer will get `LeaderNotAvailableException` while a leader is getting elected, and if the producer handles this error correctly (see next section), it will retry sending the message and the message will arrive safely to the new leader. You can lose data if the leader crashes and some messages that were successfully written to the leader and acknowledged were not replicated to the followers before the crash.

- `acks=all` means that the leader will wait until all in-sync replicas got the message before sending back an acknowledgment or an error. In conjunction with the `min.insync.replica` configuration on the broker, this lets you control how many replicas get the message before it is acknowledged. This is the safest option —the producer won't stop trying to send the message before it is fully committed. This is also the slowest option—the producer waits for all replicas to get all the messages before it can mark the message batch as "done" and carry on. The effects can be mitigated by using async mode for the producer and by sending larger batches, but this option will typically get you lower throughput.

Configuring Producer Retries

There are two parts to handling errors in the producer: the errors that the producers handle automatically for you and the errors that you as the developer using the producer library must handle.

The producer can handle *retriable* errors that are returned by the broker for you. When the producer sends messages to a broker, the broker can return either a success or an error code. Those error codes belong to two categories—errors that can be resolved after retrying and errors that won't be resolved. For example, if the broker returns the error code `LEADER_NOT_AVAILABLE`, the producer can try sending the error again—maybe a new broker was elected and the second attempt will succeed. This means that `LEADER_NOT_AVAILABLE` is a *retriable* error. On the other hand, if a broker returns an `INVALID_CONFIG` exception, trying the same message again will not change the configuration. This is an example of a *nonretriable error*.

In general, if your goal is to never lose a message, your best approach is to configure the producer to keep trying to send the messages when it encounters a retriable error. Why? Because things like lack of leader or network connectivity issues often take a few seconds to resolve—and if you just let the producer keep trying until it succeeds, you don't need to handle these issues yourself. I frequently get asked "how many times should I configure the producer to retry?" and the answer really depends on what you are planning on doing after the producer throws an exception that it retried

N times and gave up. If your answer is "I'll catch the exception and retry some more," then you definitely need to set the number of retries higher and let the producer continue trying. You want to stop retrying when the answer is either "I'll just drop the message; there's no point to continue retrying" or "I'll just write it somewhere else and handle it later." Note that Kafka's cross-DC replication tool (MirrorMaker, which we'll discuss in Chapter 8) is configured by default to retry endlessly (i.e., retries = MAX_INT)—because as a highly reliable replication tool, it should never just drop messages.

Note that retrying to send a failed message often includes a small risk that both messages were successfully written to the broker, leading to duplicates. For example, if network issues prevented the broker acknowledgment from reaching the producer, but the message was successfully written and replicated, the producer will treat the lack of acknowledgment as a temporary network issue and will retry sending the message (since it can't know that it was received). In that case, the broker will end up having the same message twice. Retries and careful error handling can guarantee that each message will be stored *at least once*, but in the current version of Apache Kafka (0.10.0), we can't guarantee it will be stored *exactly once*. Many real-world applications add a unique identifier to each message to allow detecting duplicates and cleaning them when consuming the messages. Other applications make the messages *idempotent*—meaning that even if the same message is sent twice, it has no negative impact on correctness. For example, the message "Account value is 110$" is idempotent, since sending it several times doesn't change the result. The message "Add $10 to the account" is not idempotent, since it changes the result every time you send it.

Additional Error Handling

Using the built-in producer retries is an easy way to correctly handle a large variety of errors without loss of messages, but as a developer, you must still be able to handle other types of errors. These include:

- Nonretriable broker errors such as errors regarding message size, authorization errors, etc.
- Errors that occur before the message was sent to the broker—for example, serialization errors
- Errors that occur when the producer exhausted all retry attempts or when the available memory used by the producer is filled to the limit due to using all of it to store messages while retrying

In Chapter 3 we discussed how to write error handlers for both sync and async message-sending methods. The content of these error handlers is specific to the application and its goals—do you throw away "bad messages"? Log errors? Store these messages in a directory on the local disk? Trigger a callback to another application?

These decisions are specific to your architecture. Just note that if all your error handler is doing is retrying to send the message, you are better off relying on the producer's retry functionality.

Using Consumers in a Reliable System

Now that we have learned how to produce data while taking Kafka's reliability guarantees into account, it is time to see how to consume data.

As we saw in the first part of this chapter, data is only available to consumers after it has been committed to Kafka—meaning it was written to all in-sync replicas. This means that consumers get data that is guaranteed to be consistent. The only thing consumers are left to do is make sure they keep track of which messages they've read and which messages they haven't. This is key to not losing messages while consuming them.

When reading data from a partition, a consumer is fetching a batch of events, checking the last offset in the batch, and then requesting another batch of events starting from the last offset received. This guarantees that a Kafka consumer will always get new data in correct order without missing any events.

When a consumer stops, another consumer needs to know where to pick up the work —what was the last offset that the previous consumer processed before it stopped? The "other" consumer can even be the original one after a restart. It doesn't really matter—some consumer is going to pick up consuming from that partition, and it needs to know in which offset to start. This is why consumers need to "commit" their offsets. For each partition it is consuming, the consumer stores its current location, so they or another consumer will know where to continue after a restart. The main way consumers can lose messages is when committing offsets for events they've read but didn't completely process yet. This way, when another consumer picks up the work, it will skip those events and they will never get processed. This is why paying careful attention to when and how offsets get committed is critical.

Committed Messages Versus Commited Offsets

This is different from a *committed message*, which, as discussed previously, is a message that was written to all in-sync replicas and is available to consumers. *Committed offsets* are offsets the consumer sent to Kafka to acknowledge that it received and processed all the messages in a partition up to this specific offset.

In Chapter 4 we discussed the consumer API in detail and covered the many methods for committing offsets. Here we will cover some important considerations and choices, but refer you back to Chapter 4 for details on using the APIs.

Important Consumer Configuration Properties for Reliable Processing

There are four consumer configuration properties that are important to understand in order to configure your consumer for a desired reliability behavior.

The first is `group.id`, as explained in great detail in Chapter 4. The basic idea is that if two consumers have the same group ID and subscribe to the same topic, each will be assigned a subset of the partitions in the topic and will therefore only read a subset of the messages individually (but all the messages will be read by the group as a whole). If you need a consumer to see, on its own, every single message in the topics it is subscribed to—it will need a unique `group.id`.

The second relevant configuration is `auto.offset.reset`. This parameter controls what the consumer will do when no offsets were committed (e.g., when the consumer first starts) or when the consumer asks for offsets that don't exist in the broker (Chapter 4 explains how this can happen). There are only two options here. If you choose `earliest`, the consumer will start from the beginning of the partition whenever it doesn't have a valid offset. This can lead to the consumer processing a lot of messages twice, but it guarantees to minimize data loss. If you choose `latest`, the consumer will start at the end of the partition. This minimizes duplicate processing by the consumer but almost certainly leads to some messages getting missed by the consumer.

The third relevant configuration is `enable.auto.commit`. This is a big decision: are you going to let the consumer commit offsets for you based on schedule, or are you planning on committing offsets manually in your code? The main benefit of automatic offset commits is that it's one less thing to worry about when implementing your consumers. If you do all the processing of consumed records within the consumer poll loop, then the automatic offset commit guarantees you will never commit an offset that you didn't process. (If you are not sure what the `consumer poll loop` is, refer back to Chapter 4.) The main drawbacks of automatic offset commits is that you have no control over the number of duplicate records you may need to process (because your consumer stopped after processing some records but before the automated commit kicked in). If you do anything fancy like pass records to another thread to process in the background, the automatic commit may commit offsets for records the consumer has read but perhaps did not process yet.

The fourth relevant configuration is tied to the third, and is `auto.com mit.interval.ms`. If you choose to commit offsets automatically, this configuration lets you configure how frequently they will be committed. The default is every five seconds. In general, committing more frequently adds some overhead but reduces the number of duplicates that can occur when a consumer stops.

Explicitly Committing Offsets in Consumers

If you go with the automatic offset commits, you don't need to worry about explicitly committing offsets. But you do need to think about how you will commit offsets if you decide you need more control over the timing of offset commits—either in order to minimize duplicates or because you are doing event processing outside the main consumer poll loop.

We will not go over the mechanics and APIs involved in committing offsets here, since they were covered in great depth in Chapter 4. Instead, we will review important considerations when developing a consumer to handle data reliably. We'll start with the simple and perhaps obvious points and move on to more complex patterns.

Always commit offsets after events were processed

If you do all the processing within the poll loop and don't maintain state between poll loops (e.g., for aggregation), this should be easy. You can use the auto-commit configuration or commit events at the end of the poll loop.

Commit frequency is a trade-off between performance and number of duplicates in the event of a crash

Even in the simplest case where you do all the processing within the poll loop and don't maintain state between poll loops, you can choose to commit multiple times within a loop (perhaps even after every event) or choose to only commit every several loops. Committing has some performance overhead (similar to produce with `acks=all`), so it all depends on the trade-offs that work for you.

Make sure you know exactly what offsets you are committing

A common pitfall when committing in the middle of the poll loop is accidentally committing the last offset read when polling and not the last offset processed. Remember that it is critical to always commit offsets for messages after they were processed—committing offsets for messages read but not processed can lead to the consumer missing messages. Chapter 4 has examples that show how to do just that.

Rebalances

When designing your application, remember that consumer rebalances will happen and you need to handle them properly. Chapter 4 contains a few examples, but the bigger picture is that this usually involves committing offsets before partitions are revoked and cleaning any state you maintain when you are assigned new partitions.

Consumers may need to retry

In some cases, after calling poll and processing records, some records are not fully processed and will need to be processed later. For example, you may try to write records from Kafka to a database, but find that the database is not available at that moment and you may wish to retry later. Note that unlike traditional pub/sub messaging systems, you commit offsets and not ack individual messages. This means that if you failed to process record #30 and succeeded in processing record #31, you should not commit record #31—this would result in committing all the records up to #31 including #30, which is usually not what you want. Instead, try following one of the following two patterns.

One option, when you encounter a retriable error, is to commit the last record you processed successfully. Then store the records that still need to be processed in a buffer (so the next poll won't override them) and keep trying to process the records. You may need to keep polling while trying to process all the records (refer to Chapter 4 for an explanation). You can use the consumer `pause()` method to ensure that additional polls won't return additional data to make retrying easier.

A second option is, when encountering a retriable error, to write it to a separate topic and continue. A separate consumer group can be used to handle retries from the retry topic, or one consumer can subscribe to both the main topic and to the retry topic, but pause the retry topic between retries. This pattern is similar to the dead-letter-queue system used in many messaging systems.

Consumers may need to maintain state

In some applications, you need to maintain state across multiple calls to poll. For example, if you want to calculate moving average, you'll want to update the average after every time you poll Kafka for new events. If your process is restarted, you will need to not just start consuming from the last offset, but you'll also need to recover the matching moving average. One way to do this is to write the latest accumulated value to a "results" topic at the same time you are committing the offset. This means that when a thread is starting up, it can pick up the latest accumulated value when it starts and pick up right where it left off. However, this doesn't completely solve the problem, as Kafka does not offer transactions yet. You could crash after you wrote the latest result and before you committed offsets, or vice versa. In general, this is a rather complex problem to solve, and rather than solving it on your own, we recommend looking at a library like Kafka Streams, which provides high level DSL-like APIs for aggregation, joins, windows, and other complex analytics.

Handling long processing times

Sometimes processing records takes a long time. Maybe you are interacting with a service that can block or doing a very complex calculation, for example. Remember that in some versions of the Kafka consumer, you can't stop polling for more than a few seconds (see Chapter 4 for details). Even if you don't want to process additional records, you must continue polling so the client can send heartbeats to the broker. A common pattern in these cases is to hand off the data to a thread-pool when possible with multiple threads to speed things up a bit by processing in parallel. After handing off the records to the worker threads, you can pause the consumer and keep polling without actually fetching additional data until the worker threads finish. Once they are done, you can resume the consumer. Because the consumer never stops polling, the heartbeat will be sent as planned and rebalancing will not be triggered.

Exactly-once delivery

Some applications require not just at-least-once semantics (meaning no data loss), but also exactly-once semantics. While Kafka does not provide full exactly-once support at this time, consumers have few tricks available that allow them to guarantee that each message in Kafka will be written to an external system exactly once (note that this doesn't handle duplications that may have occurred while the data was produced into Kafka).

The easiest and probably most common way to do exactly-once is by writing results to a system that has some support for unique keys. This includes all key-value stores, all relational databases, Elasticsearch, and probably many more data stores. When writing results to a system like a relational database or Elastic search, either the record itself contains a unique key (this is fairly common), or you can create a unique key using the topic, partition, and offset combination, which uniquely identifies a Kafka record. If you write the record as a value with a unique key, and later you accidentally consume the same record again, you will just write the exact same key and value. The data store will override the existing one, and you will get the same result that you would without the accidental duplicate. This pattern is called *idempotent writes* and is very common and useful.

Another option is available when writing to a system that has transactions. Relational databases are the easiest example, but HDFS has atomic renames that are often used for the same purpose. The idea is to write the records and their offsets in the same transaction so they will be in-sync. When starting up, retrieve the offsets of the latest records written to the external store and then use `consumer.seek()` to start consuming again from those offsets. Chapter 4 contains an example of how this can be done.

Validating System Reliability

Once you have gone through the process of figuring out your reliability requirements, configuring the brokers, configuring the clients, and using the APIs in the best way for your use case, you can just relax and run everything in production, confident that no event will ever be missed, right?

You could do that, but we recommend doing some validation first. We suggest three layers of validation: validate the configuration, validate the application, and monitor the application in production. Let's look at each of these steps and see what you need to validate and how.

Validating Configuration

It is easy to test the broker and client configuration in isolation from the application logic, and it is recommended to do so for two reasons:

- It helps to test if the configuration you've chosen can meet your requirements.
- It is good exercise to reason through the expected behavior of the system. This chapter was a bit theoretical, so checking your understanding of how the theory applies in practice is important.

Kafka includes two important tools to help with this validation. The `org.apache.kafka.tools` package includes `VerifiableProducer` and `Verifiable Consumer` classes. These can run as command-line tools, or be embedded in an automated testing framework.

The idea is that the verifiable producer produces a sequence of messages containing numbers from 1 to a value you choose. You can configure it the same way you configure your own producer, setting the right number of `acks`, retries, and rate at which the messages will be produced. When you run it, it will print success or error for each message sent to the broker, based on the `acks` received. The verifiable consumer performs the complementary check. It consumes events (usually those produced by the verifiable producer) and prints out the events it consumed in order. It also prints information regarding commits and rebalances.

You should also consider which tests you want to run. For example:

- Leader election: what happens if I kill the leader? How long does it take the producer and consumer to start working as usual again?
- Controller election: how long does it take the system to resume after a restart of the controller?
- Rolling restart: can I restart the brokers one by one without losing any messages?
- Unclean leader election test: what happens when we kill all the replicas for a partition one by one (to make sure each goes out of sync) and then start a broker that was out of sync? What needs to happen in order to resume operations? Is this acceptable?

Then you pick a scenario, start the verifiable producer, start the verifiable consumer, and run through the scenario—for example, kill the leader of the partition you are producing data into. If you expected a short pause and then everything to resume normally with no message loss, make sure the number of messages produced by the producer and the number of messages consumed by the consumer match.

The Apache Kafka source repository includes an extensive test suite (*https:// github.com/apache/kafka/tree/trunk/tests*). Many of the tests in the suite are based on the same principle—use the verifiable producer and consumer to make sure rolling upgrades work, for example.

Validating Applications

Once you are sure your broker and client configuration meet your requirements, it is time to test whether your application provides the guarantees you need. This will check things like your custom error-handling code, offset commits, and rebalance listeners and similar places where your application logic interacts with Kafka's client libraries.

Naturally, because it is your application, there is only so much guidance we can provide on how to test it. Hopefully you have integration tests for your application as part of your development process. However you validate your application, we recommend running tests under a variety of failure conditions:

- Clients lose connectivity to the server (your system administrator can assist you in simulating network failures)
- Leader election
- Rolling restart of brokers
- Rolling restart of consumers
- Rolling restart of producers

For each scenario, you will have *expected behavior*, which is what you planned on seeing when you developed your application, and then you can run the test to see what actually happens. For example, when planning for a rolling restart of consumers, you may plan for a short pause as consumers rebalance and then continue consumption with no more than 1,000 duplicate values. Your test will show whether the way the application commits offsets and handles rebalances actually works this way.

Monitoring Reliability in Production

Testing the application is important, but it does not replace the need to continuously monitor your production systems to make sure data is flowing as expected. Chapter 9 will cover detailed suggestions on how to monitor the Kafka cluster, but in addition to monitoring the health of the cluster, it is important to also monitor the clients and the flow of data through the system.

First, Kafka's Java clients include JMX metrics that allow monitoring client-side status and events. For the producers, the two metrics most important for reliability are error-rate and retry-rate per record (aggregated). Keep an eye on those, since error or retry rates going up can indicate an issue with the system. Also monitor the producer logs for errors that occur while sending events that are logged at WARN level, and say something along the lines of "Got error produce response with correlation id 5689 on topic-partition [topic-1,3], retrying (two attempts left). Error: ...". If you see events with 0 attempts left, the producer is running out of retries. Based on the discussion in the section "Using Producers in a Reliable System" on page 121, you may want to increase the number of retries—or solve the problem that caused the errors in the first place.

On the consumer side, the most important metric is consumer lag. This metric indicates how far the consumer is from the latest message committed to the partition on the broker. Ideally, the lag would always be zero and the consumer will always read the latest message. In practice, because calling poll() returns multiple messages and then the consumer spends time processing them before fetching more messages, the lag will always fluctuate a bit. What is important is to make sure consumers do eventually catch up rather than fall farther and farther behind. Because of the expected fluctuation in consumer lag, setting traditional alerts on the metric can be challenging. Burrow (*https://github.com/linkedin/Burrow*) is a consumer lag checker by LinkedIn and can make this easier.

Monitoring the flow of data also means making sure all produced data is consumed in a timely manner (your requirements will dictate what "timely manner" means). In order to make sure data is consumed in a timely manner, you need to know when the data was produced. Kafka assists in this: starting with version 0.10.0, all messages include a timestamp that indicates when the event was produced. If you are running clients with an earlier version, we recommend recording the timestamp, name of the app producing the message, and hostname where the message was created, for each event. This will help track down sources of issues later on.

In order to make sure all produced messages are consumed within a reasonable amount of time, you will need the application producing the code to record the number of events produced (usually as events per second). The consumers need to both record the number of events consumed (also events per second) and also record lags from the time events were produced to the time they were consumed, using the event timestamp. Then you will need a system to reconcile the events per second numbers from both the producer and the consumer (to make sure no messages were lost on the way) and to make sure the time gaps between the time events were produced in a reasonable amount of time. For even better monitoring, you can add a monitoring consumer on critical topics that will count events and compare them to the events produced, so you will get accurate monitoring of producers even if no one is consuming the events at a given point in time. These type of end-to-end monitoring systems can be challenging and time-consuming to implement. To the best of our knowledge, there is no open source implementation of this type of system, but Confluent provides a commercial implementation as part of the Confluent Control Center (*http://www.confluent.io/product/control-center*).

Summary

As we said in the beginning of the chapter, reliability is not just a matter of specific Kafka features. You need to build an entire reliable system, including your application architecture, the way your application uses the producer and consumer APIs, producer and consumer configuration, topic configuration, and broker configuration. Making the system more reliable always has trade-offs in application complexity, performance, availability, or disk-space usage. By understanding all the options and common patterns and understanding requirements for your use case, you can make informed decisions regarding how reliable your application and Kafka deployment needs to be and which trade-offs make sense for you.

## CHAPTER 7

Building Data Pipelines

When people discuss building data pipelines using Apache Kafka, they are usuallly referring to a couple of use cases. The first is building a data pipeline where Apache Kafka is one of the two end points. For example, getting data from Kafka to S3 or getting data from MongoDB into Kafka. The second use case involves building a pipeline between two different systems but using Kafka as an intermediary. An example of this is getting data from Twitter to Elasticsearch by sending the data first from Twitter to Kafka and then from Kafka to Elasticsearch.

When we added Kafka Connect to Apache Kafka in version 0.9, it was after we saw Kafka used in both use cases at LinkedIn and other large organizations. We noticed that there were specific challenges in integrating Kafka into data pipelines that every organization had to solve, and decided to add APIs to Kafka that solve some of those challenges rather than force every organization to figure them out from scratch.

The main value Kafka provides to data pipelines is its ability to serve as a very large, reliable buffer between various stages in the pipeline, effectively decoupling producers and consumers of data within the pipeline. This decoupling, combined with reliability security and efficiency, makes Kafka a good fit for most data pipelines.

Putting Data Integrating in Context

Some organizations think of Kafka as an *end point* of a pipeline. They look at problems such as "How do I get data from Kafka to Elastic?" This is a valid question to ask—especially if there is data you need in Elastic and it is currently in Kafka—and we will look at ways to do exactly this. But we are going to start the discussion by looking at the use of Kafka within a larger context that includes at least two (and possibly many more) end points that are not Kafka itself. We encourage anyone faced with a data-integration problem to consider the bigger picture and not focus only on the immediate end points. Focusing on short-term integrations is how you end up with a complex and expensive-to-maintain data integration mess.

In this chapter, we'll discuss some of the common issues that you need to take into account when building data pipelines. Those challenges are not specific to Kafka, but rather general data integration problems. Nonetheless, we will show why Kafka is a good fit for data integration use cases and how it addresses many of those challenges. We will discuss how the Kafka Connect APIs are different from the normal producer and consumer clients, and when each client type should be used. Then we'll jump into some details of Kafka Connect. While a full discussion of Kafka Connect is outside the scope of this chapter, we will show examples of basic usage to get you started and give you pointers on where to learn more. Finally, we'll discuss other data integration systems and how they integrate with Kafka.

Considerations When Building Data Pipelines

While we can't get into all the details on building data pipelines here, we would like to highlight some of the most important things to take into account when designing software architectures with the intent of integrating multiple systems.

Timeliness

Some systems expect their data to arrive in large bulks once a day; others expect the data to arrive a few milliseconds after it is generated. Most data pipelines fit somewhere in between these two extremes. Good data integration systems can support different timeliness requirements for different pipelines and also make the migration between different timetables easier as business requirements can change. Kafka, being a streaming data platform with scalable and reliable storage, can be used to support anything from near-real-time pipelines to hourly batches. Producers can write to Kafka as frequently and infrequently as needed and consumers can also read and deliver the latest events as they arrive. Or consumers can work in batches: run every hour, connect to Kafka, and read the events that accumulated during the previous hour.

A useful way to look at Kafka in this context is that it acts as a giant buffer that decouples the time-sensitivity requirements between producers and consumers. Producers can write events in real-time while consumers process batches of events, or vice versa. This also makes it trivial to apply back-pressure—Kafka itself applies back-pressure on producers (by delaying acks when needed) since consumption rate is driven entirely by the consumers.

Reliability

We want to avoid single points of failure and allow for fast and automatic recovery from all sorts of failure events. Data pipelines are often the way data arrives to business critical systems; failure for more than a few seconds can be hugely disruptive, especially when the timeliness requirement is closer to the few-milliseconds end of the spectrum. Another important consideration for reliability is delivery guarantees —some systems can afford to lose data, but most of the time there is a requirement for *at-least-once* delivery, which means every event from the source system will reach its destination, but sometimes retries will cause duplicates. Often, there is even a requirement for *exactly-once* delivery—every event from the source system will reach the destination with no possibility for loss or duplication.

We discussed Kafka's availability and reliability guarantees in depth in Chapter 6. As we discussed, Kafka can provide at-least-once on its own, and exactly-once when combined with an external data store that has a transactional model or unique keys. Since many of the end points are data stores that provide the right semantics for exactly-once delivery, a Kafka-based pipeline can often be implemented as exactly-once. It is worth highlighting that Kafka's Connect APIs make it easier for connectors to build an end-to-end exactly-once pipeline by providing APIs for integrating with the external systems when handling offsets. Indeed, many of the available open source connectors support exactly-once delivery.

High and Varying Throughput

The data pipelines we are building should be able to scale to very high throughputs as is often required in modern data systems. Even more importantly, they should be able to adapt if throughput suddenly increases.

With Kafka acting as a buffer between producers and consumers, we no longer need to couple consumer throughput to the producer throughput. We no longer need to implement a complex back-pressure mechanism because if producer throughput exceeds that of the consumer, data will accumulate in Kafka until the consumer can catch up. Kafka's ability to scale by adding consumers or producers independently allows us to scale either side of the pipeline dynamically and independently to match the changing requirements.

Kafka is a high-throughput distributed system—capable of processing hundreds of megabytes per second on even modest clusters—so there is no concern that our pipeline will not scale as demand grows. In addition, the Kafka Connect API focuses on parallelizing the work and not just scaling it out. We'll describe in the following sections how the platform allows data sources and sinks to split the work between multiple threads of execution and use the available CPU resources even when running on a single machine.

Kafka also supports several types of compression, allowing users and admins to control the use of network and storage resources as the throughput requirements increase.

Data Formats

One of the most important considerations in a data pipeline is reconciling different data formats and data types. The data types supported vary among different databases and other storage systems. You may be loading XMLs and relational data into Kafka, using Avro within Kafka, and then need to convert data to JSON when writing it to Elasticsearch, to Parquet when writing to HDFS, and to CSV when writing to S3.

Kafka itself and the Connect APIs are completely agnostic when it comes to data formats. As we've seen in previous chapters, producers and consumers can use any serializer to represent data in any format that works for you. Kafka Connect has its own in-memory objects that include data types and schemas, but as we'll soon discuss, it allows for pluggable converters to allow storing these records in any format. This means that no matter which data format you use for Kafka, it does not restrict your choice of connectors.

Many sources and sinks have a schema; we can read the schema from the source with the data, store it, and use it to validate compatibility or even update the schema in the sink database. A classic example is a data pipeline from MySQL to Hive. If someone added a column in MySQL, a great pipeline will make sure the column gets added to Hive too as we are loading new data into it.

In addition, when writing data from Kafka to external systems, Sink connectors are responsible for the format in which the data is written to the external system. Some connectors choose to make this format pluggable. For example, the HDFS connector allows a choice between Avro and Parquet formats.

It is not enough to support different types of data; a generic data integration framework should also handle differences in behavior between various sources and sinks. For example, Syslog is a source that pushes data while relational databases require the framework to pull data out. HDFS is append-only and we can only write data to it, while most systems allow us to both append data and update existing records.

Transformations

Transformations are more controversial than other requirements. There are generally two schools of building data pipelines: ETL and ELT. ETL, which stands for *Extract-Transform-Load*, means the data pipeline is responsible for making modifications to the data as it passes through. It has the perceived benefit of saving time and storage because you don't need to store the data, modify it, and store it again. Depending on the transformations, this benefit is sometimes real but sometimes shifts the burden of computation and storage to the data pipeline itself, which may or may not be desirable. The main drawback of this approach is that the transformations that happen to the data in the pipeline tie the hands of those who wish to process the data farther down the pipe. If the person who built the pipeline between MongoDB and MySQL decided to filter certain events or remove fields from records, all the users and applications who access the data in MySQL will only have access to partial data. If they require access to the missing fields, the pipeline needs to be rebuilt and historical data will require reprocessing (assuming it is available).

ELT stands for *Extract-Load-Transform* and means the data pipeline does only minimal transformation (mostly around data type conversion), with the goal of making sure the data that arrives at the target is as similar as possible to the source data. These are also called high-fidelity pipelines or data-lake architecture. In these systems, the target system collects "raw data" and all required processing is done at the target system. The benefit here is that the system provides maximum flexibility to users of the target system, since they have access to all the data. These systems also tend to be easier to troubleshoot since all data processing is limited to one system rather than split between the pipeline and additional applications. The drawback is that the transformations take CPU and storage resources at the target system. In some cases, these systems are expensive and there is strong motivation to move computation off those systems when possible.

Security

Security is always a concern. In terms of data pipelines, the main security concerns are:

- Can we make sure the data going through the pipe is encrypted? This is mainly a concern for data pipelines that cross datacenter boundaries.
- Who is allowed to make modifications to the pipelines?
- If the data pipeline needs to read or write from access-controlled locations, can it authenticate properly?

Kafka allows encrypting data on the wire, as it is piped from sources to Kafka and from Kafka to sinks. It also supports authentication (via SASL) and authorization—so you can be sure that if a topic contains sensitive information, it can't be piped into less secured systems by someone unauthorized. Kafka also provides an audit log to track access—unauthorized and authorized. With some extra coding, it is also possible to track where the events in each topic came from and who modified them, so you can provide the entire lineage for each record.

Failure Handling

Assuming that all data will be perfect all the time is dangerous. It is important to plan for failure handling in advance. Can we prevent faulty records from ever making it into the pipeline? Can we recover from records that cannot be parsed? Can bad records get fixed (perhaps by a human) and reprocessed? What if the bad event looks exactly like a normal event and you only discover the problem a few days later?

Because Kafka stores all events for long periods of time, it is possible to go back in time and recover from errors when needed.

Coupling and Agility

One of the most important goals of data pipelines is to decouple the data sources and data targets. There are multiple ways accidental coupling can happen:

Ad-hoc pipelines

Some companies end up building a custom pipeline for each pair of applications they want to connect. For example, they use Logstash to dump logs to Elasticsearch, Flume to dump logs to HDFS, GoldenGate to get data from Oracle to HDFS, Informatica to get data from MySQL and XMLs to Oracle, and so on. This tightly couples the data pipeline to the specific end points and creates a mess of integration points that requires significant effort to deploy, maintain, and monitor. It also means that every new system the company adopts will require building additional pipelines, increasing the cost of adopting new technology, and inhibiting innovation.

Loss of metadata

If the data pipeline doesn't preserve schema metadata and does not allow for schema evolution, you end up tightly coupling the software producing the data at the source and the software that uses it at the destination. Without schema information, both software products need to include information on how to parse the data and interpret it. If data flows from Oracle to HDFS and a DBA added a new field in Oracle without preserving schema information and allowing schema evolution, either every app that reads data from HDFS will break or all the developers will need to upgrade their applications at the same time. Neither option is agile. With support for schema evolution in the pipeline, each team can modify their applications at their own pace without worrying that things will break down the line.

Extreme processing

As we mentioned when discussing data transformations, some processing of data is inherent to data pipelines. After all, we are moving data between different systems where different data formats make sense and different use cases are supported. However, too much processing ties all the downstream systems to decisions made when building the pipelines. Decisions about which fields to preserve, how to aggregate data, etc. This often leads to constant changes to the pipeline as requirements of downstream applications change, which isn't agile, efficient, or safe. The more agile way is to preserve as much of the raw data as possible and allow downstream apps to make their own decisions regarding data processing and aggregation.

When to Use Kafka Connect Versus Producer and Consumer

When writing to Kafka or reading from Kafka, you have the choice between using traditional producer and consumer clients, as described in Chapters 3 and 4, or using the Connect APIs and the connectors as we'll describe below. Before we start diving into the details of Connect, it makes sense to stop and ask yourself: "When do I use which?"

As we've seen, Kafka clients are clients embedded in your own application. It allows your application to write data to Kafka or to read data from Kafka. Use Kafka clients when you can modify the code of the application that you want to connect an application to and when you want to either push data into Kafka or pull data from Kafka.

You will use Connect to connect Kafka to datastores that you did not write and whose code you cannot or will not modify. Connect will be used to pull data from the external datastore into Kafka or push data from Kafka to an external store. For datastores where a connector already exists, Connect can be used by nondevelopers, who will only need to configure the connectors.

If you need to connect Kafka to a datastore and a connector does not exist yet, you can choose between writing an app using the Kafka clients or the Connect API. Connect is recommended because it provides out-of-the-box features like configuration management, offset storage, parallelization, error handling, support for different data types, and standard management REST APIs. Writing a small app that connects Kafka to a datastore sounds simple, but there are many little details you will need to handle concerning data types and configuration that make the task nontrivial. Kafka Connect handles most of this for you, allowing you to focus on transporting data to and from the external stores.

Kafka Connect

Kafka Connect is a part of Apache Kafka and provides a scalable and reliable way to move data between Kafka and other datastores. It provides APIs and a runtime to develop and run `connector plugins`—libraries that Kafka Connect executes and which are responsible for moving the data. Kafka Connect runs as a cluster of *worker processes*. You install the connector plugins on the workers and then use a REST API to configure and manage *connectors*, which run with a specific configuration. *Connectors* start additional *tasks* to move large amounts of data in parallel and use the available resources on the worker nodes more efficiently. Source connector tasks just need to read data from the source system and provide Connect data objects to the worker processes. Sink connector tasks get connector data objects from the workers and are responsible for writing them to the target data system. Kafka Connect uses `convertors` to support storing those data objects in Kafka in different formats—JSON format support is part of Apache Kafka, and the Confluent Schema Registry provides Avro converters. This allows users to choose the format in which data is stored in Kafka independent of the connectors they use.

This chapter cannot possibly get into all the details of Kafka Connect and its many connectors. This could fill an entire book on its own. We will, however, give an overview of Kafka Connect and how to use it, and point to additional resources for reference.

Running Connect

Kafka Connect ships with Apache Kafka, so there is no need to install it separately. For production use, especially if you are planning to use Connect to move large amounts of data or run many connectors, you should run Connect on separate servers. In this case, install Apache Kafka on all the machines, and simply start the brokers on some servers and start Connect on other servers.

Starting a Connect worker is very similar to starting a broker—you call the start script with a properties file:

```
bin/connect-distributed.sh config/connect-distributed.properties
```

There are a few key configurations for Connect workers:

- `bootstrap.servers`:: A list of Kafka brokers that Connect will work with. `Connectors` will pipe their data either to or from those brokers. You don't need to specify every broker in the cluster, but it's recommended to specify at least three.

- `group.id`:: All workers with the same group ID are part of the same Connect cluster. A connector started on the cluster will run on any worker and so will its tasks.

- `key.converter` and `value.converter`:: Connect can handle multiple data formats stored in Kafka. The two configurations set the converter for the key and value part of the message that will be stored in Kafka. The default is JSON format using the JSONConverter included in Apache Kafka. These configurations can also be set to `AvroConverter`, which is part of the Confluent Schema Registry.

Some converters include converter-specific configuration parameters. For example, JSON messages can include a schema or be schema-less. To support either, you can set `key.converter.schema.enable=true` or `false`, respectively. The same configuration can be used for the value converter by setting `value.converter.schema.enable` to `true` or `false`. Avro messages also contain a schema, but you need to configure the location of the Schema Registry using `key.converter.schema.registry.url` and `value.converter.schema.registry.url`.

`rest.host.name` and `rest.port` Connectors are typically configured and monitored through the REST API of Kafka Connect. You can configure the specific port for the REST API.

Once the workers are up and you have a cluster, make sure it is up and running by checking the REST API:

```
gwen$ curl http://localhost:8083/
{"version":"0.10.1.0-SNAPSHOT","commit":"561f45d747cd2a8c"}
```

Accessing the base REST URI should return the current version you are running. We are running a snapshot of Kafka 0.10.1.0 (prerelease). We can also check which connector plugins are available:

```
gwen$ curl http://localhost:8083/connector-plugins

[{"class":"org.apache.kafka.connect.file.FileStreamSourceConnector"},
{"class":"org.apache.kafka.connect.file.FileStreamSinkConnector"}]
```

We are running plain Apache Kafka, so the only available connector plugins are the file source and file sink.

Let's see how to configure and use these example connectors, and then we'll dive into more advanced examples that require setting up external data systems to connect to.

Standalone Mode

Take note that Kafka Connect also has a standalone mode. It is similar to distributed mode—you just run `bin/connect-standalone.sh` instead of `bin/connect-distributed.sh`. You can also pass in a connector configuration file on the command line instead of through the REST API. In this mode, all the connectors and tasks run on the one standalone worker. It is usually easier to use Connect in standalone mode for development and troubleshooting as well as in cases where connectors and tasks need to run on a specific machine (e.g., `syslog` connector listens on a port, so you need to know which machines it is running on).

Connector Example: File Source and File Sink

This example will use the file connectors and JSON converter that are part of Apache Kafka. To follow along, make sure you have Zookeeper and Kafka up and running.

To start, let's run a distributed Connect worker. In a real production environment, you'll want at least two or three of these running to provide high availability. In this example, I'll only start one:

```
bin/connect-distributed.sh config/connect-distributed.properties &
```

Now it's time to start a file source. As an example, we will configure it to read the Kafka configuration file—basically piping Kafka's configuration into a Kafka topic:

```
echo '{"name":"load-kafka-config", "config":{"connector.class":"FileStream-
Source","file":"config/server.properties","topic":"kafka-config-topic"}}' |
curl -X POST -d @- http://localhost:8083/connectors --header "content-
Type:application/json"

{"name":"load-kafka-config","config":{"connector.class":"FileStream-
Source","file":"config/server.properties","topic":"kafka-config-
topic","name":"load-kafka-config"},"tasks":[]}
```

To create a connector, we wrote a JSON that includes a connector name, `load-kafka-config`, and a connector configuration map, which includes the connector class, the file we want to load, and the topic we want to load the file into.

Let's use the Kafka Console consumer to check that we have loaded the configuration into a topic:

```
gwen$ bin/kafka-console-consumer.sh --new --bootstrap-server=localhost:9092 --
topic kafka-config-topic --from-beginning
```

If all went well, you should see something along the lines of:

```
{"schema":{"type":"string","optional":false},"payload":"# Licensed to the
Apache Software Foundation (ASF) under one or more"}
```

```
<more stuff here>
```

```
{"schema":{"type":"string","optional":false},"pay-
load":"########################### Server Basics
###########################"}
{"schema":{"type":"string","optional":false},"payload":""}
{"schema":{"type":"string","optional":false},"payload":"# The id of the broker.
This must be set to a unique integer for each broker."}
{"schema":{"type":"string","optional":false},"payload":"broker.id=0"}
{"schema":{"type":"string","optional":false},"payload":""}
```

```
<more stuff here>
```

This is literally the contents of the *config/server.properties* file, as it was converted to JSON line by line and placed in kafka-config-topic by our connector. Note that by default, the JSON converter places a schema in each record. In this specific case, the schema is very simple—there is only a single column, named payload of type string, and it contains a single line from the file for each record.

Now let's use the file sink converter to dump the contents of that topic into a file. The resulting file should be completely identical to the original server.properties file, as the JSON converter will convert the JSON records back into simple text lines:

```
echo '{"name":"dump-kafka-config", "config":
{"connector.class":"FileStreamSink","file":"copy-of-server-
properties","topics":"kafka-config-topic"}}' | curl -X POST -d @- http://local-
host:8083/connectors --header "content-Type:application/json"

{"name":"dump-kafka-config","config":
{"connector.class":"FileStreamSink","file":"copy-of-server-
properties","topics":"kafka-config-topic","name":"dump-kafka-config"},"tasks":
[]}
```

Note the changes from the source configuration: the class we are using is now File StreamSink rather than FileStreamSource. We still have a file property but now it refers to the destination file rather than the source of the records, and instead of specifying a *topic*, you specify *topics*. Note the plurality—you can write multiple topics into one file with the sink, while the source only allows writing into one topic.

If all went well, you should have a file named *copy-of-server-properties*, which is completely identical to the *config/server.properties* we used to populate kafka-config-topic.

To delete a connector, you can run:

```
curl -X DELETE http://localhost:8083/connectors/dump-kafka-config
```

If you look at the Connect worker log after deleting a connector, you should see all other connectors restarting their tasks. They are restarting in order to rebalance the remaining tasks between the workers and ensure equivalent workloads after a connector was removed.

Connector Example: MySQL to Elasticsearch

Now that we have a simple example working, let's do something more useful. Let's take a MySQL table, stream it to a Kafka topic and from there load it to Elasticsearch and index its contents.

We are running tests on a MacBook. To install MySQL and Elasticsearch, we simply run:

```
brew install mysql
brew install elasticsearch
```

The next step is to make sure you have the connectors. If you are running Confluent OpenSource, you should have the connectors already installed as part of the platform. Otherwise, you can just build the connectors from GitHub:

1. Go to *https://github.com/confluentinc/kafka-connect-elasticsearch*

2. Clone the repository

3. Run mvn install to build the project

4. Repeat with the JDBC connector (*https://github.com/confluentinc/kafka-connect-jdbc*)

Now take the jars that were created under the target directory where you built each connector and copy them into Kafka Connect's class path:

```
gwen$ mkdir libs
gwen$ cp ../kafka-connect-jdbc/target/kafka-connect-jdbc-3.1.0-SNAPSHOT.jar
libs/
gwen$ cp ../kafka-connect-elasticsearch/target/kafka-connect-
elasticsearch-3.2.0-SNAPSHOT-package/share/java/kafka-connect-elasticsearch/*
libs/
```

If the Kafka Connect workers are not already running, make sure to start them, and check that the new connector plugins are listed:

```
gwen$  bin/connect-distributed.sh config/connect-distributed.properties &

gwen$  curl http://localhost:8083/connector-plugins
[{"class":"org.apache.kafka.connect.file.FileStreamSourceConnector"},
{"class":"io.confluent.connect.elasticsearch.ElasticsearchSinkConnector"},
{"class":"org.apache.kafka.connect.file.FileStreamSinkConnector"},
{"class":"io.confluent.connect.jdbc.JdbcSourceConnector"}]
```

We can see that we now have additional connector plugins available in our Connect cluster. The JDBC source requires a MySQL driver in order to work with MySQL. We downloaded the JDBC driver for MySQL from the Oracle website, unzipped the package, and copied *mysql-connector-java-5.1.40-bin.jar* to the *libs/* directory when we copied the connectors.

The next step is to create a table in MySQL that we can stream into Kafka using our JDBC connector:

```
gwen$ mysql.server restart

mysql> create database test;
Query OK, 1 row affected (0.00 sec)

mysql> use test;
Database changed
mysql> create table login (username varchar(30), login_time datetime);
Query OK, 0 rows affected (0.02 sec)

mysql> insert into login values ('gwenshap', now());
Query OK, 1 row affected (0.01 sec)

mysql> insert into login values ('tpalino', now());
Query OK, 1 row affected (0.00 sec)

mysql> commit;
Query OK, 0 rows affected (0.01 sec)
```

As you can see, we created a database, a table, and inserted a few rows as an example.

The next step is to configure our JDBC source connector. We can find out which configuration options are available by looking at the documentation, but we can also use the REST API to find the available configuration options:

```
gwen$ curl -X PUT -d "{}" localhost:8083/connector-plugins/JdbcSourceConnector/
config/validate --header "content-Type:application/json" | python -m json.tool

{
    "configs": [
        {
            "definition": {
                "default_value": "",
                "dependents": [],
                "display_name": "Timestamp Column Name",
                "documentation": "The name of the timestamp column to use
                to detect new or modified rows. This column may not be
                nullable.",
                "group": "Mode",
                "importance": "MEDIUM",
                "name": "timestamp.column.name",
                "order": 3,
                "required": false,
                "type": "STRING",
                "width": "MEDIUM"
            },
            <more stuff>
```

We basically asked the REST API to validate configuration for a connector and sent it an empty configuration. As a response, we got the JSON definition of all available configurations. We piped the output through Python to make the JSON more readable.

With this information in mind, it's time to create and configure our JDBC connector:

```
echo '{"name":"mysql-login-connector", "config":{"connector.class":"JdbcSource-
Connector","connection.url":"jdbc:mysql://127.0.0.1:3306/test?
user=root","mode":"timestamp","table.whitelist":"login","vali-
date.non.null":false,"timestamp.column.name":"login_time","topic.pre-
fix":"mysql."}}' | curl -X POST -d @- http://localhost:8083/connectors --header
"content-Type:application/json"


{"name":"mysql-login-connector","config":{"connector.class":"JdbcSourceConnec-
tor","connection.url":"jdbc:mysql://127.0.0.1:3306/test?
user=root","mode":"timestamp","table.whitelist":"login","validate.non.null":"fal
se","timestamp.column.name":"login_time","topic.prefix":"mysql.","name":"mysql-
login-connector"},"tasks":[]}
```

Let's make sure it worked by reading data from the *mysql.login* topic:

```
gwen$ bin/kafka-console-consumer.sh --new --bootstrap-server=localhost:9092 --
topic mysql.login --from-beginning

<more stuff>

{"schema":{"type":"struct","fields":
[{"type":"string","optional":true,"field":"username"},
{"type":"int64","optional":true,"name":"org.apache.kafka.connect.data.Time-
stamp","version":1,"field":"login_time"}],"optional":false,"name":"login"},"pay-
load":{"username":"gwenshap","login_time":1476423962000}}
{"schema":{"type":"struct","fields":
[{"type":"string","optional":true,"field":"username"},
{"type":"int64","optional":true,"name":"org.apache.kafka.connect.data.Time-
stamp","version":1,"field":"login_time"}],"optional":false,"name":"login"},"pay-
load":{"username":"tpalino","login_time":1476423981000}}
```

If you get errors saying the topic doesn't exist or you see no data, check the Connect worker logs for errors such as:

```
[2016-10-16 19:39:40,482] ERROR Error while starting connector mysql-login-
connector (org.apache.kafka.connect.runtime.WorkerConnector:108)
org.apache.kafka.connect.errors.ConnectException: java.sql.SQLException: Access
denied for user 'root;'@'localhost' (using password: NO)
        at io.confluent.connect.jdbc.JdbcSourceConnector.start(JdbcSourceConnec-
tor.java:78)
```

It took multiple attempts to get the connection string right. Other issues can involve the existence of the driver in the classpath or permissions to read the table.

Note that while the connector is running, if you insert additional rows in the *login* table, you should immediately see them reflected in the *mysql.login* topic.

Getting MySQL data to Kafka is useful in itself, but let's make things more fun by writing the data to Elasticsearch.

First, we start Elasticsearch and verify it is up by accessing its local port:

```
gwen$ elasticsearch &
gwen$ curl http://localhost:9200/
{
  "name" : "Hammerhead",
  "cluster_name" : "elasticsearch_gwen",
  "cluster_uuid" : "42D5GrxOQFebf83DYgNl-g",
  "version" : {
    "number" : "2.4.1",
    "build_hash" : "c67dc32e24162035d18d6fe1e952c4cbcbe79d16",
    "build_timestamp" : "2016-09-27T18:57:55Z",
    "build_snapshot" : false,
    "lucene_version" : "5.5.2"
  },
  "tagline" : "You Know, for Search"
}
```

Now let's start the connector:

```
echo '{"name":"elastic-login-connector", "config":{"connector.class":"Elastic-
searchSinkConnector","connection.url":"http://localhost:
9200","type.name":"mysql-data","topics":"mysql.login","key.ignore":true}}' |
curl -X POST -d @- http://localhost:8083/connectors --header "content-
Type:application/json"

{"name":"elastic-login-connector","config":{"connector.class":"Elasticsearch-
SinkConnector","connection.url":"http://localhost:9200","type.name":"mysql-
data","topics":"mysql.login","key.ignore":"true","name":"elastic-login-
connector"},"tasks":[{"connector":"elastic-login-connector","task":0}]}
```

There are few configurations we need to explain here. The connection.url is simply the URL of the local Elasticsearch server we configured earlier. Each topic in Kafka will become, by default, a separate Elasticsearch index, with the same name as the topic. Within the topic, we need to define a type for the data we are writing. We assume all the events in a topic will be of the same type, so we just hardcode type.name=mysql-data. The only topic we are writing to Elasticsearch is mysql.login. When we defined the table in MySQL we didn't give it a primary key. As a result, the events in Kafka have null keys. Because the events in Kafka lack keys, we need to tell the Elasticsearch connector to use the topic name, partition ID, and offset as the key for each event.

Let's check that the index with mysql.login data was created:

```
gwen$ curl 'localhost:9200/_cat/indices?v'
health status index          pri rep docs.count docs.deleted store.size
pri.store.size
yellow open   mysql.login  5   1          3            0    10.7kb
10.7kb
```

If the index isn't there, look for errors in the Connect worker log. Missing configurations or libraries are common causes for errors. If all is well, we can search the index for our records:

```
gwen$ curl -s -X "GET" "http://localhost:9200/mysql.login/_search?pretty=true"
{
  "took" : 29,
  "timed_out" : false,
  "_shards" : {
    "total" : 5,
    "successful" : 5,
    "failed" : 0
  },
  "hits" : {
    "total" : 3,
    "max_score" : 1.0,
    "hits" : [ {
      "_index" : "mysql.login",
      "_type" : "mysql-data",
      "_id" : "mysql.login+0+1",
      "_score" : 1.0,
      "_source" : {
        "username" : "tpalino",
        "login_time" : 1476423981000
      }
    }, {
      "_index" : "mysql.login",
      "_type" : "mysql-data",
      "_id" : "mysql.login+0+2",
      "_score" : 1.0,
      "_source" : {
        "username" : "nnarkede",
        "login_time" : 1476672246000
      }
    }, {
      "_index" : "mysql.login",
      "_type" : "mysql-data",
      "_id" : "mysql.login+0+0",
      "_score" : 1.0,
      "_source" : {
        "username" : "gwenshap",
        "login_time" : 1476423962000
      }
    } ]
  }
}
```

If you add new records to the table in MySQL, they will automatically appear in the *mysql.login* topic in Kafka and in the corresponding Elasticsearch index.

Now that we've seen how to build and install the JDBC source and Elasticsearch sink, we can build and use any pair of connectors that suits our use case. Confluent maintains a list of all connectors we know about (*http://www.confluent.io/product/connectors/*), including both those written and supported by companies and community connectors. You can pick any connector on the list that you wish to try out, build it from the GitHub repository, configure it—either based on the documentation or by pulling the configuration from the REST API—and run it on your Connect worker cluster.

Build Your Own Connectors

The Connector API is public and anyone can create a new connector. In fact, this is how most of the connectors became part of the Connector Hub—people built connectors and told us about them. So if the datastore you wish to integrate with is not available in the hub, we encourage you to write your own. You can even contribute it to the community so others can discover and use it. It is beyond the scope of this chapter to discuss all the details involved in building a connector, but you can learn about it in the official documentation (*http://docs.confluent.io/3.0.1/connect/devguide.html*). We also recommend looking at the existing connectors as a starting point and perhaps jumpstarting using a maven archtype (*http://bit.ly/2sc9E9q*). We always encourage you to ask for assistance or show off your latest connectors on the Apache Kafka community mailing list (*users@kafka.apache.org*).

A Deeper Look at Connect

To understand how Connect works, you need to understand three basic concepts and how they interact. As we explained earlier and demonstrated with examples, to use Connect you need to run a cluster of workers and start/stop connectors. An additional detail we did not dive into before is the handling of data by convertors—these are the components that convert MySQL rows to JSON records, which the connector wrote into Kafka.

Let's look a bit deeper into each system and how they interact with each other.

Connectors and tasks

Connector plugins implement the connector API, which includes two parts:

Connectors

The connector is responsible for three important things:

- Determining how many tasks will run for the connector
- Deciding how to split the data-copying work between the tasks
- Getting configurations for the tasks from the workers and passing it along

  For example, the JDBC source connector will connect to the database, discover the existing tables to copy, and based on that decide how many tasks are needed—choosing the lower of `max.tasks` configuration and the number of tables. Once it decides how many tasks will run, it will generate a configuration for each task—using both the connector configuration (e.g., `connection.url`) and a list of tables it assigns for each task to copy. The `taskConfigs()` method returns a list of maps (i.e., a configuration for each task we want to run). The workers are then responsible for starting the tasks and giving each one its own unique configuration so that it will copy a unique subset of tables from the database. Note that when you start the connector via the REST API, it may start on any node and subsequently the tasks it starts may also execute on any node.

Tasks

Tasks are responsible for actually getting the data in and out of Kafka. All tasks are initialized by receiving a context from the worker. Source context includes an object that allows the source task to store the offsets of source records (e.g., in the file connector, the offsets are positions in the file; in the JDBC source connector, the offsets can be primary key IDs in a table). Context for the sink connector includes methods that allow the connector to control the records it receives from Kafka—this is used for things like applying back-pressure, and retrying and storing offsets externally for exactly-once delivery. After tasks are initialized, the are started with a `Properties` object that contains the configuration the `Connector` created for the task. Once tasks are started, source tasks poll an external system and return lists of records that the worker sends to Kafka brokers. Sink tasks receive records from Kafka through the worker and are responsible for writing the records to an external system.

Workers

Kafka Connect's worker processes are the "container" processes that execute the connectors and tasks. They are responsible for handling the HTTP requests that define connectors and their configuration, as well as for storing the connector configuration, starting the connectors and their tasks, and passing the appropriate configurations along. If a worker process is stopped or crashes, other workers in a Connect cluster will recognize that (using the heartbeats in Kafka's consumer protocol) and reassign the connectors and tasks that ran on that worker to the remaining workers. If a new worker joins a Connect cluster, other workers will notice that and assign connectors or tasks to it to make sure load is balanced among all workers fairly.

Workers are also responsible for automatically committing offsets for both source and sink connectors and for handling retries when tasks throw errors.

The best way to understand workers is to realize that connectors and tasks are responsible for the "moving data" part of data integration, while the workers are responsible for the REST API, configuration management, reliability, high availability, scaling, and load balancing.

This separation of concerns is the main benefit of using Connect APIs versus the classic consumer/producer APIs. Experienced developers know that writing code that reads data from Kafka and inserts it into a database takes maybe a day or two, but if you need to handle configuration, errors, REST APIs, monitoring, deployment, scaling up and down, and handling failures, it can take a few months to get right. If you implement data copying with a connector, your connector plugs into workers that handle a bunch of complicated operational issues that you don't need to worry about.

Converters and Connect's data model

The last piece of the Connect API puzzle is the connector data model and the converters. Kafka's Connect APIs includes a data API, which includes both data objects and a schema that describes that data. For example, the JDBC source reads a column from a database and constructs a `Connect Schema` object based on the data types of the columns returned by the database. It then uses the schema to construct a `Struct` that contains all the fields in the database record. For each column, we store the column name and the value in that column. Every source connector does something similar—read an event from the source system and generate a pair of `Schema` and `Value`. Sink connectors do the opposite—get a `Schema` and `Value` pair and use the `Schema` to parse the values and insert them into the target system.

Though source connectors know how to generate objects based on the Data API, there is still a question of how `Connect` workers store these objects in Kafka. This is where the converters come in. When users configure the worker (or the connector), they choose which converter they want to use to store data in Kafka. At the moment the available choices are Avro, JSON, or strings. The JSON converter can be configured to either include a schema in the result record or not include one—so we can support both structured and semistructured data. When the connector returns a Data API record to the worker, the worker then uses the configured converter to convert the record to either an Avro object, JSON object, or a string, and the result is then stored into Kafka.

The opposite process happens for sink connectors. When the Connect worker reads a record from Kafka, it uses the configured converter to convert the record from the format in Kafka (i.e., Avro, JSON, or string) to the Connect Data API record and then passes it to the sink connector, which inserts it into the destination system.

This allows the Connect API to support different types of data stored in Kafka, independent of the connector implementation (i.e., any connector can be used with any record type, as long as a converter is available).

Offset management

Offset management is one of the convenient services the workers perform for the connectors (in addition to deployment and configuration management via the REST API). The idea is that connectors need to know which data they have already processed, and they can use APIs provided by Kafka to maintain information on which events were already processed.

For source connectors, this means that the records the connector returns to the Connect workers include a logical partition and a logical offset. Those are not Kafka partitions and Kafka offsets, but rather partitions and offsets as needed in the source system. For example, in the file source, a partition can be a file and an offset can be a line number or character number in the file. In a JDBC source, a partition can be a database table and the offset can be an ID of a record in the table. One of the most important design decisions involved in writing a source connector is deciding on a good way to partition the data in the source system and to track offsets—this will impact the level of parallelism the connector can achieve and whether it can deliver at-least-once or exactly-once semantics.

When the source connector returns a list of records, which includes the source partition and offset for each record, the worker sends the records to Kafka brokers. If the brokers successfully acknowledge the records, the worker then stores the offsets of the records it sent to Kafka. The storage mechanism is pluggable and is usually a Kafka topic. This allows connectors to start processing events from the most recently stored offset after a restart or a crash.

Sink connectors have an opposite but similar workflow: they read Kafka records, which already have a topic, partition, and offset identifiers. Then they call the `connector put()` method that should store those records in the destination system. If the connector reports success, they commit the offsets they've given to the connector back to Kafka, using the usual consumer commit methods.

Offset tracking provided by the framework itself should make it easier for developers to write connectors and guarantee some level of consistent behavior when using different connectors.

Alternatives to Kafka Connect

So far we've looked at Kafka's Connect APIs in great detail. While we love the convenience and reliability the Connect APIs provide, they are not the only method for getting data in and out of Kafka. Let's look at other alternatives and when they are commonly used.

Ingest Frameworks for Other Datastores

While we like to think that Kafka is the center of the universe, some people disagree. Some people build most of their data architectures around systems like Hadoop or Elasticsearch. Those systems have their own data ingestion tools—Flume for Hadoop and Logstash or Fluentd for Elasticsearch. We recommend Kafka's Connect APIs when Kafka is an integral part of the architecture and when the goal is to connect large numbers of sources and sinks. If you are actually building an Hadoop-centric or Elastic-centric system and Kafka is just one of many inputs into that system, then using Flume or Logstash makes sense.

GUI-Based ETL Tools

From old-school systems like Informatica, open source alternatives like Talend and Pentaho, and even newer alternatives such as Apache NiFi and StreamSets, support Apache Kafka as both a data source and a destination. Using these systems makes sense if you are already using them—if you already do everything using Pentaho, for example, you may not be interested in adding another data integration system just for Kafka. They also make sense if you are using a GUI-based approach to building ETL pipelines. The main drawback of these systems is that they are usually built for involved workflows and will be a somewhat heavy and involved solution if all you want to do is get data in and out of Kafka. As mentioned in the section "Transformations" on page 139, we believe that data integration should focus on faithful delivery of messages under all conditions, while most ETL tools add unnecessary complexity.

We do encourage you to look at Kafka as a platform that can handle both data integration (with Connect), application integration (with producers and consumers), and stream processing. Kafka could be a viable replacement for an ETL tool that only integrates data stores.

Stream-Processing Frameworks

Almost all stream-processing frameworks include the ability to read events from Kafka and write them to a few other systems. If your destination system is supported and you already intend to use that stream-processing framework to process events from Kafka, it seems reasonable to use the same framework for data integration as well. This often saves a step in the stream-processing workflow (no need to store processed events in Kafka—just read them out and write them to another system), with the drawback that it can be more difficult to troubleshoot things like lost and corrupted messages.

Summary

In this chapter we discussed the use of Kafka for data integration. Starting with reasons to use Kafka for data integration, we covered general considerations for data integration solutions. We showed why we think Kafka and its Connect APIs are a good fit. We then gave several examples of how to use Kafka Connect in different scenarios, spent some time looking at how Connect works, and then discussed a few alternatives to Kafka Connect.

Whatever data integration solution you eventually land with, the most important feature will always be its ability to deliver all messages under all failure conditions. We believe that Kafka Connect is extremely reliable—based on its integration with Kafka's tried and true reliability features—but it is important that you test the system of your choice, just like we do. Make sure your data integration system of choice can survive stopped processes, crashed machines, network delays, and high loads without missing a message. After all, data integration systems only have one job—delivering those messages.

Of course, while reliability is usually the most important requirement when integrating data systems, it is only one requirement. When choosing a data system, it is important to first review your requirements (refer to "Considerations When Building Data Pipelines" on page 136 for examples) and then make sure your system of choice satisfies them. But this isn't enough—you must also learn your data integration solution well enough to be certain that you are using it in a way that supports your requirements. It isn't enough that Kafka supports at-least-once semantics; you must be sure you aren't accidentally configuring it in a way that may end up with less than complete reliability.

## CHAPTER 8

Cross-Cluster Data Mirroring

For most of the book we discuss the setup, maintenance, and use of a single Kafka cluster. There are, however, a few scenarios in which an architecture may need more than one cluster.

In some cases, the clusters are completely separated. They belong to different departments or different use cases and there is no reason to copy data from one cluster to another. Sometimes, different SLAs or workloads make it difficult to tune a single cluster to serve multiple use cases. Other times, there are different security requirements. Those use cases are fairly easy—managing multiple distinct clusters is the same as running a single cluster multiple times.

In other use cases, the different clusters are interdependent and the administrators need to continuously copy data between the clusters. In most databases, continuously copying data between database servers is called *replication*. Since we've used "replication" to describe movement of data between Kafka nodes that are part of the same cluster, we'll call copying of data between Kafka clusters *mirroring*. Apache Kafka's built-in cross-cluster replicator is called *MirrorMaker*.

In this chapter we will discuss cross-cluster mirroring of all or part of the data. We'll start by discussing some of the common use cases for cross-cluster mirroring. Then we'll show a few architectures that are used to implement these use cases and discuss the pros and cons of each architecture pattern. We'll then discuss MirrorMaker itself and how to use it. We'll share operational tips, including deployment and performance tuning. We'll finish by discussing a few alternatives to MirrorMaker.

Use Cases of Cross-Cluster Mirroring

The following is a list of examples of when cross-cluster mirroring would be used.

Regional and central clusters

In some cases, the company has one or more datacenters in different geographical regions, cities, or continents. Each datacenter has its own Kafka cluster. Some applications can work just by communicating with the local cluster, but some applications require data from multiple datacenters (otherwise, you wouldn't be looking at cross data-center replication solutions). There are many cases when this is a requirement, but the classic example is a company that modifies prices based on supply and demand. This company can have a datacenter in each city in which it has a presence, collects information about local supply and demand, and adjusts prices accordingly. All this information will then be mirrored to a central cluster where business analysts can run company-wide reports on its revenue.

Redundancy (DR)

The applications run on just one Kafka cluster and don't need data from other locations, but you are concerned about the possibility of the entire cluster becoming unavailable for some reason. You'd like to have a second Kafka cluster with all the data that exists in the first cluster, so in case of emergency you can direct your applications to the second cluster and continue as usual.

Cloud migrations

Many companies these days run their business in both an on-premise datacenter and a cloud provider. Often, applications run on multiple regions of the cloud provider, for redundancy, and sometimes multiple cloud providers are used. In these cases, there is often at least one Kafka cluster in each on-premise datacenter and each cloud region. Those Kafka clusters are used by applications in each datacenter and region to transfer data efficiently between the datacenters. For example, if a new application is deployed in the cloud but requires some data that is updated by applications running in the on-premise datacenter and stored in an on-premise database, you can use Kafka Connect to capture database changes to the local Kafka cluster and then mirror these changes to the cloud Kafka cluster where the new application can use them. This helps control the costs of cross-datacenter traffic as well as improve governance and security of the traffic.

Multicluster Architectures

Now that we've seen a few use cases that require multiple Kafka clusters, let's look at some common architectural patterns that we've successfully used when implementing these use cases. Before we go into the architectures, we'll give a brief overview of the realities of cross-datacenter communications. The solutions we'll discuss may seem overly complicated without understanding that they represent trade-offs in the face of specific network conditions.

Some Realities of Cross-Datacenter Communication

The following is a list of some things to consider when it comes to cross-datacenter communication:

High latencies
> Latency of communication between two Kafka clusters increases as the distance and the number of network hops between the two clusters increase.

Limited bandwidth
> Wide area networks (WANs) typically have far lower available bandwidth than what you'll see inside a single datacenter, and the available bandwidth can vary minute to minute. In addition, higher latencies make it more challenging to utilize all the available bandwith.

Higher costs
> Regardless of whether you are running Kafka on-premise or in the cloud, there are higher costs to communicate between clusters. This is partly because the bandwidth is limited and adding bandwidth can be prohibitively expensive, and also because of the prices vendors charge for transferring data between datacenters, regions, and clouds.

Apache Kafka's brokers and clients were designed, developed, tested, and tuned all within a single datacenter. We assumed low latency and high bandwidth between brokers and clients. This is apparent in default timeouts and sizing of various buffers. For this reason, it is not recommended (except in specific cases, which we'll discuss later) to install some Kafka brokers in one datacenter and others in another datacenter.

In most cases, it's best to avoid producing data to a remote datacenter, and when you do, you need to account for higher latency and the potential for more network errors. You can handle the errors by increasing the number of producer retries and handle the higher latency by increasing the size of the buffers that hold records between attempts to send them.

If we need any kind of replication between clusters and we ruled out inter-broker communication and producer-broker communication, then we must allow for broker-consumer communication. Indeed, this is the safest form of cross-cluster communication because in the event of network partition that prevents a consumer from reading data, the records remain safe inside the Kafka brokers until communications resume and consumers can read them. There is no risk of accidental data loss due to network partitions. Still, because bandwidth is limited, if there are multiple applications in one datacenter that need to read data from Kafka brokers in another datacenter, we prefer to install a Kafka cluster in each datacenter and mirror the necessary data between them once rather than have multiple applications consume the same data across the WAN.

We'll talk more about tuning Kafka for cross-datacenter communication, but the following principles will guide most of the architectures we'll discuss next:

- No less than one cluster per datacenter
- Replicate each event exactly once (barring retries due to errors) between each pair of datacenters
- When possible, consume from a remote datacenter rather than produce to a remote datacenter

Hub-and-Spokes Architecture

This architecture is intended for the case where there are multiple local Kafka clusters and one central Kafka cluster. See Figure 8-1.

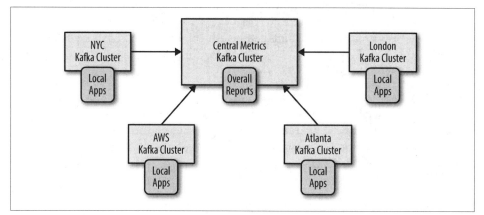

Figure 8-1. The hub-and-spokes architecture

There is also a simpler variation of this architecture with just two clusters—a leader and a follower. See Figure 8-2.

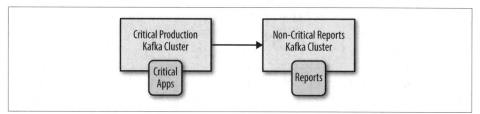

Figure 8-2. A simpler version of the hub-and-spokes architecture

This architecture is used when data is produced in multiple datacenters and some consumers need access to the entire data set. The architecture also allows for applications in each datacenter to only process data local to that specific datacenter. But it does not give access to the entire data set from each datacenter.

The main benefit of this architecture is that data is always produced to the local datacenter and that events from each datacenter are only mirrored once—to the central datacenter. Applications that process data from a single datacenter can be located at that datacenter. Applications that need to process data from multiple datacenters will be located at the central datacenter where all the events are mirrored. Because replication always goes in one direction and because each consumer always reads from the same cluster, this architecture is simple to deploy, configure, and monitor.

The main drawbacks of this architecture are the direct results of its benefits and simplicity. Processors in one regional datacenter can't access data in another. To understand better why this is a limitation, let's look at an example of this architecture.

Suppose that we are a large bank and have branches in multiple cities. Let's say that we decide to store user profiles and their account history in a Kafka cluster in each city. We replicate all this information to a central cluster that is used to run the bank's business analytics. When users connect to the bank website or visit their local branch, they are routed to send events to their local cluster and read events from the same local cluster. However, suppose that a user visits a branch in a different city. Because the user information doesn't exist in the city he is visiting, the branch will be forced to interact with a remote cluster (not recommended) or have no way to access the user's information (really embarrassing). For this reason, use of this pattern is usually limited to only parts of the data set that can be completely separated between regional datacenters.

When implementing this architecture, for each regional datacenter you need at least one mirroring process on the central datacenter. This process will consume data from each remote regional cluster and produce it to the central cluster. If the same topic exists in multiple datacenters, you can write all the events from this topic to one topic with the same name in the central cluster, or write events from each datacenter to a separate topic.

Active-Active Architecture

This architecture is used when two or more datacenters share some or all of the data and each datacenter is able to both produce and consume events. See Figure 8-3.

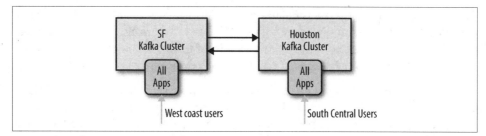

Figure 8-3. The active-active architecture model

The main benefits of this architecture are the ability to serve users from a nearby datacenter, which typically has performance benefits, without sacrificing functionality due to limited availability of data (as we've seen happen in the hub-and-spokes architecture). A secondary benefit is redundancy and resilience. Since every datacenter has all the functionality, if one datacenter is unavailable you can direct users to a remaining datacenter. This type of failover only requires network redirects of users, typically the easiest and most transparent type of failover.

The main drawback of this architecture is the challenges in avoiding conflicts when data is read and updated asynchronously in multiple locations. This includes technical challenges in mirroring events—for example, how do we make sure the same event isn't mirrored back and forth endlessly? But more important, maintaining data consistency between the two datacenters will be difficult. Here are few examples of the difficulties you will encounter:

- If a user sends an event to one datacenter and reads events from another datacenter, it is possible that the event they wrote hasn't arrived the second datacenter yet. To the user, it will look like he just added a book to his wish list, clicked on the wish list, but the book isn't there. For this reason, when this architecture is used, the developers usually find a way to "stick" each user to a specific datacenter and make sure they use the same cluster most of the time (unless they connect from a remote location or the datacenter becomes unavailable).

- An event from one datacenter says user ordered book A and an event from more or less the same time at a second datacenter says that the same user ordered book B. After mirroring, both datacenters have both events and thus we can say that each datacenter has two conflicting events. Applications on both datacenters need to know how to deal with this situation. Do we pick one event as the "correct" one? If so, we need consistent rules on how to pick one so applications on both datacenters will arrive at the same conclusion. Do we decide that both are true and simply send the user two books and have another department deal with returns? Amazon used to resolve conflicts that way, but organizations dealing with stock trades, for example, can't. The specific method for minimizing conflicts and handling them when they occur is specific to each use case. It is important to keep in mind that if you use this architecture, you *will* have conflicts and will need to deal with them.

If you find ways to handle the challenges of asynchronous reads and writes to the same data set from multiple locations, then this architecture is highly recommended. It is the most scalable, resilient, flexible, and cost-effective option we are aware of. So it is well worth the effort to figure out solutions for avoiding replication cycles, keeping users mostly in the same datacenter, and handling conflicts when they occur.

Part of the challenge of active-active mirroring, especially with more than two datacenters, is that you will need a mirroring process for each pair of datacenters and each direction. With five datacenters, you need to maintain at least 20 mirroring processes —and more likely 40, since each process needs redundancy for high availability.

In addition, you will want to avoid loops in which the same event is mirrored back-and-forth endlessly. You can do this by giving each "logical topic" a separate topic for each datacenter and making sure to avoid replicating topics that originated in remote datacenters. For example, logical topic *users* will be topic *SF.users* in one datacenter and *NYC.users* in another datacenter. The mirroring processes will mirror topic *SF.users* from SF to NYC and topic *NYC.users* from NYC to SF. As a result, each event will only be mirrored once, but each datacenter will contain both *SF.users* and *NYC.users*, which means each datacenter will have information for all the users. Consumers will need to consume events from *.users* if they wish to consume all user events. Another way to think of this setup is to see it as a separate namespace for each datacenter that contains all the topics for the specific datacenter. In our example, we'll have the NYC and the SF namespaces.

Note that in the near future (and perhaps before you read this book), Apache Kafka will add record headers. This will allow tagging events with their originating datacenter and using this header information to avoid endless mirroring loops and also to allow processing events from different datacenters separately. You can still implement this feature by using a structured data format for the record values (Avro is our favorite example) and use this to include tags and headers in the event itself. However, this does require extra effort when mirroring, since none of the existing mirroring tools will support your specific header format.

Active-Standby Architecture

In some cases, the only requirement for multiple clusters is to support some kind of disaster scenario. Perhaps you have two clusters in the same datacenter. You use one cluster for all the applications, but you want a second cluster that contains (almost) all the events in the original cluster that you can use if the original cluster is completely unavailable. Or perhaps you need geographic resiliency. Your entire business is running from a datacenter in California, but you need a second datacenter in Texas that usually doesn't do much and that you can use in case of an earthquake. The Texas datacenter will probably have an inactive ("cold") copy of all the applications that admins can start up in case of emergency and that will use the second cluster (Figure 8-4). This is often a legal requirement rather than something that the business is actually planning on doing—but you still need to be ready.

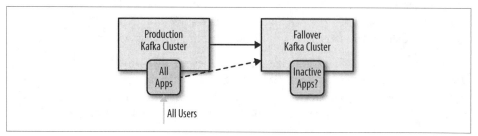

Figure 8-4. The active-standby architecture

The benefits of this setup is simplicity in setup and the fact that it can be used in pretty much any use case. You simply install a second cluster and set up a mirroring process that streams all the events from one cluster to another. No need to worry about access to data, handling conflicts, and other architectural complexities.

The disadvantages are waste of a good cluster and the fact that failover between Kafka clusters is, in fact, much harder than it looks. The bottom line is that it is currently not possible to perform cluster failover in Kafka without either losing data or having duplicate events. Often both. You can minimize them, but never fully eliminate them.

It should be obvious that a cluster that does nothing except wait around for a disaster is a waste of resources. Since disasters are (or should be) rare, most of the time we are looking at a cluster of machines that does nothing at all. Some organizations try to fight this issue by having a DR (disaster recovery) cluster that is much smaller than the production cluster. But this is a risky decision because you can't be sure that this minimally sized cluster will hold up during an emergency. Other organizations prefer to make the cluster useful during non-disasters by shifting some read-only workloads to run on the DR cluster, which means they are really running a small version of a hub-and-spoke architecture with a single spoke.

The more serious issue is, how do you failover to a DR cluster in Apache Kafka?

First, it should go without saying that whichever failover method you choose, your SRE team must practice it on a regular basis. A plan that works today may stop working after an upgrade, or perhaps new use cases make the existing tooling obsolete. Once a quarter is usually the bare minimum for failover practices. Strong SRE teams practice far more frequently. Netflix's famous Chaos Monkey, a service that randomly causes disasters, is the extreme—any day may become failover practice day.

Now, let's take a look at what is involved in a failover.

Data loss and inconsistencies in unplanned failover

Because Kafka's various mirroring solutions are all asynchronous (we'll discuss a synchronous solution in the next section), the DR cluster will not have the latest messages from the primary cluster. You should always monitor how far behind the DR cluster is and never let it fall too far behind. But in a busy system you should expect the DR cluster to be a few hundred or even a few thousand messages behind the primary. If your Kafka cluster handles 1 million messages a second and there is a 5 millisecond lag between the primary and the DR cluster is 5 milliseconds, your DR cluster will be 5,000 messages behind the primary in the best-case scenario. So prepare for unplanned failover to include some data loss. In planned failover, you can stop the primary cluster and wait for the mirroring process to mirror the remaining messages before failing over applications to the DR cluster, thus avoiding this data loss. When unplanned failover occurs and you lose a few thousand messages, note that Kafka currently has no concept of transactions, which means that if some events in multiple topics are related to each other (e.g., sales and line-items), you can have some events arrive to the DR site in time for the failover and others that don't. Your applications will need to be able to handle a line item without a corresponding sale after you failover to the DR cluster.

Start offset for applications after failover

Perhaps the most challenging part in failing over to another cluster is making sure applications know where to start consuming data. There are several common approaches. Some are simple but can cause additional data loss or duplicate processing; others are more involved but minimize additional data loss and reprocessing. Let's take a look at a few:

Auto offset reset

Apache Kafka consumers have a configuration for how to behave when they don't have a previously committed offset—they either start reading from the beginning of the partition or from the end of the partition. If you are using old consumers that are committing offsets to Zookeeper and you are not somehow mirroring these offsets as part of the DR plan, you need to choose one of these options. Either start reading from the beginning of available data and handle large amounts of duplicates or skip to the end and miss an unknown (and hopefully small) number of events. If your application handles duplicates with no issues, or missing some data is no big deal, this option is by far the easiest. Simply skipping to the end of the topic on failover is probably still the most popular failover method.

Replicate offsets topic

If you are using new (0.9 and above) Kafka consumers, the consumers will commit their offsets to a special topic: __consumer_offsets. If you mirror this topic to your DR cluster, when consumers start consuming from the DR cluster they will be able to pick up their old offsets and continue from where they left off. It is simple, but there is a long list of caveats involved.

First, there is no guarantee that offsets in the primary cluster will match those in the secondary cluster. Suppose you only store data in the primary cluster for three days and you start mirroring a topic a week after it was created. In this case the first offset available in the primary cluster may be offset 57000000 (older events were from the first 4 days and were removed already), but the first offset in the DR cluster will be 0. So a consumer that tries to read offset 57000003 (because that's its next event to read) from the DR cluster will fail to do this.

Second, even if you started mirroring immediately when the topic was first created and both the primary and the DR topics start with 0, producer retries can cause offsets to diverge. Simply put, there is no existing Kafka mirroring solution that preserves offsets between primary and DR clusters.

Third, even if the offsets were perfectly preserved, because of the lag between primary and DR clusters and because Kafka currently lacks transactions, an offset committed by a Kafka consumer may arrive ahead or behind the record with this offset. A consumer that fails over may find committed offsets without matching records. Or it may find that the latest committed offset in the DR site is older than the latest committed offset in the primary site. See Figure 8-5.

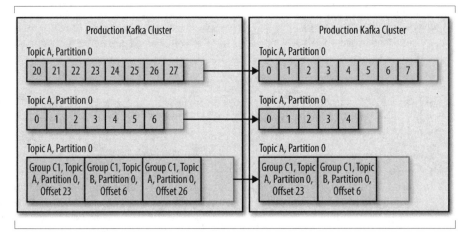

Figure 8-5. A fail over causes committed offsets without matching records

In these cases, you need to accept some duplicates if the latest committed offset in the DR site is older than the one committed on the primary or if the offsets in the records in the DR site are ahead of the primary due to retries. You will also need to figure out how to handle cases where the latest committed offset in the

DR site doesn't have a matching record—do you start processing from the beginning of the topic, or skip to the end?

As you can see, this approach has its limitations. Still, this option lets you failover to another DR with a reduced number of duplicated or missing events compared to other approaches, while still being simple to implement.

Time-based failover

If you are using really new (0.10.0 and above) Kafka consumers, each message includes a timestamp indicating the time the message was sent to Kafka. In really new Kafka versions (0.10.1.0 and above), the brokers include an index and an API for looking up offsets by the timestamp. So, if you failover to the DR cluster and you know that your trouble started at 4:05 A.M., you can tell consumers to start processing data from 4:03 A.M. There will be some duplicates from those two minutes, but it is probably better than other alternatives and the behavior is much easier to explain to everyone in the company—"We failed back to 4:03 A.M." sounds better than "We failed back to what may or may not be the latest committed offsets." So this is often a good compromise. The only question is: how do we tell consumers to start processing data from 4:03 A.M.?

One option is to bake it right into your app. Have a user-configurable option to specify the start time for the app. If this is configured, the app can use the new APIs to fetch offset by time, seek to that time, and start consuming from the right point, committing offsets as usual.

This option is great if you wrote all your applications this way in advance. But what if you didn't? It is fairly straightforward to write a small tool that will take a timestamp, use the new APIs to fetch offsets for this timestamp, and then commit these offsets for a list of topics and partitions as a specific consumer group. We hope to add this tool to Kafka in the near future, but it is possible to write one yourself. The consumer group should be stopped while running this type of tool and started immediately after.

This option is recommended for those using new versions of Kafka who like some certainty in their failover and are willing to write a bit of custom tooling around the process.

External offset mapping

When discussing mirroring the offsets topic, one of the biggest challenges with that approach is the fact that offsets in primary and DR clusters can diverge. With this in mind, some organizations choose to use an external data store, such as Apache Cassandra, to store mapping of offsets from one cluster to another. They build their Kafka mirroring tool so that whenever an event is produced to the DR cluster, both offsets are sent to the external datastore. Or they only store both offsets whenever the difference between the two offsets changed. For example, if offset 495 on primary mapped to offset 500 on the DR cluster, we'll record (495,500) in the external store. If the difference changes later due to duplicates and offset 596 is mapped to 600, then we'll record the new mapping (596,600). There is no need to store all the offset mappings between 495 and 596; we just assume that the difference remains the same and so offset 550 in the primary cluster will map to 555 in the DR. Then when failover occurs, instead of mapping timestamps (which are always a bit inaccurate) to offsets, they map primary offsets to DR offsets and use those. They use one of the two techniques listed above to force consumers to start using the new offsets from the mapping. This still has an issue with offset commits that arrived ahead of the records themselves and offset commits that didn't get mirrored to the DR on time, but it covers some cases.

This solution is quite complex and in my opinion almost never worth the extra effort. It dates back to before time indexes existed and could be used for failover. These days I'd opt to upgrade the cluster and use the time-based solution rather than go through the effort of mapping offsets, which still doesn't cover all failover cases.

After the failover

Let's say that failover was successful. Everything is working just fine on the DR cluster. Now we need to do something with the primary cluster. Perhaps turn it into a DR.

It is tempting to simply modify the mirroring processes to reverse their direction and simply start mirroring from the new primary to the old one. However, this leads to two important questions:

- How do we know where to start mirroring? We need to solve the same problem we have for all our consumers for the mirroring application itself. And remember that all our solutions have cases where they either cause duplicates or miss data—often both.
- In addition, for reasons we discussed above, it is likely that your original primary will have events that the DR cluster does not. If you just start mirroring new data back, the extra history will remain and the two clusters will be inconsistent.

For this reason, the simplest solution is to first scrape the original cluster—delete all the data and committed offsets and then start mirroring from the new primary back to what is now the new DR cluster. This gives you a clean slate that is identical to the new primary.

A few words on cluster discovery

One of the important points to consider when planning a standby cluster is that in the event of failover, your applications will need to know how to start communicating with the failover cluster. If you hardcoded the hostnames of your primary cluster brokers in the producer and consumer properties, this will be challenging. Most organizations keep it simple and create a DNS name that usually points to the primary brokers. In case of an emergency, the DNS name can be pointed to the standby cluster. The discovery service (DNS or other) doesn't need to include all the brokers —Kafka clients only need to access a single broker successfully in order to get metadata about the cluster and discover the other brokers. So including just three brokers is usually fine. Regardless of the discovery method, most failover scenarios do require bouncing consumer applications after failover so they can find the new offsets they need to start consuming.

Stretch Clusters

Active-standby architectures are used to protect the business against the failure of a Kafka cluster, by moving applications to communicate with another cluster in case of cluster failure. Stretch clusters are intended to protect the Kafka cluster from failure in the event an entire datacenter failed. They do this by installing a single Kafka cluster across multiple datacenters.

Stretch clusters are fundamentally different from other multi-datacenter scenarios. To start with, they are not multicluster—it is just one cluster. As a result, we don't need a mirroring process to keep two clusters in sync. Kafka's normal replication mechanism is used, as usual, to keep all brokers in the cluster in sync. This setup can include synchronous replication. Producers normally receive an acknowledgment from a Kafka broker after the message was successfully written to Kafka. In the Stretch cluster case, we can configure things so the acknowledgment will be sent after the message is written successfully to Kafka brokers in two datacenters. This involves using rack definitions to make sure each partition has replicas in multiple datacenters and the use of `min.isr` and `acks=all` to ensure that every write is acknowledged from at least two datacenters.

The advantages of this architecture are in the synchronous replication—some types of business simply require that their DR site is always 100% synchronized with the primary site. This is often a legal requirement and is applied to any data-store across the company—Kafka included. The other advantage is that both datacenters and all brokers in the cluster are used. There is no waste like the one we saw in active-standby architectures.

This architecture is limited in the type of disasters it protects against. It only protects from datacenter failures, not any kind of application or Kafka failures. The operational complexity is also limited. This architecture demands physical infrastructure that not all companies can provide.

This architecture is feasible if you can install Kafka (and Zookeeper) in at least three datacenters with high bandwidth and low latency between them. This can be done if your company owns three buildings on the same street, or—more commonly—by using three availability zones inside one region of your cloud provider.

The reason three datacenters are important is because Zookeeper requires an uneven number of nodes in a cluster and will remain available if a majority of the nodes are available. With two datacenters and an uneven number of nodes, one datacenter will always contain a majority, which means that if this datacenter is unavailable, Zookeeper is unavailable, and Kafka is unavailable. With three datacenters, you can easily allocate nodes so no single datacenter has a majority. So if one datacenter is unavailable, a majority of nodes exist in the other two datacenters and the Zookeeper cluster will remain available. Therefore, so will the Kafka cluster.

It is possible to run Zookeeper and Kafka in two datacenters using a Zookeeper group configuration that allows for manual failover between two datacenters. However, this setup is uncommon.

Apache Kafka's MirrorMaker

Apache Kafka contains a simple tool for mirroring data between two datacenters. It is called MirrorMaker and at its core, it is a collection of consumers (called *streams* in MirrorMaker documentation, for historical reasons), which are all part of the same consumer group and read data from the set of topics you chose to replicate. Each MirrorMaker process has a single producer. The workflow is pretty simple: MirrorMaker runs a thread for each consumer. Each consumer consumes events from the topics and partitions it was assigned on the source cluster and uses the shared producer to send those events to the target cluster. Every 60 seconds (by default), the consumers will tell the producer to send all the events it has to Kafka and wait until Kafka acknowledges these events. Then the consumers contact the source Kafka cluster to commit the offsets for those events. This guarantees no data loss (messages are acknowledged by Kafka before offsets are committed to the source) and there is no more than 60 seconds' worth of duplicates if the MirrorMaker process crashes. See Figure 8-6.

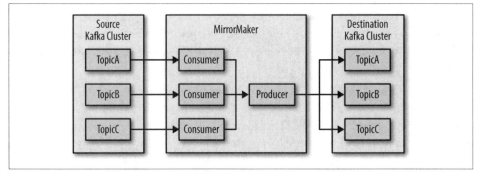

Figure 8-6. The MirrorMaker process in Kafka

More about MirrorMaker

MirrorMaker sounds very simple, but because we were trying to be very efficient and get very close to exactly-once delivery, it turned out to be tricky to implement correctly. By release 0.10.0.0 of Apache Kafka, MirrorMaker had been rewritten four times. Additional writes may happen in the future as well. The description here and the details in the following sections apply to MirrorMaker as it existed from release 0.9.0.0 to release 0.10.2.0.

How to Configure

MirrorMaker is highly configurable. First, it uses one producer and multiple consumers, so every configuration property of producers and consumers can be used when configuring MirrorMaker. In addition, MirrorMaker itself has a sizable list of configuration options, sometimes with complex dependencies between them. We will show a few examples here and highlight some of the important configuration options, but exhaustive documentation of MirrorMaker is outside our scope.

With that in mind, let's take a look at a MirrorMaker example:

```
bin/kafka-mirror-maker --consumer.config etc/kafka/consumer.properties --
producer.config etc/kafka/producer.properties --new.consumer --num.streams=2 --
whitelist ".*"
```

Let's look at MirrorMaker's basic command-line arguments one by one:

`consumer.config`

This is the configuration for all the consumers that will be fetching data from the source cluster. They all share one configuration file, which means you can only have one source cluster and one `group.id`. So all the consumers will be part of the same consumer group, which is exactly what we want. The mandatory configurations in the file are the `bootstrap.servers` (for the source cluster) and the `group.id`. But you can use any additional configuration you want for the consumers. The one configuration you don't want to touch is `auto.com mit.enable=false`. MirrorMaker depends on its ability to commit its own offsets after they safely arrive to the target Kafka cluster. Changing this setting can result in data loss. One configuration you do want to change is `auto.offset.reset`. This defaults to `latest`, which means MirrorMaker will only mirror events that arrived to the source cluster after MirrorMaker started. If you want to mirror existing data as well, change this to `earliest`. We will discuss additional configuration properties in the section "Tuning MirrorMaker" on page 175.

`producer.config`

The configuration for the producer used by MirrorMaker to write to the target cluster. The only mandatory configuration is `bootstrap.servers` (for the target cluster). We will discuss additional configuration properties in the section "Tuning MirrorMaker" on page 175.

`new.consumer`

MirrorMaker can use the 0.8 consumer or the new 0.9 consumer. We recommend the 0.9 consumer because it is more stable at this point.

`num.streams`

As we explained previously, each stream is another consumer reading from the source cluster. Remember that all consumers in the same MirrorMaker process share the same producers. It will take multiple streams to saturate a producer. If you need additional throughput after this point, you'll need another Mirror-Maker process.

`whitelist`

A regular expression for the topic names that will be mirrored. All topic names that match the regular expression will be mirrored. In this example, we chose to replicate every topic, but it is often good practice to use something like *prod.** and avoid replicating test topics. Or in active-active architecture, MirrorMaker replicating from a NYC datacenter to a SF datacenter will configure `white list="NYC.\*"` and avoid replicating back topics that originated in SF.

Deploying MirrorMaker in Production

In the previously given example, we ran MirrorMaker as a command-line utility. Usually when running MirrorMaker in a production environment, you will want to run MirrorMaker as a service, running in the background with `nohup` and redirecting its console output to a log file. Technically, the tool has `-daemon` as a command-line option that should do all of the above for you, but in practice, this hasn't worked as expected in recent releases.

Most companies that use MirrorMaker have their own startup scripts that also include the configuration parameters they use. Production deployment systems like Ansible, Puppet, Chef, and Salt are often used to automate deployment and manage the many configuration options and files.

A more advanced deployment option that is becoming very popular is to run Mirror-Maker inside a Docker container. MirrorMaker is completely stateless and doesn't require any disk storage (all the data and state is stored in Kafka itself). Wrapping MirrorMaker in Docker also allows running multiple instances on a single machine. Since a single MirrorMaker instance is limited to the throughput of a single producer, this is often important to launch multiple instances of MirrorMaker, and Docker makes it much easier. It also makes it easier to scale up and down—spin additional containers when more throughput is needed at peak time and spin them down when there is less traffic. If you are running MirrorMaker in a cloud environment, you can even spin up additional servers on which to run the containers based on throughput and demand.

If at all possible, run MirrorMaker at the destination datacenter. So if you are sending data from NYC to SF, MirrorMaker should run in SF and consume data across the US from NYC. The reason for this is that long-distance networks can be a bit less reliable than those inside a datacenter. If there is a network partition and you lose connectivity between the datacenters, having a consumer that is unable to connect to a cluster is much safer than a producer that can't connect. If the consumer can't connect, it simply won't be able to read events, but the events will still be stored in the source Kafka cluster and can remain there for a long time. There is no risk of losing events. On the other hand, if the events were already consumed and MirrorMaker can't produce them due to network partition, there is always a risk that these events will accidentally get lost by MirrorMaker. So remote consuming is safer than remote producing.

When do you have to consume locally and produce remotely? The answer is when you need to encrypt the data while it is transferred between the datacenters but you don't need to encrypt the data inside the datacenter. Consumers take a significant performance hit when connecting to Kafka with SSL encryption—much more so than producers. And this performance hit also affects the Kafka brokers themselves. If your cross datacenter traffic requires encryption, you are better off placing Mirror-Maker at the source datacenter, having it consume unencrypted data locally, and then producing it to the remote datacenter through an SSL encrypted connection. This way, the producer connects to Kafka with SSL but not the consumer, which doesn't impact performance as much. If you use this consume locally and produce remotely, make sure MirrorMaker is configured to never lose events by configuring it with acks=all and a sufficient number of retries. Also, configure MirrorMaker to exit when it fails to send events, which is typically safer to do than to continue and risk data loss.

If having very low lag between the source and target clusters is important, you will probably want to run at least two MirrorMaker instances on two different servers and have both use the same consumer group. If one server is stopped for whatever reason, the MirrorMaker instance can continue mirroring the data.

When deploying MirrorMaker in production, it is important to remember to monitor it as follows:

Lag monitoring

You will definitely want to know if the destination cluster is falling behind the source. The lag is the difference in offsets between the latest message in the source Kafka and the latest message in the destination. See Figure 8-7.

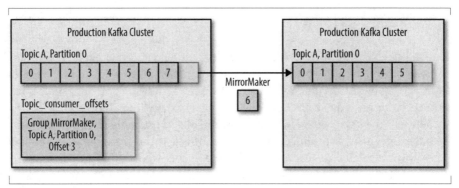

Figure 8-7. Monitoring the lag difference in offsets

In Figure 8-7, the last offset in the source cluster is 7 and the last offset in the destination is 5—meaning there is a lag of 2 messages.

There are two ways to track this lag, and neither is perfect:

- Check the latest offset committed by MirrorMaker to the source Kafka cluster. You can use the `kafka-consumer-groups` tool to check for each partition MirrorMaker is reading— the offset of the last event in the partition, the last offset MirrorMaker committed, and the lag between them. This indicator is not 100% accurate because MirrorMaker doesn't commit offsets all the time. It commits offsets every minute by default so you will see the lag grow for a minute and then suddenly drop. In the diagram, the real lag is 2, but the `kafka-consumer-groups` tool will report a lag of 4 because MirrorMaker hasn't committed offsets for more recent messages yet. LinkedIn's Burrow monitors the same information but has a more sophisticated method to determine whether the lag represents a real problem, so you won't get false alerts.

- Check the latest offset read by MirrorMaker (even if it isn't committed). The consumers embedded in MirrorMaker publish key metrics in JMX. One of them is the consumer maximum lag (over all the partitions it is consuming). This lag is also not 100% accurate because it is updated based on what the consumer read but doesn't take into account whether the producer managed to send those messages to the destination Kafka cluster and whether they were acknowledged successfully. In this example, the MirrorMaker consumer will report a lag of 1 message rather than 2, because it already read message 6—even though the message wasn't produced to the destination yet.

Note that if MirrorMaker skips or drops messages, neither method will detect an issue because they just track the latest offset. Confluent's Control Center monitors message counts and checksums and closes this monitoring gap.

Metrics monitoring

> MirrorMaker contains a producer and a consumer. Both have many available metrics and we recommend collecting and tracking them. Kafka documentation (*http://bit.ly/2sMfZWf*) lists all the available metrics. Here are a few metrics that proved useful in tuning MirrorMaker performance:

> *Consumer*
>> `fetch-size-avg`, `fetch-size-max`, `fetch-rate`, `fetch-throttle-time-avg`, and `fetch-throttle-time-max`

> *Producer*
>> `batch-size-avg`, `batch-size-max`, `requests-in-flight`, and `record-retry-rate`

> *Both*
>> `io-ratio` and `io-wait-ratio`

Canary

> If you monitor everything else, a canary isn't strictly necessary, but we like to add it in for multiple layers of monitoring. It provides a process that, every minute, sends an event to a special topic in the source cluster and tries to read the event from the destination cluster. It also alerts you if the event takes more than an acceptable amount of time to arrive. This can mean MirrorMaker is lagging or that it isn't around at all.

Tuning MirrorMaker

Sizing of the MirrorMaker cluster depends on the throughput you need and the lag you can tolerate. If you can't tolerate any lag, you have to size MirrorMaker with enough capacity to keep up with your top throughput. If you can tolerate some lag, you can size MirrorMaker to be 75-80% utilized 95-99% of the time. Then, expect some lag to develop when you are at peak throughput. Because MirrorMaker has spare capacity most of the time, it will catch up once the peak is over.

Then you want to measure the throughput you get from MirrorMaker with a different number of consumer threads—configured with `num.streams` parameter. We can give you some ballpark numbers (LinkedIn gets 6MB/s with 8 consumer threads and 12MB/s with 16), but since this depends a lot on your hardware, datacenter, or cloud provider, you will want to run your own tests. Kafka ships with the `kafka-performance-producer` tool. Use it to generate load on a source cluster and then connect MirrorMaker and start mirroring this load. Test MirrorMaker with 1, 2, 4, 8, 16, 24, and 32 consumer threads. Watch where performance tapers off and set `num.streams` just below this point. If you are consuming or producing compressed events (recommended, since bandwidth is the main bottleneck for cross-datacenter mirroring), MirrorMaker will have to decompress and recompress the events. This uses a lot of CPU, so keep an eye on CPU utilization as you increase the number of threads. Using this process, you will find the maximum throughput you can get with a single MirrorMaker instance. If it is not enough, you will want to experiment with additional instances and after that, additional servers.

In addition, you may want to separate sensitive topics—those that absolutely require low latency and where the mirror must be as close to the source as possible—to a separate MirrorMaker cluster with its own consumer group. This will prevent a bloated topic or an out of control producer from slowing down your most sensitive data pipeline.

This is pretty much all the tuning you can do to MirrorMaker itself. However, you can still increase the throughput of each consumer thread and each MirrorMaker instance.

If you are running MirrorMaker across datacenters, you want to optimize the network configuration in Linux as follows:

- Increase TCP buffer size (`net.core.rmem_default`, `net.core.rmem_max`, `net.core.wmem_default`, `net.core.wmem_max`, `net.core.optmem_max`)
- Enable automatic window scaling (`sysctl -w net.ipv4.tcp_window_scaling=1` or add `net.ipv4.tcp_window_scaling=1` to `/etc/sysctl.conf`)
- Reduce the TCP slow start time (set `/proc/sys/net/ipv4/tcp_slow_start_after_idle` to 0)

Note that tuning the Linux network is a large and complex topic. To understand more about these parameters and others, we recommend reading a network tuning guide such as *Performance Tuning for Linux Servers* by Sandra K. Johnson, et al. (IBM Press).

In addition, you may want to tune the producers and consumers that are running in MirrorMaker. First, you will want decide whether the producer or the consumer is the bottleneck—is the producer waiting for the consumer to bring more data or the other way around? One way to decide is to look at the producer and consumer metrics you are monitoring. If one process is idle while the other is fully utilized, you know which one needs tuning. Another method is to do several thread dumps (using jstack) and see if the MirrorMaker threads are spending most of the time in poll or in send—more time spent polling usually means the consumer is the bottleneck, while more time spent sending shift points to the producer.

If you need to tune the producer, the following configuration settings can be useful:

`max.in.flight.requests.per.connection`
> By default, MirrorMaker only allows one in-flight request. This means every request that was sent by the producer has to be acknowledged by the destination cluster before the next message will be sent. This can limit throughput, especially if there is significant latency before the brokers acknowledge the messages. The reason MirrorMaker limits the number of in-flight requests is because this is the only way to guarantee that Kafka will preserve message order in the event that some messages will require multiple retries before they are successfully acknowledged. If message order is not critical for your use case, increasing `max.in.flight.requests.per.connection` can significantly increase your throughput.

`linger.ms` *and* `batch.size`
> If your monitoring shows that the producer consistently sends partially empty batches (i.e., `batch-size-avg` and `batch-size-max` metrics are lower than configured `batch.size`), you can increase throughput by introducing a bit of latency. Increase `latency.ms` and the producer will wait a few milliseconds for the batches to fill up before sending them. If you are sending full batches and have memory to spare, you can increase `batch.size` and send larger batches.

The following consumer configurations can increase throughput for the consumer:

- The partition assignment strategy in MirrorMaker (i.e., the algorithm that decides which consumer is assigned which partitions) defaults to `range`. There are benefits to `range` strategy, which is why it is the normal default for consumers, but it can lead to uneven assignment of partitions to consumers. For MirrorMaker, it is usually better to change the strategy to round robin, especially when mirroring a large number of topics and partitions. You set this by adding `parti tion.assignment.strategy=org.apache.kafka.clients.consumer.RoundRobi nAssignor` to the consumer properties file.

- `fetch.max.bytes`—if the metrics you are collecting show that `fetch-size-avg` and `fetch-size-max` are close to the `fetch.max.bytes` configuration, the consumer is reading as much data from the broker as it is allowed. If you have available memory, try increasing `fetch.max.bytes` to allow the consumer to read more data in each request.

- `fetch.min.bytes` and `fetch.max.wait`—if you see in the consumer metrics that `fetch-rate` is high, the consumer is sending too many requests to the brokers and not receiving enough data in each request. Try increasing both `fetch.min.bytes` and `fetch.max.wait` so the consumer will receive more data in each request and the broker will wait until enough data is available before responding to the consumer request.

Other Cross-Cluster Mirroring Solutions

We looked in depth at MirrorMaker because this mirroring software arrives as part of Apache Kafka. However, MirrorMaker also has some limitations when used in practice. It is worthwhile to look at some of the alternatives to MirrorMaker and the ways they address MirrorMaker limitations and complexities.

Uber uReplicator

Uber ran MirrorMaker at very large scale, and as the number of topics and partitions grew and the cluster throughput increased, they started running into the following problems:

Rebalancing delays

MirrorMaker consumers are just consumers. Adding MirrorMaker threads, adding MirrorMaker instances, bouncing MirrorMaker instances, or even adding new topics that match the regular expression used in the whitelist all cause consumers to rebalance. As we saw in Chapter 4, rebalancing stops all the consumers until new partitions can be assigned to each consumer. With a very large number of topics and partitions, this can take a while. This is especially true when using old consumers like Uber did. In some cases this caused 5-10 minutes of inactivity, causing mirroring to fall behind and accumulate a large backlog of events to mirror, which can take a long time to recover from. This caused very high latency for consumers reading events from the destination cluster.

Difficulty adding topics

Using a regular expression as the topic whitelist means that MirrorMaker will rebalance every time someone adds a matching topic to the source cluster. We've already seen that rebalances were particularly painful for Uber. To avoid this, they decided to simply list every topic they need to mirror and avoid surprise rebalances. But this means that they need to manually add new topics that they want to mirror to the whitelist on all MirrorMaker instances and bounce the instances, which leads to rebalances. At least those rebalances happen on scheduled maintenance and not every time someone adds a topic, but it is still lots of maintenance. This also means that if the maintenance isn't done correctly and different instances have different topic lists, MirrorMaker will start and endlessly rebalance as the consumers won't be able to agree on the topics they subscribe to.

Given these issues, Uber decided to write their own MirrorMaker clone, called uReplicator. They decided to use Apache Helix as a central (but highly available) controller that will manage the topic list and the partitions assigned to each uReplicator instance. Administrators use a REST API to add new topics to the list in Helix and uReplicator is responsible for assigning partitions to the different consumers. To achieve this, Uber replaced the Kafka consumers used in MirrorMaker with a Kafka consumer they wrote themselves called Helix consumer. This consumer takes its partition assignment from the Apache Helix controller rather than as a result of an agreement between the consumers (see Chapter 4 for details on how this is done in Kafka). As a result, the Helix consumer can avoid rebalances and instead listen to changes in the assigned partitions that arrive from Helix.

Uber wrote a blog post (*https://eng.uber.com/ureplicator/*) describing the architecture in more detail and showing the improvements they experienced. At the time of writing, we are not aware of any company besides Uber that uses the uReplicator. This is possibly because most companies don't operate at Uber's scale and don't run into the same issues, or perhaps because the dependency on Apache Helix introduces a completely new component to learn and manage, which adds complexity to the entire project.

Confluent's Replicator

At the same time that Uber developed their uReplicator, Confluent independently developed Replicator. Despite the similarities in names, the projects have almost nothing in common—they are different solutions to two different sets of Mirror-Maker problems. Confluent's Replicator was developed to address issues their enterprise customers encountered when using MirrorMaker to manage their multicluster deployments.

Diverging cluster configuration

> While MirrorMaker keeps data in sync between source and destination, this is the only thing it keeps in sync. Topics can end up with different numbers of partitions, replication factors, and topic-level settings. Increasing topic retention from one to three weeks on the source cluster and forgetting about the DR cluster can lead to a rather nasty surprise when you failover to the second cluster and discover that a few weeks of data are now missing. Trying to manually keep all these settings in sync is error-prone and can cause downstream applications, or even replication itself, to fail if the systems fall out of sync.

Cluster management challenges

> We've already seen that MirrorMaker is typically deployed as a cluster of multiple instances. This means yet another cluster to figure out how to deploy, monitor, and manage. With two configuration files and a large number of parameters, configuration management for MirrorMaker itself can be a challenge. This increases if there are more than two clusters and one-direction replication. If you have three active-active clusters, you have six MirrorMaker clusters to deploy,

monitor, and configure, and each of those likely has at least three instances. With five active-active clusters, the number of MirrorMaker clusters increases to 20.

With the goal of minimizing administration overhead for busy enterprise IT departments, Confluent decided to implement Replicator as a source connector for the Kafka Connect framework, a source connector that reads data from another Kafka cluster rather than from a database. If you recall the Kafka Connect architecture from Chapter 7, you remember that each connector divides the work between a configurable number of tasks. In Replicator, each task is a consumer and a producer pair. The Connect framework assigns those tasks to different Connect worker nodes as needed —so you may have multiple tasks on one server or have the tasks spread out to multiple servers. This replaces the manual work of figuring out how many MirrorMaker streams should run per instance and how many instances per machine. Connect also has a REST API to centrally manage the configuration for the connectors and tasks. If we assume that most Kafka deployments include Kafka Connect for other reasons (sending database change events into Kafka is a very popular use case), then by running Replicator inside Connect, we can cut down on the number of clusters we need to manage. The other significant improvement is that the Replicator connector, in addition to replicating data from a list of Kafka topics, also replicates the configuration for those topics from Zookeeper.

Summary

We started the chapter by describing the reasons you may need to manage more than a single Kafka cluster and then proceeded to describe several common multicluster architectures, ranging from the simple to the very complex. We went into the details of implementing failover architecture for Kafka and compared the different options currently available. Then we proceeded to discuss the available tools. Starting with Apache Kafka's MirrorMaker, we went into many details of using it in production. We finished by reviewing two alternative options that solve some of the issues you might encounter with MirrorMaker.

Whichever architecture and tools you end up using—remember that multicluster configuration and mirroring pipelines should be monitored and tested just like everything else you take into production. Because multicluster management in Kafka can be easier than it is with relational databases, some organizations treat it as an afterthought and neglect to apply proper design, planning, testing, deployment automation, monitoring, and maintenance. By taking multicluster management seriously, preferably as part of a holistic disaster or geodiversity plan for the entire organization that involves mutliple applications and datastores, you will greatly increase the chances of successfully managing multiple Kafka clusters.

## CHAPTER 9

Administering Kafka

Kafka provides several command-line interface (CLI) utilities that are useful for making administrative changes to your clusters. The tools are implemented in Java classes, and a set of scripts are provided to call those classes properly. These tools provide basic functions, but you may find they are lacking for more complex operations. This chapter will describe the tools that are available as part of the Apache Kafka open source project. More information about advanced tools that have been developed in the community, outside of the core project, can be found on the Apache Kafka website (*https://kafka.apache.org/*).

Authorizing Admin Operations

While Apache Kafka implements authentication and authorization to control topic operations, most cluster operations are not yet supported. This means that these CLI tools can be used without any authentication required, which will allow operations such as topic changes to be executed with no security check or audit. This functionality is under development and should be added soon.

Topic Operations

The kafka-topics.sh tool provides easy access to most topic operations (configuration changes have been deprecated and moved to the kafka-configs.sh tool). It allows you to create, modify, delete, and list information about topics in the cluster. To use this command, you are required to provide the Zookeeper connect string for the cluster with the --zookeeper argument. In the examples that follow, the Zookeeper connect string is assumed to be zoo1.example.com:2181/kafka-cluster.

Check the Version

Many of the command-line tools for Kafka operate directly on the metadata stored in Zookeeper rather than connecting to the brokers themselves. For this reason, it is important to make sure the version of the tools that you are using matches the version of the brokers in the cluster. The safest approach is to run the tools on the Kafka brokers themselves, using the deployed version.

Creating a New Topic

You need three arguments to create a new topic in a cluster (these arguments must be provided, even though some of them have broker-level defaults configured already):

Topic name
> The name of the topic that you wish to create.

Replication Factor
> The number of replicas of the topic to maintain within the cluster.

Partitions
> The number of partitions to create for the topic.

Specifying Topic Configurations

It is also possible to explicitly set the replicas for a topic during creation, or set configuration overrides for the topic. Neither of these operations will be covered here. Configuration overrides can be found later in this chapter, and they can be provided to `kafka-topics.sh` using the `--config` command-line parameter. Partiton reassignment is also covered later in this chapter.

Topic names may contain alphanumeric characters, as well as underscores, dashes, and periods.

Naming Topics

It is permitted, but not recommended, to have topic names that start with two underscores. Topics of this form are considered internal topics for the cluster (such as the `__consumer_offsets` topic for the consumer group offset storage). It is also not recommended to use both periods and underscores in a single cluster because when the topic names are used in metric names inside Kafka, periods are changed to underscores (e.g., "topic.1" becomes "topic_1" in metrics).

Execute `kafka-topics.sh` as follows:

```
kafka-topics.sh --zookeeper <zookeeper connect> --create --topic <string>
--replication-factor <integer> --partitions <integer>
```

The command will cause the cluster to create a topic with the specified name and number of partitions. For each partition, the cluster will select the specified number of replicas appropriately. This means that if the cluster is set up for rack-aware replica assignment, the replicas for each partition will be in separate racks. If rack-aware assignment is not desired, specify the `--disable-rack-aware` command-line argument.

For example, create a topic named "my-topic" with eight partitions that have two replicas each:

```
# kafka-topics.sh --zookeeper zoo1.example.com:2181/kafka-cluster --create
--topic my-topic --replication-factor 2 --partitions 8
Created topic "my-topic".
#
```

Skipping Errors for Existing Topics

When using this script in automation, you may want to use the `--if-not-exists` argument, which will not return an error if the topic already exists.

Adding Partitions

It is sometimes necessary to increase the number of partitions for a topic. Partitions are the way topics are scaled and replicated across a cluster, and the most common reason to increase the partition count is to spread out a topic further, or decrease the throughput for a single partition. Topics may also be increased if a consumer needs to expand to run more copies in a single group, as a partition can only be consumed by a single member in a group.

Adjusting Keyed Topics

Topics that are produced with keyed messages can be very difficult to add partitions to from a consumer's point of view. This is because the mapping of keys to partitions will change when the number of partitions is changed. For this reason, it is advisable to set the number of partitions for a topic that will contain keyed messages once, when the topic is created, and avoid resizing the topic.

Skipping Errors for Nonexistent Topics

While an `--if-exists` argument is provided for the `--alter` command, using it is not recommended. Using this argument will cause the command to not return an error if the topic being changed does not exist. This can mask problems where a topic does not exist that should have been created.

For example, increase the number of partitions for a topic named "my-topic" to 16:

```
# kafka-topics.sh --zookeeper zoo1.example.com:2181/kafka-cluster
--alter --topic my-topic --partitions 16
WARNING: If partitions are increased for a topic that has a key,
the partition logic or ordering of the messages will be affected
Adding partitions succeeded!
#
```

Reducing Partition Counts

It is not possible to reduce the number of partitions for a topic. The reason this is not supported is because deleting a partition from a topic would cause part of the data in that topic to be deleted as well, which would be inconsistent from a client point of view. In addition, trying to redistribute the data to remaining partitions would be difficult and result in out-of-order messages. Should you need to reduce the number of partitions, you will need to delete the topic and recreate it.

Deleting a Topic

Even a topic with no messages in it uses cluster resources, including disk space, open filehandles, and memory. If a topic is no longer needed, it can be deleted in order to free up these resources. In order to perform this action, the brokers in the cluster must have been configured with the `delete.topic.enable` option set to true. If this option has been set to false, then the request to delete the topic will be ignored.

Data Loss Ahead

Deleting a topic will also delete all its messages. This is not a reversible operation, so make sure it executed carefully.

For example, delete the topic named "my-topic":

```
# kafka-topics.sh --zookeeper zoo1.example.com:2181/kafka-cluster
--delete --topic my-topic
Topic my-topic is marked for deletion.
```

```
Note: This will have no impact if delete.topic.enable is not set
to true.
#
```

Listing All Topics in a Cluster

The topics tool can list all topics in a cluster. The list is formatted with one topic per line, in no particular order.

For example, list topics in the cluster:

```
# kafka-topics.sh --zookeeper zoo1.example.com:2181/kafka-cluster
--list
my-topic - marked for deletion
other-topic
#
```

Describing Topic Details

It is also possible to get detailed information on one or more topics in the cluster. The output includes the partition count, topic configuration overrides, and a listing of each partition with its replica assignments. This can be limited to a single topic by providing a --topic argument to the command.

For example, describe all topics in the cluster:

```
# kafka-topics.sh --zookeeper zoo1.example.com:2181/kafka-cluster --describe
Topic:other-topic       PartitionCount:8        ReplicationFactor:2 Configs:
Topic:other-topic       Partition: 0    ...  Replicas: 1,0    Isr: 1,0
Topic:other-topic       Partition: 1    ...  Replicas: 0,1    Isr: 0,1
Topic:other-topic       Partition: 2    ...  Replicas: 1,0    Isr: 1,0
Topic:other-topic       Partition: 3    ...  Replicas: 0,1    Isr: 0,1
Topic:other-topic       Partition: 4    ...  Replicas: 1,0    Isr: 1,0
Topic:other-topic       Partition: 5    ...  Replicas: 0,1    Isr: 0,1
Topic:other-topic       Partition: 6    ...  Replicas: 1,0    Isr: 1,0
Topic:other-topic       Partition: 7    ...  Replicas: 0,1    Isr: 0,1
#
```

The describe command also has several useful options for filtering the output. These can be helpful for diagnosing cluster issues. For each of these, do not specify the --topic argument (because the intention is to find all topics or partitions in a cluster that match the criteria). These options will not work with the list command (detailed in the previous section).

In order to find all topics that have configuration overrides, use the --topics-with-overrides argument. This will describe only the topics that have configurations that differ from the cluster defaults.

There are two filters used to find partitions that have problems. The `--under-replicated-partitions` argument will show all partitions where one or more of the replicas for the partition are not in-sync with the leader. The `--unavailable-partitions` argument shows all partitions without a leader. This is a more serious situation that means that the partition is currently offline and unavailable for produce or consume clients.

For example, show under-replicated partitions:

```
# kafka-topics.sh --zookeeper zoo1.example.com:2181/kafka-cluster
--describe --under-replicated-partitions
        Topic: other-topic     Partition: 2    Leader: 0       Replicas: 1,0
        Isr: 0
        Topic: other-topic     Partition: 4    Leader: 0       Replicas: 1,0
        Isr: 0
#
```

Consumer Groups

Consumer groups in Kafka are managed in two places: for older consumers, the information is maintained in Zookeeper, whereas for the new consumer it is maintained within the Kafka brokers. The `kafka-consumer-groups.sh` tool can be used to list and describe both types of groups. It can also be used to delete consumer groups and offset information, but only for groups running under the old consumer (maintained in Zookeeper). When working with older consumer groups, you will access the Kafka cluster by specifying the `--zookeeper` command-line parameter for the tool. For new consumer groups, you will need to use the `--bootstrap-server` parameter with the hostname and port number of the Kafka broker to connect to instead.

List and Describe Groups

To list consumer groups using the older consumer clients, execute with the `--zookeeper` and `--list` parameters. For the new consumer, use the `--bootstrap-server`, `--list`, and `--new-consumer` parameters.

For example, list old consumer groups:

```
# kafka-consumer-groups.sh --zookeeper
zoo1.example.com:2181/kafka-cluster --list
console-consumer-79697
myconsumer
#
```

For example, list new consumer groups:

```
# kafka-consumer-groups.sh --new-consumer --bootstrap-server
kafka1.example.com:9092/kafka-cluster --list
kafka-python-test
```

```
my-new-consumer
#
```

For any group listed, you can get more details by changing the `--list` parameter to `--describe` and adding the `--group` parameter. This will list all the topics that the group is consuming, as well as the offsets for each topic partition.

For example, get consumer group details for the old consumer group named "testgroup":

```
# kafka-consumer-groups.sh --zookeeper zoo1.example.com:2181/kafka-cluster
--describe --group testgroup
GROUP                          TOPIC                          PARTITION
CURRENT-OFFSET  LOG-END-OFFSET  LAG             OWNER
myconsumer                     my-topic                       0
1688            1688            0
myconsumer_host1.example.com-1478188622741-7dab5ca7-0
myconsumer                     my-topic                       1
1418            1418            0
myconsumer_host1.example.com-1478188622741-7dab5ca7-0
myconsumer                     my-topic                       2
1314            1315            1
myconsumer_host1.example.com-1478188622741-7dab5ca7-0
myconsumer                     my-topic                       3
2012            2012            0
myconsumer_host1.example.com-1478188622741-7dab5ca7-0
myconsumer                     my-topic                       4
1089            1089            0
myconsumer_host1.example.com-1478188622741-7dab5ca7-0
myconsumer                     my-topic                       5
1429            1432            3
myconsumer_host1.example.com-1478188622741-7dab5ca7-0
myconsumer                     my-topic                       6
1634            1634            0
myconsumer_host1.example.com-1478188622741-7dab5ca7-0
myconsumer                     my-topic                       7
2261            2261            0
myconsumer_host1.example.com-1478188622741-7dab5ca7-0
#
```

Table 9-1 shows the fields provided in the output.

Table 9-1. Fields provided for old consumer group named "testgroup"

Field	Description
GROUP	The name of the consumer group.
TOPIC	The name of the topic being consumed.
PARTITION	The ID number of the partition being consumed.
CURRENT-OFFSET	The last offset committed by the consumer group for this topic partition. This is the position of the consumer within the partition.

Field	Description
LOG-END-OFFSET	The current high-water mark offset from the broker for the topic partition. This is the offset of the last message produced and committed to the cluster.
LAG	The difference between the consumer Current-Offset and the broker Log-End-Offset for this topic partition.
OWNER	The member of the consumer group that is currently consuming this topic partition. This is an arbitrary ID provided by the group member, and does not necessarily contain the hostname of the consumer.

Delete Group

Deletion of consumer groups is only supported for old consumer clients. This will remove the entire group from Zookeeper, including all stored offsets for all topics that the group is consuming. In order to perform this action, all consumers in the group should be shut down. If this step is not performed first, you may have undefined behavior from the consumer as the Zookeeper metadata for the group will be removed while it is using it.

For example, delete the consumer group named "testgroup":

```
# kafka-consumer-groups.sh --zookeeper
zoo1.example.com:2181/kafka-cluster --delete --group testgroup
Deleted all consumer group information for group testgroup in
zookeeper.
#
```

It is also possible to use the same command to delete offsets for a single topic that the group is consuming without deleting the entire group. Again, it is recommended that the consumer group be stopped, or configured to not consume the topic to be deleted, before performing this action.

For example, delete the offsets for the topic "my-topic" from the consumer group named "testgroup":

```
# kafka-consumer-groups.sh --zookeeper
zoo1.example.com:2181/kafka-cluster --delete --group testgroup
--topic my-topic
Deleted consumer group information for group testgroup topic
my-topic in zookeeper.
#
```

Offset Management

In addition to displaying and deleting the offsets for a consumer group using the old consumer client, it is also possible to retrieve the offsets and store new offsets in a batch. This is useful for resetting the offsets for a consumer when there is a problem that requires messages to be reread, or for advancing offsets past a message that the consumer is having a problem with (e.g., if there is a badly formatted message that the consumer cannot handle).

Managing Offsets Committed to Kafka

There is currently no tool available to manage the offsets for a consumer client that is committing offsets to Kafka. This function is only available for consumers that are committing offsets to Zookeeper. In order to manage offsets for a group that is committing to Kafka, you must use the APIs available in the client to commit offsets for the group.

Export Offsets

There is no named script to export offsets, but we are able to use the `kafka-run-class.sh` script to execute the underlying Java class for the tool in the proper environment. Exporting offsets will produce a file that contains each topic partition for the group and its offsets in a defined format that the import tool can read. The file that is created will have one topic partition per line, with the following format: /consumers/GROUPNAME/offsets/topic/TOPICNAME/PARTITIONID-0:OFFSET.

For example, export the offsets for the consumer group named "testgroup" to a file named *offsets*:

```
# kafka-run-class.sh kafka.tools.ExportZkOffsets
--zkconnect zoo1.example.com:2181/kafka-cluster --group testgroup
--output-file offsets
# cat offsets
/consumers/testgroup/offsets/my-topic/0:8905
/consumers/testgroup/offsets/my-topic/1:8915
/consumers/testgroup/offsets/my-topic/2:9845
/consumers/testgroup/offsets/my-topic/3:8072
/consumers/testgroup/offsets/my-topic/4:8008
/consumers/testgroup/offsets/my-topic/5:8319
/consumers/testgroup/offsets/my-topic/6:8102
/consumers/testgroup/offsets/my-topic/7:12739
#
```

Import Offsets

The import offset tool is the opposite of exporting. It takes the file produced by exporting offsets in the previous section and uses it to set the current offsets for the consumer group. A common practice is to export the current offsets for the consumer group, make a copy of the file (such that you preserve a backup), and edit the copy to replace the offsets with the desired values. Note that for the import command, the `--group` option is not used. This is because the consumer group name is embedded in the file to be imported.

Stop Consumers First

Before performing this step, it is important that all consumers in the group are stopped. They will not read the new offsets if they are written while the consumer group is active. The consumers will just overwrite the imported offsets.

For example, import the offsets for the consumer group named "testgroup" from a file named *offsets*:

```
# kafka-run-class.sh kafka.tools.ImportZkOffsets --zkconnect
zoo1.example.com:2181/kafka-cluster --input-file offsets
#
```

Dynamic Configuration Changes

Configurations can be overridden while the cluster is running for topics and for client quotas. There is the intention to add more dynamic configurations in the future, which is why these changes have been put in a separate CLI tool, `kafka-configs.sh`. This allows you to set configurations for specific topics and client IDs. Once set, these configurations are permanent for the cluster. They are stored in Zookeeper, and they are read by each broker when it starts. In tools and documentation, dynamic configurations like this are referred to as *per-topic* or *per-client* configurations, as well as *overrides*.

As with the previous tools, you are required to provide the Zookeeper connect string for the cluster with the `--zookeeper` argument. In the examples that follow, the Zookeeper connect string is assumed to be `zoo1.example.com:2181/kafka-cluster`.

Overriding Topic Configuration Defaults

There are many configurations that apply to topics that can be changed for individual topics in order to accommodate different use cases within a single cluster. Most of these configurations have a default specified in the broker configuration, which will apply unless an override is set.

The format of the command to change a topic configuration is:

```
kafka-configs.sh --zookeeper zoo1.example.com:2181/kafka-cluster
--alter --entity-type topics --entity-name <topic name>
--add-config <key>=<value>[,<key>=<value>...]
```

Table 9-2 shows the valid configurations (keys) for topics.

Table 9-2. Valid keys for topics

Configuration Key	Description
cleanup.policy	If set to compact, the messages in this topic will be discarded such that only the most recent message with a given key is retained (log compacted).
compression.type	The compression type used by the broker when writing message batches for this topic to disk. Current values are gzip, snappy, and lz4.
delete.retention.ms	How long, in milliseconds, deleted tombstones will be retained for this topic. Only valid for log compacted topics.
file.delete.delay.ms	How long, in milliseconds, to wait before deleting log segments and indices for this topic from disk.
flush.messages	How many messages are received before forcing a flush of this topic's messages to disk.
flush.ms	How long, in milliseconds, before forcing a flush of this topic's messages to disk.
index.interval.bytes	How many bytes of messages can be produced between entries in the log segment's index.
max.message.bytes	The maximum size of a single message for this topic, in bytes.
message.format.version	The message format version that the broker will use when writing messages to disk. Must be a valid API version number (e.g., "0.10.0").
message.timestamp. difference.max.ms	The maximum allowed difference, in milliseconds, between the message timestamp and the broker timestamp when the message is received. This is only valid if the message.timestamp.type is set to CreateTime.
message.timestamp.type	Which timestamp to use when writing messages to disk. Current values are CreateTime for the timestamp specified by the client and LogAppendTime for the time when the message is written to the partition by the broker.
min.cleana ble.dirty.ratio	How frequently the log compactor will attempt to compact partitions for this topic, expressed as a ratio of the number of uncompacted log segments to the total number of log segments. Only valid for log compacted topics.
min.insync.replicas	The minimum number of replicas that must be in-sync for a partition of the topic to be considered available.
preallocate	If set to true, log segments for this topic should be preallocated when a new segment is rolled.
retention.bytes	The amount of messages, in bytes, to retain for this topic.
retention.ms	How long messages should be retained for this topic, in milliseconds.
segment.bytes	The amount of messages, in bytes, that should be written to a single log segment in a partition.
segment.index.bytes	The maximum size, in bytes, of a single log segment index.
segment.jitter.ms	A maximum number of milliseconds that is randomized and added to segment.ms when rolling log segments.
segment.ms	How frequently, in milliseconds, the log segment for each partition should be rotated.
unclean.leader. election.enable	If set to false, unclean leader elections will not be permitted for this topic.

For example, set the retention for the topic named "my-topic" to 1 hour (3,600,000 ms):

```
# kafka-configs.sh --zookeeper zoo1.example.com:2181/kafka-cluster
--alter --entity-type topics --entity-name my-topic --add-config
retention.ms=3600000
Updated config for topic: "my-topic".
#
```

Overriding Client Configuration Defaults

For Kafka clients, the only configurations that can be overridden are the producer and consumer quotas. These are both a rate, in bytes per second, that all clients with the specified client ID are allowed to either produce or consume on a per-broker basis. This means that if you have five brokers in a cluster, and you specify a producer quota of 10 MB/sec for a client, that client will be allowed to produce 10 MB/sec on each broker at the same time for a total of 50 MB/sec.

Client ID Versus Consumer Group

The client ID is not necessarily the same as the consumer group name. Consumers can set their own client ID, and you may have many consumers that are in different groups that specify the same client ID. It is considered a best practice to set the client ID for each consumer group to something unique that identifies that group. This allows a single consumer group to share a quota, and it makes it easier to identify in logs what group is responsible for requests.

The format of the command to change a client configuration is:

```
kafka-configs.sh --zookeeper zoo1.example.com:2181/kafka-cluster
--alter --entity-type clients --entity-name <client ID>
--add-config <key>=<value>[,<key>=<value>...]
```

Table 9-3 shows the configurations (keys) for clients.

Table 9-3. The configurations (keys) for clients

Configuration Key	Description
producer_bytes_rate	The amount of messages, in bytes, that a singe client ID is allowed to produce to a single broker in one second.
consumer_bytes_rate	The amount of messages, in bytes, that a single client ID is allowed to consume from a single broker in one second.

Describing Configuration Overrides

All configuration overrides can be listed using the command-line tool. This will allow you to examine the specific configuration for a topic or client. Similar to other tools, this is done using the --describe command.

For example, show all configuration overrides for the topic named "my-topic":

```
# kafka-configs.sh --zookeeper zoo1.example.com:2181/kafka-cluster
--describe --entity-type topics --entity-name my-topic
Configs for topics:my-topic are
retention.ms=3600000,segment.ms=3600000
#
```

Topic Overrides Only

The configuration description will only show overrides—it does not include the cluster default configurations. Currently, there is no way to dynamically discover, either via Zookeeper or the Kafka protocol, the configuration of the brokers themselves. This means that when using this tool to discover topic or client settings in automation, the tool must have separate knowledge of the cluster default configuration.

Removing Configuration Overrides

Dynamic configurations can be removed entirely, which will cause the entity to revert back to the cluster defaults. To delete a configuration override, use the `--alter` command along with the `--delete-config` parameter.

For example, delete a configuration override for `retention.ms` for a topic named "my-topic":

```
# kafka-configs.sh --zookeeper zoo1.example.com:2181/kafka-cluster
--alter --entity-type topics --entity-name my-topic
--delete-config retention.ms
Updated config for topic: "my-topic".
#
```

Partition Management

The Kafka tools contain two scripts for working with the management of partitions—one allows for the reelection of leader replicas, and the other is a low-level utility for assigning partitions to brokers. Together, these tools can assist with the proper balancing of message traffic within a cluster of Kafka brokers.

Preferred Replica Election

As described in Chapter 6, partitions can have multiple replicas for reliability. However, only one of these replicas can be the leader for the partition, and all produce and consume operations happen on that broker. This is defined by Kafka internals as the first in-sync replica in the replica list, but when a broker is stopped and restarted, it does not resume leadership of any partitions automatically.

Automatic Leader Rebalancing

There is a broker configuration for automatic leader rebalancing, but it is not recommended for production use. There are significant performance impacts caused by the automatic balancing module, and it can cause a lengthy pause in client traffic for larger clusters.

One way to cause brokers to resume leadership is to trigger a preferred replica election. This tells the cluster controller to select the ideal leader for partitions. The operation is generally nonimpacting, as the clients can track leadership changes automatically. This can be manually ordered using the `kafka-preferred-replica-election.sh` utility.

For example, start a preferred replica election for all topics in a cluster with one topic that has eight partitions:

```
# kafka-preferred-replica-election.sh --zookeeper
zoo1.example.com:2181/kafka-cluster
Successfully started preferred replica election for partitions
Set([my-topic,5], [my-topic,0], [my-topic,7], [my-topic,4],
[my-topic,6], [my-topic,2], [my-topic,3], [my-topic,1])
#
```

For clusters with a large number of partitions, it is possible that a single preferred replica election will not be able to run. The request must be written to a Zookeeper znode within the cluster metadata, and if the request is larger than the size for a znode (by default, 1 MB), it will fail. In this case, you will need to create a file that contains a JSON object listing the partitions to elect for and break the request into multiple steps. The format for the JSON file is:

```
{
    "partitions": [
        {
            "partition": 1,
            "topic": "foo"
        },
        {
            "partition": 2,
            "topic": "foobar"
        }
    ]
}
```

For example, start a preferred replica election with a specified list of partitions in a file named "partitions.json":

```
# kafka-preferred-replica-election.sh --zookeeper
zoo1.example.com:2181/kafka-cluster --path-to-json-file
partitions.json
```

```
Successfully started preferred replica election for partitions
Set([my-topic,1], [my-topic,2], [my-topic,3])
#
```

Changing a Partition's Replicas

From time to time, it may be necessary to change the replica assignments for a partition. Some examples of when this might be needed are:

- If a topic's partitions are not balanced across the cluster, causing uneven load on brokers
- If a broker is taken offline and the partition is under-replicated
- If a new broker is added and needs to receive a share of the cluster load

The `kafka-reassign-partitions.sh` can be used to perform this operation. This tool must be used in at least two steps. The first step uses a broker list and a topic list to generate a set of moves. The second step executes the moves that were generated. There is an optional third step that uses the generated list to verify the progress or completion of the partition reassignments.

To generate a set of partition moves, you must create a file that contains a JSON object listing the topics. The JSON object is formatted as follows (the version number is currently always 1):

```
{
    "topics": [
        {
            "topic": "foo"
        },
        {
            "topic": "foo1"
        }
    ],
    "version": 1
}
```

For example, generate a set of partition moves to move the topics listed in the file "topics.json" to the brokers with IDs 0 and 1:

```
# kafka-reassign-partitions.sh --zookeeper
zoo1.example.com:2181/kafka-cluster --generate
--topics-to-move-json-file topics.json --broker-list 0,1
Current partition replica assignment

{"version":1,"partitions":[{"topic":"my-topic","partition":5,"replicas":[0,1]},
{"topic":"my-topic","partition":10,"replicas":[1,0]},{"topic":"my-
topic","partition":1,"replicas":[0,1]},{"topic":"my-topic","partition":4,"repli
cas":[1,0]},{"topic":"my-topic","partition":7,"replicas":[0,1]},{"topic":"my-
topic","partition":6,"replicas":[1,0]},{"topic":"my-topic","partition":
```

```
3,"replicas":[0,1]},{"topic":"my-topic","partition":15,"replicas":[0,1]},
{"topic":"my-topic","partition":0,"replicas":[1,0]},{"topic":"my-
topic","partition":11,"replicas":[0,1]},{"topic":"my-topic","partition":8,"repli
cas":[1,0]},{"topic":"my-topic","partition":12,"replicas":[1,0]},{"topic":"my-
topic","partition":2,"replicas":[1,0]},{"topic":"my-topic","partition":
13,"replicas":[0,1]},{"topic":"my-topic","partition":14,"replicas":[1,0]},
{"topic":"my-topic","partition":9,"replicas":[0,1]}]}
Proposed partition reassignment configuration

{"version":1,"partitions":[{"topic":"my-topic","partition":5,"replicas":[0,1]},
{"topic":"my-topic","partition":10,"replicas":[1,0]},{"topic":"my-
topic","partition":1,"replicas":[0,1]},{"topic":"my-topic","partition":4,"repli
cas":[1,0]},{"topic":"my-topic","partition":7,"replicas":[0,1]},{"topic":"my-
topic","partition":6,"replicas":[1,0]},{"topic":"my-topic","partition":
15,"replicas":[0,1]},{"topic":"my-topic","partition":0,"replicas":[1,0]},
{"topic":"my-topic","partition":3,"replicas":[0,1]},{"topic":"my-
topic","partition":11,"replicas":[0,1]},{"topic":"my-topic","partition":8,"repli
cas":[1,0]},{"topic":"my-topic","partition":12,"replicas":[1,0]},{"topic":"my-
topic","partition":13,"replicas":[0,1]},{"topic":"my-topic","partition":
2,"replicas":[1,0]},{"topic":"my-topic","partition":14,"replicas":[1,0]},
{"topic":"my-topic","partition":9,"replicas":[0,1]}]}
#
```

The broker list is provided on the tool command line as a comma-separated list of
broker IDs. The tool will output, on standard output, two JSON objects describing
the current partition assignment for the topics and the proposed partition assignment. The format of these JSON objects is: {"partitions": [{"topic": "*my-
topic*", "partition": *0*, "replicas": [*1,2*] }], "version":_1_}.

The first JSON object can be saved in case the reassignment needs to be reverted. The
second JSON object—the one that shows the proposed assignment—should be saved
to a new file. This file is then provided back to the kafka-reassign-partitions.sh
tool for the second step.

For example, execute a proposed partition reassignment from the file "reassign.json".

```
# kafka-reassign-partitions.sh --zookeeper
zoo1.example.com:2181/kafka-cluster --execute
--reassignment-json-file reassign.json
Current partition replica assignment

{"version":1,"partitions":[{"topic":"my-topic","partition":5,"replicas":[0,1]},
{"topic":"my-topic","partition":10,"replicas":[1,0]},{"topic":"my-
topic","partition":1,"replicas":[0,1]},{"topic":"my-topic","partition":4,"repli
cas":[1,0]},{"topic":"my-topic","partition":7,"replicas":[0,1]},{"topic":"my-
topic","partition":6,"replicas":[1,0]},{"topic":"my-topic","partition":
3,"replicas":[0,1]},{"topic":"my-topic","partition":15,"replicas":[0,1]},
{"topic":"my-topic","partition":0,"replicas":[1,0]},{"topic":"my-
topic","partition":11,"replicas":[0,1]},{"topic":"my-topic","partition":8,"repli
cas":[1,0]},{"topic":"my-topic","partition":12,"replicas":[1,0]},{"topic":"my-
topic","partition":2,"replicas":[1,0]},{"topic":"my-topic","partition":
```

```
13,"replicas":[0,1]},{"topic":"my-topic","partition":14,"replicas":[1,0]},
{"topic":"my-topic","partition":9,"replicas":[0,1]}]}

Save this to use as the --reassignment-json-file option during
rollback
Successfully started reassignment of partitions {"version":1,"partitions":
[{"topic":"my-topic","partition":5,"replicas":[0,1]},{"topic":"my-
topic","partition":0,"replicas":[1,0]},{"topic":"my-topic","partition":7,"repli
cas":[0,1]},{"topic":"my-topic","partition":13,"replicas":[0,1]},{"topic":"my-
topic","partition":4,"replicas":[1,0]},{"topic":"my-topic","partition":
12,"replicas":[1,0]},{"topic":"my-topic","partition":6,"replicas":[1,0]},
{"topic":"my-topic","partition":11,"replicas":[0,1]},{"topic":"my-
topic","partition":10,"replicas":[1,0]},{"topic":"my-topic","partition":9,"repli
cas":[0,1]},{"topic":"my-topic","partition":2,"replicas":[1,0]},{"topic":"my-
topic","partition":14,"replicas":[1,0]},{"topic":"my-topic","partition":
3,"replicas":[0,1]},{"topic":"my-topic","partition":1,"replicas":[0,1]},
{"topic":"my-topic","partition":15,"replicas":[0,1]},{"topic":"my-
topic","partition":8,"replicas":[1,0]}]}
#
```

This will start the reassignment of the specified partition replicas to the new brokers.
The cluster controller performs this action by adding the new replicas to the replica
list for each partition (increasing the replication factor). The new replicas will then
copy all existing messages for each partition from the current leader. Depending on
the size of the partitions on disk, this can take a significant amount of time as the data
is copied across the network to the new replicas. Once replication is complete, the
controller removes the old replicas from the replica list (reducing the replication factor to the original size).

Improving Network Utilization When Reassigning Replicas

When removing many partitions from a single broker, such as if
that broker is being removed from the cluster, it is a best practice to
shut down and restart the broker before starting the reassignment.
This will move leadership for the partitions on that particular
broker to other brokers in the cluster (as long as automatic leader
elections are not enabled). This can significantly increase the performance of reassignments and reduce the impact on the cluster as
the replication traffic will be distributed to many brokers.

While the reassignment is running, and after it is complete, the kafka-reassign-
partitions.sh tool can be used to verify the status of the reassignment. This will
show what reassignments are currently in progress, what reassignments have completed, and, if there was an error, what reassignments have failed. In order to do this, you
must have the file with the JSON object that was used in the execute step.

For example, verify a running partition reassignment from the file "reassign.json":

```
# kafka-reassign-partitions.sh --zookeeper
zoo1.example.com:2181/kafka-cluster --verify
--reassignment-json-file reassign.json
Status of partition reassignment:
Reassignment of partition [my-topic,5] completed successfully
Reassignment of partition [my-topic,0] completed successfully
Reassignment of partition [my-topic,7] completed successfully
Reassignment of partition [my-topic,13] completed successfully
Reassignment of partition [my-topic,4] completed successfully
Reassignment of partition [my-topic,12] completed successfully
Reassignment of partition [my-topic,6] completed successfully
Reassignment of partition [my-topic,11] completed successfully
Reassignment of partition [my-topic,10] completed successfully
Reassignment of partition [my-topic,9] completed successfully
Reassignment of partition [my-topic,2] completed successfully
Reassignment of partition [my-topic,14] completed successfully
Reassignment of partition [my-topic,3] completed successfully
Reassignment of partition [my-topic,1] completed successfully
Reassignment of partition [my-topic,15] completed successfully
Reassignment of partition [my-topic,8] completed successfully
#
```

Batching Reassignments

Partition reassignments have a big impact on the performance of your cluster, as they will cause changes in the consistency of the memory page cache and use network and disk I/O. Breaking reassignments into many small steps is a good idea to keep this to a minimum.

Changing Replication Factor

There is an undocumented feature of the partition reassignment tool that will allow you to increase or decrease the replication factor for a partition. This may be necessary in situations where a partition was created with the wrong replication factor (such as if there were not enough brokers available when the topic was created). This can be done by creating a JSON object with the format used in the execute step of partition reassignment that adds or removes replicas to set the replication factor correctly. The cluster will complete the reassignment and keep the replication factor at the new size.

For example, consider the current assignment for a topic named "my-topic" with one partition and a replication factor of 1:

```
{
    "partitions": [
        {
            "topic": "my-topic",
            "partition": 0,
```

```
            "replicas": [
                1
            ]
        }
    ],
    "version": 1
}
```

Providing the following JSON object in the execute step of partition reassignment will result in the replication factor being increased to 2:

```
{
    "partitions": [
        {
            "partition": 0,
            "replicas": [
                1,
                2
            ],
            "topic": "my-topic"
        }
    ],
    "version": 1
}
```

Similarly, the replication factor for a partition can be reduced by providing a JSON object with a smaller list of replicas.

Dumping Log Segments

If you have to go looking for the specific content of a message, perhaps because you ended up with a "poison pill" message in your topic that the consumer cannot handle, there is a helper tool you can use to decode the log segments for a partition. This will allow you to view individual messages without needing to consume and decode them. The tool takes a comma-separated list of log segment files as an argument and can print out either message summary information or detailed message data.

For example, decode the log segment file named *00000000000052368601.log*, showing the message summaries:

```
# kafka-run-class.sh kafka.tools.DumpLogSegments --files
00000000000052368601.log
Dumping 00000000000052368601.log
Starting offset: 52368601
offset: 52368601 position: 0 NoTimestampType: -1 isvalid: true
payloadsize: 661 magic: 0 compresscodec: GZIPCompressionCodec crc:
1194341321
offset: 52368603 position: 687 NoTimestampType: -1 isvalid: true
payloadsize: 895 magic: 0 compresscodec: GZIPCompressionCodec crc:
278946641
offset: 52368604 position: 1608 NoTimestampType: -1 isvalid: true
payloadsize: 665 magic: 0 compresscodec: GZIPCompressionCodec crc:
3767466431
offset: 52368606 position: 2299 NoTimestampType: -1 isvalid: true
payloadsize: 932 magic: 0 compresscodec: GZIPCompressionCodec crc:
2444301359
...
```

For example, decode the log segment file named *00000000000052368601.log*, showing the message data:

```
# kafka-run-class.sh kafka.tools.DumpLogSegments --files
00000000000052368601.log --print-data-log
offset: 52368601 position: 0 NoTimestampType: -1 isvalid: true
payloadsize: 661 magic: 0 compresscodec: GZIPCompressionCodec crc:
1194341321 payload: test message 1
offset: 52368603 position: 687 NoTimestampType: -1 isvalid: true
payloadsize: 895 magic: 0 compresscodec: GZIPCompressionCodec crc:
278946641 payload: test message 2
offset: 52368604 position: 1608 NoTimestampType: -1 isvalid: true
payloadsize: 665 magic: 0 compresscodec: GZIPCompressionCodec crc:
3767466431 payload: test message 3
offset: 52368606 position: 2299 NoTimestampType: -1 isvalid: true
payloadsize: 932 magic: 0 compresscodec: GZIPCompressionCodec crc:
2444301359 payload: test message 4
...
```

It is also possible to use this tool to validate the index file that goes along with a log segment. The index is used for finding messages within a log segment, and if corrupted will cause errors in consumption. Validation is performed whenever a broker starts up in an unclean state (i.e., it was not stopped normally), but it can be performed manually as well. There are two options for checking indices, depending on how much checking you want to do. The option --index-sanity-check will just check that the index is in a useable state, while --verify-index-only will check for mismatches in the index without printing out all the index entries.

For example, validate that the index file for the log segment file named *00000000000052368601.log* is not corrupted:

```
# kafka-run-class.sh kafka.tools.DumpLogSegments --files
00000000000052368601.index,00000000000052368601.log
```

```
--index-sanity-check
Dumping 00000000000052368601.index
00000000000052368601.index passed sanity check.
Dumping 00000000000052368601.log
Starting offset: 52368601
offset: 52368601 position: 0 NoTimestampType: -1 isvalid: true
payloadsize: 661 magic: 0 compresscodec: GZIPCompressionCodec crc:
1194341321
offset: 52368603 position: 687 NoTimestampType: -1 isvalid: true
payloadsize: 895 magic: 0 compresscodec: GZIPCompressionCodec crc:
278946641
offset: 52368604 position: 1608 NoTimestampType: -1 isvalid: true
payloadsize: 665 magic: 0 compresscodec: GZIPCompressionCodec crc:
3767466431
...
```

Replica Verification

Partition replication works similar to a regular Kafka consumer client: the follower broker starts replicating at the oldest offset and checkpoints the current offset to disk periodically. When replication stops and restarts, it picks up from the last checkpoint. It is possible for previously replicated log segments to get deleted from a broker, and the follower will not fill in the gaps in this case.

To validate that the replicas for a topic's partitions are the same across the cluster, you can use the `kafka-replica-verification.sh` tool for verification. This tool will fetch messages from all the replicas for a given set of topic partitions and check that all messages exist on all replicas. You must provide the tool with a regular expression that matches the topics you wish to validate. If none is provided, all topics are validated. You must also provide an explicit list of brokers to connect to.

Caution: Cluster Impact Ahead

The replica verification tool will have an impact on your cluster similar to reassigning partitions, as it must read all messages from the oldest offset in order to verify the replica. In addition, it reads from all replicas for a partition in parallel, so it should be used with caution.

For example, verify the replicas for the topics starting with "my-" on brokers 1 and 2:

```
# kafka-replica-verification.sh --broker-list
kafka1.example.com:9092,kafka2.example.com:9092 --topic-white-list 'my-.*'
2016-11-23 18:42:08,838: verification process is started.
2016-11-23 18:42:38,789: max lag is 0 for partition [my-topic,7]
at offset 53827844 among 10 partitions
2016-11-23 18:43:08,790: max lag is 0 for partition [my-topic,7]
at offset 53827878 among 10 partitions
```

Consuming and Producing

While working with Apache Kafka, you will often find it is necessary to manually consume messages, or produce some sample messages, in order to validate what's going on with your applications. There are two utilities provided to help with this: `kafka-console-consumer.sh` and `kafka-console-producer.sh`. These are wrappers around the Java client libraries that allow you to interact with Kafka topics without having to write an entire application to do it.

Piping Output to Another Application

While it is possible to write applications that wrap around the console consumer or producer (e.g., to consume messages and pipe them to another application for processing), this type of application is quite fragile and should be avoided. It is difficult to interact with the console consumer in a way that does not lose messages. Likewise, the console producer does not allow for using all features, and properly sending bytes is tricky. It is best to use either the Java client libraries directly, or a third-party client library for other languages that use the Kafka protocol directly.

Console Consumer

The `kafka-console-consumer.sh` tool provides a means to consume messages out of one or more topics in your Kafka cluster. The messages are printed in standard output, delimited by a new line. By default, it outputs the raw bytes in the message with no formatting (using the `DefaultFormatter`). The required options are described in the following paragraphs.

Checking Tool Versions

It is very important to use a consumer that is the same version as your Kafka cluster. Older console consumers can potentially damage the cluster by interacting with Zookeeper in incorrect ways.

The first option that is required is to specify whether or not to use the new consumer, and for the configuration to point to the Kafka cluster itself. When using the older consumer, the only argument required for this is the `--zookeeper` option followed by the connect string for the cluster. From the above examples, this might be `--zookeeper zoo1.example.com:2181/kafka-cluster`. If you are using the new consumer, you must specify both the `--new-consumer` flag as well as the `--broker-list` option followed by a comma-separated broker list, such as `--broker-list kafka1.example.com:9092,kafka2.example.com:9092`.

Next, you must specify the topics to consume. Three options are provided for this: `--topic`, `--whitelist`, and `--blacklist`. One, and only one, may be provided. The `--topic` option specifies a single topic to consume. The `--whitelist` and `--blacklist` options each are followed by a regular expression (remember to properly escape the regular expression so that it is not changed by the shell command line). The whitelist will consume all topics that match the regular expression, whereas the blacklist will consume all topics *except* those matched by the regular expression.

For example, consume a single topic named "my-topic" using the old consumer:

```
# kafka-console-consumer.sh --zookeeper
zoo1.example.com:2181/kafka-cluster --topic my-topic
sample message 1
sample message 2
^CProcessed a total of 2 messages
#
```

In addition to the basic command-line options, it is possible to pass any normal consumer configuration options to the console consumer as well. This can be done in two ways, depending on how many options you need to pass and how you prefer to do it. The first is to provide a consumer configuration file by specifying `--consumer.config CONFIGFILE`, where _CONFIGFILE_ is the full path to a file that contains the configuration options. The other way is to specify the options on the command line with one or more arguments of the form `--consumer-property KEY=VALUE`, where _KEY_ is the configuration option name and _VALUE_ is the value to set it to. This can be useful for consumer options like setting the consumer group ID.

Confusing Command-Line Options

There is a `--property` command-line option for both the console consumer and the console producer, but this should not be confused with the `--consumer-property` and `--producer-property` options. The `--property` option is only used for passing configurations to the message formatter, and not the client itself.

There are a few other commonly used options for the console consumer that you should know:

`--formatter CLASSNAME`
Specifies a message formatter class to be used to decode the messages. This defaults to `kafka.tools.DefaultFormatter`.

`--from-beginning`
Consume messages in the topic(s) specified from the oldest offset. Otherwise, consumption starts from the latest offset.

`--max-messages` *NUM*
> Consume at most *NUM* messages before exiting.

`--partition` *NUM*
> Consume only from the partition with ID *NUM* (requires the new consumer).

Message formatter options

There are three message formatters available to use besides the default:

`kafka.tools.LoggingMessageFormatter`
> Outputs messages using the logger, rather than standard out. Messages are printed at the INFO level, and include the timestamp, key, and value.

`kafka.tools.ChecksumMessageFormatter`
> Prints only message checksums.

`kafka.tools.NoOpMessageFormatter`
> Consumes messages but does not output them at all.

The `kafka.tools.DefaultMessageFormatter` also has several useful options that can be passed using the `--property` command-line option:

`print.timestamp`
> Set to "true" to display the timestamp of each message (if available).

`print.key`
> Set to "true" to display the message key in addition to the value.

`key.separator`
> Specify the delimiter character to use between the message key and message value when printing.

`line.separator`
> Specify the delimiter character to use between messages.

`key.deserializer`
> Provide a class name that is used to deserialize the message key before printing.

`value.deserializer`
> Provide a class name that is used to deserialize the message value before printing.

The deserializer classes must implement `org.apache.kafka.common.serialization.Deserializer` and the console consumer will call the `toString` method on them to get the output to display. Typically, you would implement these deserializers as a Java class that you would insert into the classpath for the console consumer by setting the `CLASSPATH` environment variable before executing `kafka_console_consumer.sh`.

Consuming the offsets topics

It is sometimes useful to see what offsets are being committed for the cluster's consumer groups. You may want to see if a particular group is committing offsets at all, or how often offsets are being committed. This can be done by using the console consumer to consume the special internal topic called __consumer_offsets. All consumer offsets are written as messages to this topic. In order to decode the messages in this topic, you must use the formatter class kafka.coordinator.GroupMeta dataManager$OffsetsMessageFormatter.

For example, consume a single message from the offsets topic:

```
# kafka-console-consumer.sh --zookeeper
zoo1.example.com:2181/kafka-cluster --topic __consumer_offsets
--formatter 'kafka.coordinator.GroupMetadataManager$OffsetsMessage
Formatter' --max-messages 1
[my-group-name,my-topic,0]::[OffsetMetadata[481690879,NO_METADATA]
,CommitTime 1479708539051,ExpirationTime 1480313339051]
Processed a total of 1 messages
#
```

Console Producer

Similar to the console consumer, the kakfa-console-producer.sh tool can be used to write messages into a Kafka topic in your cluster. By default, messages are read one per line, with a tab character separating the key and the value (if no tab character is present, the key is null).

Changing Line-Reading Behavior

You can provide your own class for reading lines in order to do custom things. The class that you create must extend kafka.com mon.MessageReader and will be responsible for creating the Produ cerRecord. Specify your class on the command line with the --line-reader option, and make sure the JAR containing your class is in the classpath.

The console producer requires that two arguments are provided at a minimum. The parameter --broker-list specifies one or more brokers, as a comma-separated list of hostname:port entries for your cluster. The other required parameter is the --topic option to specify the topic that you are producing messages to. When you are done producing, send an end-of-file (EOF) character to close the client.

For example, produce two messages to a topic named "my-topic":

```
# kafka-console-producer.sh --broker-list
kafka1.example.com:9092,kafka2.example.com:9092 --topic my-topic
sample message 1
sample message 2
^D
#
```

Just like the console consumer, it is possible to pass any normal producer configuration options to the console producer as well. This can be done in two ways, depending on how many options you need to pass and how you prefer to do it. The first is to provide a producer configuration file by specifying `--producer.config` *CONFIGFILE*, where *CONFIGFILE* is the full path to a file that contains the configuration options. The other way is to specify the options on the command line with one or more arguments of the form `--producer-property` *KEY=VALUE*, where *KEY* is the configuration option name and *VALUE* is the value to set it to. This can be useful for producer options like message-batching configurations (such as `linger.ms` or `batch.size`).

The console producer has many command-line arguments available for adjusting its behavior. Some of the more useful options are:

`--key-serializer` *CLASSNAME*
> Specifies a message encoder class to be used to serialize the message key. This defaults to `kafka.serializer.DefaultEncoder`.

`--value-serializer` *CLASSNAME*
> Specifies a message encoder class to be used to serialize the message value. This defaults to `kafka.serializer.DefaultEncoder`.

`--compression-codec` *STRING*
> Specify the type of compression to be used when producing messages. This can be one of `none`, `gzip`, `snappy`, or `lz4`. The default value is `gzip`.

`--sync`
> Produce messages synchronously, waiting for each message to be acknowledged before sending the next one.

Creating a Custom Serializer

Custom serializers must extend `kafka.serializer.Encoder`. This can be used to take the strings from standard input and convert them to an encoding, such as Avro or Protobuf, which is appropriate for the topic.

Line-Reader Options

The `kafka.tools.LineMessageReader` class, which is responsible for reading standard input and creating producer records, also has several useful options that can be passed to the console producer using the `--property` command-line option:

`ignore.error`
> Set to "false" to throw an exception when `parse.key` is set to `true` and a key separator is not present. Defaults to `true`.

`parse.key`
> Set to `false` to always set the key to null. Defaults to `true`.

`key.separator`
> Specify the delimiter character to use between the message key and message value when reading. Defaults to a tab character.

When producing messages, the `LineMessageReader` will split the input on the first instance of the `key.separator`. If there are no characters remaining after that, the value of the message will be empty. If no key separator character is present on the line, or if `parse.key` is false, the key will be null.

Client ACLs

There is a command-line tool, `kafka-acls.sh`, provided for interacting with access controls for Kafka clients. Additional documentation on ACLs and security is provided on the Apache Kafka website (*https://kafka.apache.org/*).

Unsafe Operations

There are some administrative tasks that are technically possible to do but should not be attempted except in the most extreme situations. Often this is when you are diagnosing a problem and have run out of options, or you have found a specific bug that you need to work around temporarily. These tasks are usually undocumented, unsupported, and pose some amount of risk to your application.

Several of the more common of these tasks are documented here so that in an emergency situation, there is a potential option for recovery. Their use is not recommended under normal cluster operations, and should be considered carefully before being executed.

Danger: Here Be Dragons

The operations in this section involve working with the cluster metadata stored in Zookeeper directly. This can be a very dangerous operation, so you must be very careful to not modify the information in Zookeeper directly, except as noted.

Moving the Cluster Controller

Every Kafka cluster has a controller, which is a thread running within one of the brokers. The controller is responsible for overseeing cluster operations, and from time to time it is desirable to forcibly move the controller to a different broker. One such example is when the controller has suffered an exception or other problem that has left it running but not functional. Moving the controller in these situations does not have a high risk, but it is not a normal task and should not be performed regularly.

The broker that is currently the controller registers itself using a Zookeeper node at the top level of the cluster path that is named /controller. Deleting this Zookeeper node manually will cause the current controller to resign, and the cluster will select a new controller.

Killing a Partition Move

The normal operational flow for a partition reassignment is:

1. Reassignment is requested (Zookeeper node is created).
2. Cluster controller adds partitions to new brokers being added.
3. New brokers begin replicating each partition until it is in-sync.
4. Cluster controller removes the old brokers from the partition replica list.

Because all the reassignments are started in parallel when requested, there is normally no reason to attempt to cancel an in-progress reassignment. One of the exceptions is when a broker fails in the middle of a reassignment and cannot immediately be restarted. This results in a reassignment that will never finish, which precludes starting any additional reassignments (such as to remove partitions from the failed broker and assign them to other brokers). In a case like this, it is possible to make the cluster forget about the existing reassignment.

To remove an in-progress partition reassignment:

1. Remove the /admin/reassign_partitions Zookeeper node from the Kafka cluster path.

2. Force a controller move (see "Moving the Cluster Controller" on page 208 for more detail).

Checking Replication Factors

When removing an in-progress partition move, any partitions that have not yet completed will not go through the step of having the old brokers removed from the replica list. This means that the replication factor for some partitions may be greater than intended. The broker will not allow some admin operations for topics that have partitions with inconsistent replication factors (such as increasing partitions). It is advisable to review the partitions that were still in progress and make sure their replication factor is correct with another partition reassignment.

Removing Topics to Be Deleted

When using the command-line tools to delete a topic, a Zookeeper node requests that the deletion is created. Under normal circumstances, this is executed by the cluster immediately. However, the command-line tool has no way of knowing whether topic deletion is enabled in the cluster. As a result, it will request deletion of topics regardless, which can result in a surprise if deletion is disabled. It is possible to delete the requests pending for deletion of topics to avoid this.

Topics are requested for deletion by creating a Zookeeper node as a child under /admin/delete_topic, which is named with the topic name. Deleting these Zookeeper nodes (but not the parent /admin/delete_topic node) will remove the pending requests.

Deleting Topics Manually

If you are running a cluster with delete topics disabled, or if you find yourself in need of deleting some topics outside of the normal flow of operations, it is possible to manually delete them from the cluster. This requires a full shutdown of all brokers in the cluster, however, and cannot be done while any of the brokers in the cluster are running.

Shut Down Brokers First

Modifying the cluster metadata in Zookeeper when the cluster is online is a very dangerous operation, and can put the cluster into an unstable state. Never attempt to delete or modify topic metadata in Zookeeper while the cluster is online.

To delete a topic from the cluster:

1. Shut down all brokers in the cluster.
2. Remove the Zookeeper path `/brokers/topics/`*TOPICNAME* from the Kafka cluster path. Note that this node has child nodes that must be deleted first.
3. Remove the partition directories from the log directories on each broker. These will be named *TOPICNAME-NUM*, where *NUM* is the partition ID.
4. Restart all brokers.

Summary

Running a Kafka cluster can be a daunting endeavor, with numerous configurations and maintenance tasks to keep the systems running at peak performance. In this chapter, we discussed many of the routine tasks, such as managing topic and client configurations that you will need to handle frequently. We also covered some of the more esoteric tasks that you'll need for debugging problems, like examining log segments. Finally, we covered a few of the operations that, while not safe or routine, can be used to get you out of a sticky situation. All together, these tools will help you to manage your Kafka cluster.

Of course, managing the cluster is impossible without proper monitoring in place. Chapter 10 will discuss ways to monitor broker and cluster health and operations so you can be sure Kafka is working well (and know when it isn't). We will also offer best practices for monitoring your clients, including both producers and consumers.

CHAPTER 10

Monitoring Kafka

The Apache Kafka applications have numerous measurements for their operation—
so many, in fact, that it can easily become confusing as to what is important to watch
and what can be set aside. These range from simple metrics about the overall rate of
traffic, to detailed timing metrics for every request type, to per-topic and per-
partition metrics. They provide a detailed view into every operation in the broker, but
they can also make you the bane of whomever is responsible for managing your monitoring system.

This section will detail the most critical metrics to monitor all the time, and how to
respond to them. We'll also describe some of the more important metrics to have on
hand when debugging problems. This is not an exhaustive list of the metrics that are
available, however, because the list changes frequently, and many will only be informative to a hardcode Kafka developer.

Metric Basics

Before getting into the specific metrics provided by the Kafka broker and clients, let's
discuss the basics of how to monitor Java applications and some best practices around
monitoring and alerting. This will provide a basis for understanding how to monitor
the applications and why the specific metrics described later in this chapter have been
chosen as the most important.

Where Are the Metrics?

All of the metrics exposed by Kafka can be accessed via the Java Management Extensions (JMX) interface. The easiest way to use them in an external monitoring system
is to use a collection agent provided by your monitoring system and attach it to the
Kafka process. This may be a separate process that runs on the system and connects

to the JMX interface, such as with the Nagios XI check_jmx plugin or jmxtrans. You can also utilize a JMX agent that runs directly in the Kafka process to access metrics via an HTTP connection, such as Jolokia or MX4J.

An in-depth discussion of how to set up monitoring agents is outside the scope of this chapter, and there are far too many choices to do justice to all of them. If your organization does not currently have experience with monitoring Java applications, it may be worthwhile to instead consider monitoring as a service. There are many companies that offer monitoring agents, metrics collection points, storage, graphing, and alerting in a services package. They can assist you further with setting up the monitoring agents required.

Finding the JMX Port

To aid with configuring applications that connect to JMX on the Kafka broker directly, such as monitoring systems, the broker sets the configured JMX port in the broker information that is stored in Zookeeper. The /brokers/ids/<ID> znode contains JSON-formatted data for the broker, including hostname and jmx_port keys.

Internal or External Measurements

Metrics provided via an interface such as JMX are internal metrics: they are created and provided by the application that is being monitored. For many internal measurements, such as timing of individual request stages, this is the best choice. Nothing other than the application itself has that level of detail. There are other metrics, such as the overall time for a request or the availability of a particular request type, that can be measured externally. This would mean that a Kafka client, or some other third-party application, provides the metrics for the server (the broker, in our case). These are often metrics like availability (is the broker reachable?) or latency (how long does a request take?). These provide an external view of the application that is often more informative.

A familiar example for the value of external measurements is monitoring the health of a website. The web server is running properly, and all of the metrics it is reporting say that it is working. However, there is a problem with the network between your web server and your external users, which means that none of your users can reach the web server. External monitoring, which is running outside your network, that checks the accessibility of the website would detect this and alert you to the situation.

Application Health Checks

No matter how you collect metrics from Kafka, you should make sure that you have a way to also monitor the overall health of the application process via a simple health-check. This can be done in two ways:

- An external process that reports whether the broker is up or down (health check)
- Alerting on the lack of metrics being reported by the Kafka broker (sometimes called *stale metrics*)

Though the second method works, it can make it difficult to differentiate between a failure of the Kafka broker and a failure of the monitoring system itself.

For the Kafka broker, this can simply be connecting to the external port (the same port that clients use to connect to the broker) to check that it responds. For client applications, it can be more complex, ranging from a simple check of whether the process is running to an internal method that determines application health.

Metric Coverage

Especially when considering the number of measurements exposed by Kafka, it is important to pick and choose what you look at. This becomes even more important when defining alerts based on those measurements. It is far too easy to succumb to "alert fatigue," where there are so many alerts going off that it is difficult to know how severe the problem is. It is also hard to properly define thresholds for every metric and keep them up-to-date. When the alerts are overwhelming or often incorrect, we begin to not trust that the alerts are correctly describing the state of our applications.

It is more advantageous to have a few alerts that have high-level coverage. For example, you could have one alert that indicates that there is a big problem but you may have to gather additional data to determine the exact nature of that problem. Think of this like the Check Engine light on a car. It would be confusing to have 100 different indicators on the dashboard that show individual problems with the air filter, oil, exhaust, and so on. Instead, one indicator tells you that there is a problem, and there is a way to find out more detailed information to tell you exactly what the problem is. Throughout this chapter, we will identify the metrics that will provide the highest amount of coverage to keep your alerting simple.

Kafka Broker Metrics

There are many Kafka broker metrics. Many of them are low-level measurements, added by developers when investigating a specific issue or in anticipation of needing information for debugging purposes later. There are metrics providing information about nearly every function within the broker, but the most common ones provide the information needed to run Kafka on a daily basis.

Who Watches the Watchers?

Many organizations use Kafka for collecting application metrics, system metrics, and logs for consumption by a central monitoring system. This is an excellent way to decouple the applications from the monitoring system, but it presents a specific concern for Kafka itself. If you use this same system for monitoring Kafka itself, it is very likely that you will never know when Kafka is broken because the data flow for your monitoring system will be broken as well.

There are many ways that this can be addressed. One way is to use a separate monitoring system for Kafka that does not have a dependency on Kafka. Another way, if you have multiple datacenters, is to make sure that the metrics for the Kafka cluster in datacenter A are produced to datacenter B, and vice versa. However you decide to handle it, make sure that the monitoring and alerting for Kafka does not depend on Kafka working.

In this section, we'll start by discussing the underreplicated partitions metric as an overall performance measurement, as well as how to respond to it. The other metrics discussed will round out the view of the broker at a high level. This is by no means an exhaustive list of broker metrics, but rather several "must have" metrics for checking on the health of the broker and the cluster. We'll wrap up with a discussion on logging before moving on to client metrics.

Under-Replicated Partitions

If there is only one metric that you are able to monitor from the Kafka broker, it should be the number of under-replicated partitions. This measurement, provided on each broker in a cluster, gives a count of the number of partitions for which the broker is the leader replica, where the follower replicas are not caught up. This single measurement provides insight into a number of problems with the Kafka cluster, from a broker being down to resource exhaustion. With the wide variety of problems that this metric can indicate, it is worthy of an in depth look at how to respond to a value other than zero. Many of the metrics used in diagnosing these types of problems will be described later in this chapter. See Table 10-1 for more details on under-replicated partitions.

Table 10-1. Metrics and their corresponding under-replicated partitions

Metric name	Under-replicated partitions
JMX MBean	kafka.server:type=ReplicaManager,name=UnderReplicatedPartitions
Value range	Integer, zero or greater

A steady (unchanging) number of under-replicated partitions reported by many of the brokers in a cluster normally indicates that one of the brokers in the cluster is off-line. The count of under-replicated partitions across the entire cluster will equal the number of partitions that are assigned to that broker, and the broker that is down will not report a metric. In this case, you will need to investigate what has happened to that broker and resolve that situation. This is often a hardware failure, but could also be an OS or Java issue that has caused the problem.

Preferred Replica Elections

The first step before trying to diagnose a problem further is to assure that you have run a preferred replica election (see Chapter 9) recently. Kafka brokers do not automatically take partition leadership back (unless auto leader rebalance is enabled, but this configuration is not recommended) after they have released leadership (e.g., when the broker has failed or been shut down). This means that it's very easy for leader replicas to become unbalanced in a cluster. The preferred replica election is safe and easy to run, so it's a good idea to do that first and see if the problem goes away.

If the number of underreplicated partitions is fluctuating, or if the number is steady but there are no brokers offline, this typically indicates a performance issue in the cluster. These types of problems are much harder to diagnose due to their variety, but there are several steps you can work through to narrow it down to the most likely causes. The first step to try and determine if the problem relates to a single broker or to the entire cluster. This can sometimes be a difficult question to answer. If the under-replicated partitions are on a single broker, then that broker is typically the problem. The error shows that other brokers are having a problem replicating messages from that one.

If several brokers have under-replicated partitions, it could be a cluster problem, but it might still be a single broker. In that case, it would be because a single broker is having problems replicating messages from everywhere, and you'll have to figure out which broker it is. One way to do this is to get a list of under-replicated partitions for the cluster and see if there is a specific broker that is common to all of the partitions that are under-replicated. Using the kafka-topics.sh tool (discussed in detail in

Chapter 9), you can get a list of under-replicated partitions to look for a common thread.

For example, list under-replicated partitions in a cluster:

```
# kafka-topics.sh --zookeeper zoo1.example.com:2181/kafka-cluster --describe
--under-replicated
    Topic: topicOne    Partition: 5    Leader: 1    Replicas: 1,2 Isr: 1
    Topic: topicOne    Partition: 6    Leader: 3    Replicas: 2,3 Isr: 3
    Topic: topicTwo    Partition: 3    Leader: 4    Replicas: 2,4 Isr: 4
    Topic: topicTwo    Partition: 7    Leader: 5    Replicas: 5,2 Isr: 5
    Topic: topicSix    Partition: 1    Leader: 3    Replicas: 2,3 Isr: 3
    Topic: topicSix    Partition: 2    Leader: 1    Replicas: 1,2 Isr: 1
    Topic: topicSix    Partition: 5    Leader: 6    Replicas: 2,6 Isr: 6
    Topic: topicSix    Partition: 7    Leader: 7    Replicas: 7,2 Isr: 7
    Topic: topicNine   Partition: 1    Leader: 1    Replicas: 1,2 Isr: 1
    Topic: topicNine   Partition: 3    Leader: 3    Replicas: 2,3 Isr: 3
    Topic: topicNine   Partition: 4    Leader: 3    Replicas: 3,2 Isr: 3
    Topic: topicNine   Partition: 7    Leader: 3    Replicas: 2,3 Isr: 3
    Topic: topicNine   Partition: 0    Leader: 3    Replicas: 2,3 Isr: 3
    Topic: topicNine   Partition: 5    Leader: 6    Replicas: 6,2 Isr: 6
#
```

In this example, the common broker is number 2. This indicates that this broker is having a problem with message replication, and will lead us to focus our investigation on that one broker. If there is no common broker, there is likely a cluster-wide problem.

Cluster-level problems

Cluster problems usually fall into one of two categories:

- Unbalanced load
- Resource exhaustion

The first problem, unbalanced partitions or leadership, is the easiest to find even though fixing it can be an involved process. In order to diagnose this problem, you will need several metrics from the brokers in the cluster:

- Partition count
- Leader partition count
- All topics bytes in rate
- All topics messages in rate

Examine these metrics. In a perfectly balanced cluster, the numbers will be even across all brokers in the cluster, as in Table 10-2.

Table 10-2. Utilization Metrics

Broker	Partitions	Leaders	Bytes in	Bytes out
1	100	50	3.56 MB/s	9.45 MB/s
2	101	49	3.66 MB/s	9.25 MB/s
3	100	50	3.23 MB/s	9.82 MB/s

This indicates that all the brokers are taking approximately the same amount of traffic. Assuming you have already run a preferred replica election, a large deviation indicates that the traffic is not balanced within the cluster. To resolve this, you will need to move partitions from the heavily loaded brokers to the less heavily loaded brokers. This is done using the `kafka-reassign-partitions.sh` tool described in Chapter 9.

Helpers for Balancing Clusters

The Kafka broker itself does not provide for automatic reassignment of partitions in a cluster. This means that balancing traffic within a Kafka cluster can be a mind-numbing process of manually reviewing long lists of metrics and trying to come up with a replica assignment that works. In order to help with this, some organizations have developed automated tools for performing this task. One example is the `kafka-assigner` tool that LinkedIn has released in the open source kafka-tools (*https://github.com/linkedin/kafka-tools*) repository on GitHub. Some enterprise offerings for Kafka support also provide this feature.

Another common cluster performance issue is exceeding the capacity of the brokers to serve requests. There are many possible bottlenecks that could slow things down: CPU, disk IO, and network throughput are a few of the most common. Disk utilization is not one of them, as the brokers will operate properly right up until the disk is filled, and then this disk will fail abruptly. In order to diagnose a capacity problem, there are many metrics you can track at the OS level, including:

- CPU utilization
- Inbound network throughput
- Outbound network throughput
- Disk average wait time
- Disk percent utilization

Exhausting any of these resources will typically show up as the same problem: under-replicated partitions. It's critical to remember that the broker replication process operates in exactly the same way that other Kafka clients do. If your cluster is having problems with replication, then your customers are having problems with producing and consuming messages as well. It makes sense to develop a baseline for these metrics when your cluster is operating correctly and then set thresholds that indicate a developing problem long before you run out of capacity. You will also want to review the trend for these metrics as the traffic to your cluster increases over time. As far as Kafka broker metrics are concerned, the `All Topics Bytes In Rate` is a good guideline to show cluster usage.

Host-level problems

If the performance problem with Kafka is not present in the entire cluster and can be isolated to one or two brokers, it's time to examine that server and see what makes it different from the rest of the cluster. These types of problems fall into several general categories:

- Hardware failures
- Conflicts with another process
- Local configuration differences

Typical Servers and Problems

A server and its OS is a complex machine with thousands of components, any of which could have problems and cause either a complete failure or just a performance degradation. It's impossible for us to cover everything that can fail in this book—numerous volumes have been written, and will continue to be, on this subject. But we can discuss some of the most common problems that are seen. This section will focus on issues with a typical server running a Linux OS.

Hardware failures are sometimes obvious, like when the server just stops working, but it's the less obvious problems that cause performance issues. These are usually soft failures that allow the system to keep running but degrade operation. This could be a bad bit of memory, where the system has detected the problem and bypassed that segment (reducing the overall available memory). The same can happen with a CPU failure. For problems such as these, you should be using the facilities that your hardware provides, such as an intelligent platform management interface (IPMI) to monitor hardware health. When there's an active problem, looking at the kernel ring buffer using `dmesg` will help you to see log messages that are getting thrown to the system console.

The more common type of hardware failure that leads to a performance degradation in Kafka is a disk failure. Apache Kafka is dependent on the disk for persistence of messages, and producer performance is directly tied to how fast your disks commit those writes. Any deviation in this will show up as problems with the performance of the producers and the replica fetchers. The latter is what leads to under-replicated partitions. As such, it is important to monitor the health of the disks at all times and address any problems quickly.

One Bad Egg

A single disk failure on a single broker can destroy the performance of an entire cluster. This is because the producer clients will connect to all brokers that lead partitions for a topic, and if you have followed best practices, those partitions will be evenly spread over the entire cluster. If one broker starts performing poorly and slowing down produce requests, this will cause back-pressure in the producers, slowing down requests to all brokers.

To begin with, make sure you are monitoring hardware status information for the disks from the IPMI, or the interface provided by your hardware. In addition, within the OS you should be running SMART (Self-Monitoring, Analysis and Reporting Technology) tools to both monitor and test the disks on a regular basis. This will alert you to a failure that is about to happen. It is also important to keep an eye on the disk controller, especially if it has RAID functionality, whether you are using hardware RAID or not. Many controllers have an onboard cache that is only used when the controller is healthy and the battery backup unit (BBU) is working. A failure of the BBU can result in the cache being disabled, degrading disk performance.

Networking is another area where partial failures will cause problems. Some of these problems are hardware issues, such as a bad network cable or connector. Some are configuration issues, which is usually a change in the speed or duplex settings for the connection, either on the server side or upstream on the networking hardware. Network configuration problems could also be OS issues, such as having the network buffers undersized, or too many network connections taking up too much of the overall memory footprint. One of the key indicators of problems in this area will be the number of errors detected on the network interfaces. If the error count is increasing, there is probably an unaddressed issue.

If there are no hardware problems, another common problem to look for is another application running on the system that is consuming resources and putting pressure on the Kafka broker. This could be something that was installed in error, or it could be a process that is supposed to be running, such as a monitoring agent, but is having problems. Use the tools on your system, such as top, to identify if there is a process that is using more CPU or memory than expected.

If the other options have been exhausted and you have not yet found the source of the discrepancy on the host, a configuration difference has likely crept in, either with the broker or the system itself. Given the number of applications that are running on any single server and the number of configuration options for each of them, it can be a daunting task to find a discrepancy. This is why it is crucial that you utilize a configuration management system, such as Chef (*https://www.chef.io/*) or Puppet (*https://puppet.com/*), in order to maintain consistent configurations across your OSes and applications (including Kafka).

Broker Metrics

In addition to underreplicated partitions, there are other metrics that are present at the overall broker level that should be monitored. While you may not be inclined to set alert thresholds for all of them, they provide valuable information about your brokers and your cluster. They should be present in any monitoring dashboard you create.

Active controller count

The *active controller count* metric indicates whether the broker is currently the controller for the cluster. The metric will either be 0 or 1, with 1 showing that the broker is currently the controller. At all times, only one broker should be the controller, and one broker must always be the controller in the cluster. If two brokers say that they are currently the controller, this means that you have a problem where a controller thread that should have exited has become stuck. This can cause problems with not being able to execute administrative tasks, such as partition moves, properly. To remedy this, you will need to restart both brokers at the very least. However, when there is an extra controller in the cluster, there will often be problems performing a controlled shutdown of a broker. See Table 10-3 for more details on active controller count.

Table 10-3. Acive controller count metric

Metric name	Active controller count
JMX MBean	`kafka.controller:type=KafkaController,name=ActiveControllerCount`
Value range	Zero or one

If no broker claims to be the controller in the cluster, the cluster will fail to respond properly in the face of state changes, including topic or partition creation, or broker failures. In this situation, you must investigate further to find out why the controller threads are not working properly. For example, a network partition from the Zookeeper cluster could result in a problem like this. Once that underlying problem is fixed, it is wise to restart all the brokers in the cluster in order to reset state for the controller threads.

Request handler idle ratio

Kafka uses two thread pools for handling all client requests: network handlers and request handlers. The network handler threads are responsible for reading and writing data to the clients across the network. This does not require significant processing, which means that exhaustion of the network handlers is less of a concern. The request handler threads, however, are responsible for servicing the client request itself, which includes reading or writing the messages to disk. As such, as the brokers get more heavily loaded, there is a significant impact on this thread pool. See Table 10-4 for more details on the request handler idle ratio.

Table 10-4. Request handler idle ratio

Metric name	Request handler average idle percentage
JMX MBean	`kafka.server:type=KafkaRequestHandlerPool,name=RequestHandlerAvgIdlePercent`
Value range	Float, between zero and one inclusive

> **Intelligent Thread Usage**
>
> While it may seem like you will need hundreds of request handler threads, in reality you do not need to configure any more threads than you have CPUs in the broker. Apache Kafka is very smart about the way it uses the request handlers, making sure to offload requests that will take a long time to process to purgatory. This is used, for example, when requests are being quoted or when more than one acknowledgment of produce requests is required.

The request handler idle ratio metric indicates the percentage of time the request handlers are not in use. The lower this number, the more loaded the broker is. Experience tells us that idle ratios lower than 20% indicate a potential problem, and lower than 10% is usually an active performance problem. Besides the cluster being undersized, there are two reasons for high thread utilization in this pool. The first is that there are not enough threads in the pool. In general, you should set the number of request handler threads equal to the number of processors in the system (including hyperthreaded processors).

The other common reason for high request handler thread utilization is that the threads are doing unnecessary work for each request. Prior to Kafka 0.10, the request handler thread was responsible for decompressing every incoming message batch, validating the messages and assigning offsets, and then recompressing the message batch with offsets before writing it to disk. To make matters worse, the compression methods were all behind a synchronous lock. As of version 0.10, there is a new message format that allows for relative offsets in a message batch. This means that newer producers will set relative offsets prior to sending the message batch, which allows the broker to skip recompression of the message batch. One of the single largest performance improvements you can make is to ensure that all producer and consumer clients support the 0.10 message format, and to change the message format version on the brokers to 0.10 as well. This will greatly reduce the utilization of the request handler threads.

All topics bytes in

The all topics bytes in rate, expressed in bytes per second, is useful as a measurement of how much message traffic your brokers are receiving from producing clients. This is a good metric to trend over time to help you determine when you need to expand the cluster or do other growth-related work. It is also useful for evaluating if one broker in a cluster is receiving more traffic than the others, which would indicate that it is necessary to rebalance the partitions in the cluster. See Table 10-5 for more details.

Table 10-5. Details on all topics bytes in metric

Metric name	Bytes in per second
JMX MBean	`kafka.server:type=BrokerTopicMetrics,name=BytesInPerSec`
Value range	Rates as doubles, count as integer

As this is the first rate metric discussed, it is worth a short discussion of the attributes that are provided by these types of metrics. All of the rate metrics have seven attributes, and choosing which ones to use depends on what type of measurement you want. The attributes provide a discrete count of events, as well as an average of the number of events over various periods of time. Make sure to use the metrics appropriately, or you will end up with a flawed view of the broker.

The first two attributes are not measurements, but they will help you understand the metric you are looking at:

EventType
:   This is the unit of measurement for all the attributes. In this case, it is "bytes."

RateUnit
:   For the rate attributes, this is the time period for the rate. In this case, it is "SECONDS."

These two descriptive attributes tell us that the rates, regardless of the period of time they average over, are presented as a value of bytes per second. There are four rate attributes provided with different granularities:

OneMinuteRate
:   An average over the previous 1 minute.

FiveMinuteRate

> An average over the previous 5 minutes.

FifteenMinuteRate

> An average over the previous 15 minutes.

MeanRate

> An average since the broker was started.

The `OneMinuteRate` will fluctuate quickly and provides more of a "point in time" view of the measurement. This is useful for seeing short spikes in traffic. The `MeanRate` will not vary much at all and provides an overall trend. Though `MeanRate` has its uses, it is probably not the metric you want to be alerted on. The `FiveMinuteRate` and `Fifteen MinuteRate` provide a compromise between the two.

In addition to the rate attributes, there is a `Count` attribute as well. This is a constantly increasing value for the metric since the time the broker was started. For this metric, all topics bytes in, the `Count` represents the total number of bytes produced to the broker since the process was started. Utilized with a metrics system that supports countermetrics, this can give you an absolute view of the measurement instead of an averaged rate.

All topics bytes out

The all topics bytes out rate, similar to the bytes in rate, is another overall growth metric. In this case, the bytes out rate shows the rate at which consumers are reading messages out. The outbound bytes rate may scale differently than the inbound bytes rate, thanks to Kafka's capacity to handle multiple consumers with ease. There are many deployments of Kafka where the outbound rate can easily be six times the inbound rate! This is why it is important to observe and trend the outbound bytes rate separately. See Table 10-6 for more details.

Table 10-6. Details on all topics bytes out metric

Metric name	Bytes out per second
JMX MBean	`kafka.server:type=BrokerTopicMetrics,name=BytesOutPerSec`
Value range	Rates as doubles, count as integer

Replica Fetchers Included

The outbound bytes rate *also* includes the replica traffic. This means that if all of the topics are configured with a replication factor of 2, you will see a bytes out rate equal to the bytes in rate when there are no consumer clients. If you have one consumer client reading all the messages in the cluster, then the bytes out rate will be twice the bytes in rate. This can be confusing when looking at the metrics if you're not aware of what is counted.

All topics messages in

While the bytes rates described previously show the broker traffic in absolute terms of bytes, the messages in rate shows the number of individual messages, regardless of their size, produced per second. This is useful as a growth metric as a different measure of producer traffic. It can also be used in conjunction with the bytes in rate to determine an average message size. You may also see an imbalance in the brokers, just like with the bytes in rate, that will alert you to maintenance work that is needed. See Table 10-7 for more details.

Table 10-7. Details on all topics messages in metric

Metric name	Messages in per second
JMX MBean	`kafka.server:type=BrokerTopicMetrics,name=MessagesInPerSec`
Value range	Rates as doubles, count as integer

Why No Messages Out?

People often ask why there is no messages out metric for the Kafka broker. The reason is that when messages are consumed, the broker just sends the next batch to the consumer without expanding it to find out how many messages are inside. Therefore, the broker doesn't really know how many messages were sent out. The only metric that can be provided is the number of fetches per second, which is a request rate, not a messages count.

Partition count

The partition count for a broker generally doesn't change that much, as it is the total number of partitions assigned to that broker. This includes every replica the broker has, regardless of whether it is a leader or follower for that partition. Monitoring this is often more interesting in a cluster that has automatic topic creation enabled, as that can leave the creation of topics outside of the control of the person running the cluster. See Table 10-8 for more details.

Table 10-8. Details on partition count metric

Metric name	Partition count
JMX MBean	`kafka.server:type=ReplicaManager,name=PartitionCount`
Value range	Integer, zero or greater

Leader count

The leader count metric shows the number of partitions that the broker is currently the leader for. As with most other measurements in the brokers, this one should be generally even across the brokers in the cluster. It is much more important to check the leader count on a regular basis, possibly alerting on it, as it will indicate when the cluster is imbalanced even if the number of replicas are perfectly balanced in count and size across the cluster. This is because a broker can drop leadership for a partition for many reasons, such as a Zookeeper session expiration, and it will not automatically take leadership back once it recovers (except if you have enabled automatic leader rebalancing). In these cases, this metric will show fewer leaders, or often zero, which indicates that you need to run a preferred replica election to rebalance leadership in the cluster. See Table 10-9 for more details.

Table 10-9. Details on leader count metric

Metric name	Leader count
JMX MBean	`kafka.server:type=ReplicaManager,name=LeaderCount`
Value range	Integer, zero or greater

A useful way to consume this metric is to use it along with the partition count to show a percentage of partitions that the broker is the leader for. In a well-balanced cluster that is using a replication factor of 2, all brokers should be leaders for approximately 50% of their partitions. If the replication factor in use is 3, this percentage drops to 33%.

Offline partitions

Along with the under-replicated partitions count, the offline partitions count is a critical metric for monitoring (see Table 10-10). This measurement is only provided by the broker that is the controller for the cluster (all other brokers will report 0), and shows the number of partitions in the cluster that currently have no leader. Partitions without leaders can happen for two main reasons:

- All brokers hosting replicas for this partition are down
- No in-sync replica can take leadership due to message-count mismatches (with unclean leader election disabled)

Table 10-10. Offline partitions count metric

Metric name	Offline partitions count
JMX MBean	`kafka.controller:type=KafkaController,name=OfflinePartitionsCount`
Value range	Integer, zero or greater

In a production Kafka cluster, an offline partition may be impacting the producer clients, losing messages or causing back-pressure in the application. This is most often a "site down" type of problem and will need to be addressed immediately.

Request metrics

The Kafka protocol, described in Chapter 5, has many different requests. Metrics are provided for how each of those requests performs. The following requests have metrics provided:

- `ApiVersions`
- `ControlledShutdown`
- `CreateTopics`
- `DeleteTopics`
- `DescribeGroups`
- `Fetch`
- `FetchConsumer`
- `FetchFollower`
- `GroupCoordinator`
- `Heartbeat`
- `JoinGroup`
- `LeaderAndIsr`
- `LeaveGroup`
- `ListGroups`
- `Metadata`
- `OffsetCommit`
- `OffsetFetch`
- `Offsets`
- `Produce`
- `SaslHandshake`

- StopReplica

- SyncGroup

- UpdateMetadata

For each of these requests, there are eight metrics provided, providing insight into each of the phases of the request processing. For example, for the Fetch request, the metrics shown in Table 10-11 are available.

Table 10-11. Request Metrics

Name	JMX MBean
Total time	kafka.network:type=RequestMetrics,name=TotalTimeMs,request=Fetch
Request queue time	kafka.network:type=RequestMetrics,name=RequestQueueTimeMs,request=Fetch
Local time	kafka.network:type=RequestMetrics,name=LocalTimeMs,request=Fetch
Remote time	kafka.network:type=RequestMetrics,name=RemoteTimeMs,request=Fetch
Throttle time	kafka.network:type=RequestMetrics,name=ThrottleTimeMs,request=Fetch
Response queue time	kafka.network:type=RequestMetrics,name=ResponseQueueTimeMs,request=Fetch
Response send time	kafka.network:type=RequestMetrics,name=ResponseSendTimeMs,request=Fetch
Requests per second	kafka.network:type=RequestMetrics,name=RequestsPerSec,request=Fetch

The requests per second metric is a rate metric, as discussed earlier, and shows the total number of that type of request that has been received and processed over the time unit. This provides a view into the frequency of each request time, though it should be noted that many of the requests, such as StopReplica and UpdateMetadata, are infrequent.

The seven *time* metrics each provide a set of percentiles for requests, as well as a discrete Count attribute, similar to rate metrics. The metrics are all calculated since the broker was started, so keep that in mind when looking at metrics that do not change for long periods of time, the longer your broker has been running, the more stable the numbers will be. The parts of request processing they represent are:

Total time

Measures the total amount of time the broker spends processing the request, from receiving it to sending the response back to the requestor.

Request queue time

The amount of time the request spends in queue after it has been received but before processing starts.

Local time

The amount of time the partition leader spends processing a request, including sending it to disk (but not necessarily flushing it).

Remote time

The amount of time spent waiting for the followers before request processing can complete.

Throttle time

The amount of time the response must be held in order to slow the requestor down to satisfy client quota settings.

Response queue time

The amount of time the response to the request spends in the queue before it can be sent to the requestor.

Response send time

The amount of time spent actually sending the response.

The attributes provided for each metric are:

Percentiles

50thPercentile, 75thPercentile, 95thPercentile, 98thPercentile, 99thPercentile, 999thPercentile

Count

Absolute count of number of requests since process start

Min

Minimum value for all requests

Max

Maximum value for all requests

Mean

Average value for all requests

StdDev

The standard deviation of the request timing measurements as a whole

What Is a Percentile?

Percentiles are a common way of looking at timing measurement. A 99th percentile measurement tells us that 99% of all values in the sample group (request timings, in this case) are less than the value of the metric. This means that 1% of the values are greater than the value specified. A common pattern is to view the average value and the 99% or 99.9% value. In this way, you can understand how the average request performs and what the outliers are.

Out of all of these metrics and attributes for requests, which are the important ones to monitor? At a minimum, you should collect at least the average and one of the higher percentiles (either 99% or 99.9%) for the total time metric, as well as the requests per second metric, for every request type. This gives a view into the overall performance of requests to the Kafka broker. If you can, you should also collect those measurements for the other six timing metrics for each request type, as this will allow you to narrow down any performance problems to a specific phase of request processing.

For setting alert thresholds, the timing metrics can be difficult. The timing for a Fetch request, for example, can vary wildly depending on many factors, including settings on the client for how long it will wait for messages, how busy the particular topic being fetched is, and the speed of the network connection between the client and the broker. It can be very useful, however, to develop a baseline value for the 99.9th percentile measurement for at least the total time, especially for Produce requests, and alert on this. Much like the under-replicated partitions metric, a sharp increase in the 99.9th percentile for Produce requests can alert you to a wide range of performance problems.

Topic and Partition Metrics

In addition to the many metrics available on the broker that describe the operation of the Kafka broker in general, there are topic- and partition-specific metrics. In larger clusters these can be numerous, and it may not be possible to collect all of them into a metrics system as a matter of normal operations. However, they are quite useful for debugging specific issues with a client. For example, the topic metrics can be used to identify a specific topic that is causing a large increase in traffic to the cluster. It also may be important to provide these metrics so that users of Kafka (the producer and consumer clients) are able to access them. Regardless of whether you are able to collect these metrics regularly, you should be aware of what is useful.

For all the examples in Table 10-12, we will be using the example topic name TOPIC NAME, as well as partition 0. When accessing the metrics described, make sure to substitute the topic name and partition number that are appropriate for your cluster.

Per-topic metrics

For all the per-topic metrics, the measurements are very similar to the broker metrics described previously. In fact, the only difference is the provided topic name, and that the metrics will be specific to the named topic. Given the sheer number of metrics available, depending on the number of topics present in your cluster, these will almost certainly be metrics that you will not want to set up monitoring and alerts for. They are useful to provide to clients, however, so that they can evaluate and debug their own usage of Kafka.

Table 10-12. Metrics for Each Topic

Name	JMX MBean
Bytes in rate	`kafka.server:type=BrokerTopicMetrics,name=BytesInPerSec,topic=`*TOPIC NAME*
Bytes out rate	`kafka.server:type=BrokerTopicMetrics,name=BytesOutPerSec,topic=`*TOPICNAME*
Failed fetch rate	`kafka.server:type=BrokerTopicMetrics,name=FailedFetchRequestsPerSec,topic=`*TOPICNAME*
Failed produce rate	`kafka.server:type=BrokerTopicMetrics,name=FailedProduceRequestsPerSec,topic=`*TOPICNAME*
Messages in rate	`kafka.server:type=BrokerTopicMetrics,name=MessagesInPerSec,topic=`*TOPICNAME*
Fetch request rate	`kafka.server:type=BrokerTopicMetrics,name=TotalFetchRequestsPerSec,topic=`*TOPICNAME*
Produce request rate	`kafka.server:type=BrokerTopicMetrics,name=TotalProduceRequestsPerSec,topic=`*TOPICNAME*

Per-partition metrics

The per-partition metrics tend to be less useful on an ongoing basis than the per-topic metrics. Additionally, they are quite numerous as hundreds of topics can easily be thousands of partitions. Nevertheless, they can be useful in some limited situations. In particular, the partition-size metric indicates the amount of data (in bytes) that is currently being retained on disk for the partition (Table 10-13). Combined, these will indicate the amount of data retained for a single topic, which can be useful in allocating costs for Kafka to individual clients. A discrepancy between the size of two partitions for the same topic can indicate a problem where the messages are not evenly distributed across the key that is being used when producing. The log-segment count metric shows the number of log-segment files on disk for the partition. This may be useful along with the partition size for resource tracking.

Table 10-13. Metrics for Each Topic

Name	JMX MBean
Partition size	`kafka.log:type=Log,name=Size,topic=`*`TOPICNAME`*`,partition=0`
Log segment count	`kafka.log:type=Log,name=NumLogSegments,topic=`*`TOPICNAME`*`,partition=0`
Log end offset	`kafka.log:type=Log,name=LogEndOffset,topic=`*`TOPICNAME`*`,partition=0`
Log start offset	`kafka.log:type=Log,name=LogStartOffset,topic=`*`TOPICNAME`*`,partition=0`

The log end offset and log start offset metrics are the highest and lowest offsets for messages in that partition, respectively. It should be noted, however, that the difference between these two numbers does not necessarily indicate the number of messages in the partition, as log compaction can result in "missing" offsets that have been removed from the partition due to newer messages with the same key. In some environments, it could be useful to track these offsets for a partition. One such use case is to provide a more granular mapping of timestamp to offset, allowing for consumer clients to easily roll back offsets to a specific time (though this is less important with time-based index searching, introduced in Kafka 0.10.1).

Under-replicated Partition Metrics

There is a per-partition metric provided to indicate whether or not the partition is underreplicated. In general, this is not very useful in day-to-day operations, as there are too many metrics to gather and watch. It is much easier to monitor the broker-wide under-replicated partition count and then use the command-line tools (described in Chapter 9) to determine the specific partitions that are under-replicated.

JVM Monitoring

In addition to the metrics provided by the Kafka broker, you should be monitoring a standard suite of measurements for all of your servers, as well as the Java Virtual Machine (JVM) itself. These will be useful to alert you to a situation, such as increasing garbage collection activity, that will degrade the performance of the broker. They will also provide insight into why you see changes in metrics downstream in the broker.

Garbage collection

For the JVM, the critical thing to monitor is the status of garbage collection (GC). The particular beans that you must monitor for this information will vary depending on the particular Java Runtime Environment (JRE) that you are using, as well as the specific GC settings in use. For an Oracle Java 1.8 JRE running with G1 garbage collection, the beans to use are shown in Table 10-14.

Table 10-14. G1 Garbage Collection Metrics

Name	JMX MBean
Full GC cycles	`java.lang:type=GarbageCollector,name=G1 Old Generation`
Young GC cycles	`java.lang:type=GarbageCollector,name=G1 Young Generation`

Note that in the semantics of GC, "Old" and "Full" are the same thing. For each of these metrics, the two attributes to watch are `CollectionCount` and `CollectionTime`. The `CollectionCount` is the number of GC cycles of that type (full or young) since the JVM was started. The `CollectionTime` is the amount of time, in milliseconds, spent in that type of GC cycle since the JVM was started. As these measurements are counters, they can be used by a metrics system to tell you an absolute number of GC cycles and time spent in GC per unit of time. They can also be used to provide an average amount of time per GC cycle, though this is less useful in normal operations.

Each of these metrics also has a `LastGcInfo` attribute. This is a composite value, made up of five fields, that gives you information on the last GC cycle for the type of GC described by the bean. The important value to look at is the `duration` value, as this tells you how long, in milliseconds, the last GC cycle took. The other values in the composite (`GcThreadCount`, `id`, `startTime`, and `endTime`) are informational and not very useful. It's important to note that you will not be able to see the timing of every GC cycle using this attribute, as young GC cycles in particular can happen frequently.

Java OS monitoring

The JVM can provide you with some information on the OS through the `java.lang:type=OperatingSystem` bean. However, this information is limited and does not represent everything you need to know about the system running your broker. The two attributes that can be collected here that are of use, which are difficult to collect in the OS, are the `MaxFileDescriptorCount` and `OpenFileDescriptorCount` attributes. `MaxFileDescriptorCount` will tell you the maximum number of file descriptors (FDs) that the JVM is allowed to have open. The `OpenFileDescriptorCount` attribute tells you the number of FDs that are currently open. There will be FDs open for every log segment and network connection, and they can add up quickly. A problem closing network connections properly could cause the broker to rapidly exhaust the number allowed.

OS Monitoring

The JVM cannot provide us with all the information that we need to know about the system it is running on. For this reason, we must not only collect metrics from the broker but also from the OS itself. Most monitoring systems will provide agents that will collect more OS information than you could possibly be interested in. The main areas that are necessary to watch are CPU usage, memory usage, disk usage, disk IO, and network usage.

For CPU utilization, you will want to look at the system load average at the very least. This provides a single number that will indicate the relative utilization of the processors. In addition, it may also be useful to capture the percent usage of the CPU broken down by type. Depending on the method of collection and your particular OS, you may have some or all of the following CPU percentage breakdowns (provided with the abbreviation used):

us

The time spent in user space.

sy

The time spent in kernel space.

ni

The time spent on low-priority processes.

id

The time spent idle.

wa

The time spent in wait (on disk).

hi

The time spent handling hardware interrupts.

si

The time spent handling software interrupts.

st

The time waiting for the hypervisor.

What Is System Load?

While many know that system load is a measure of CPU usage on a system, most people misunderstand how it is measured. The load average is a count of the number of processes that are runnable and are waiting for a processor to execute on. Linux also includes threads that are in an uninterruptable sleep state, such as waiting for the disk. The load is presented as three numbers, which is the count averaged over the last minute, 5 minutes, and 15 minutes. In a single CPU system, a value of 1 would mean the system is 100% loaded, with a thread always waiting to execute. This means that on a multiple CPU system, the load average number that indicates 100% is equal to the number of CPUs in the system. For example, if there are 24 processors in the system, 100% would be a load average of 24.

The Kafka broker uses a significant amount of processing for handling requests. For this reason, keeping track of the CPU utilization is important when monitoring Kafka. Memory is less important to track for the broker itself, as Kafka will normally be run with a relatively small JVM heap size. It will use a small amount of memory outside of the heap for compression functions, but most of the system memory will be left to be used for cache. All the same, you should keep track of memory utilization to make sure other applications do not infringe on the broker. You will also want to make sure that swap memory is not being used by monitoring the amount of total and free swap memory.

Disk is by far the most important subsystem when it comes to Kafka. All messages are persisted to disk, so the performance of Kafka depends heavily on the performance of the disks. Monitoring usage of both disk space and inodes (inodes are the file and directory metadata objects for Unix filesystems) is important, as you need to assure that you are not running out of space. This is especially true for the partitions where Kafka data is being stored. It is also necessary to monitor the disk IO statistics, as this will tell us that the disk is being used efficiently. For at least the disks where Kafka data is stored, monitor the reads and writes per second, the average read and write queue sizes, the average wait time, and the utilization percentage of the disk.

Finally, monitor the network utilization on the brokers. This is simply the amount of inbound and outbound network traffic, normally reported in bits per second. Keep in mind that every bit inbound to the Kafka broker will be a number of bits outbound equal to the replication factor of the topics, with no consumers. Depending on the number of consumers, inbound network traffic could easily become an order of magnitude larger on outbound traffic. Keep this in mind when setting thresholds for alerts.

Logging

No discussion of monitoring is complete without a word about logging. Like many applications, the Kafka broker will fill disks with log messages in minutes if you let it. In order to get useful information from logging, it is important to enable the right loggers at the right levels. By simply logging all messages at the INFO level, you will capture a significant amount of important information about the state of the broker. It is useful to separate a couple of loggers from this, however, in order to provide a cleaner set of log files.

There are two loggers writing to separate files on disk. The first is kafka.controller, still at the INFO level. This logger is used to provide messages specifically regarding the cluster controller. At any time, only one broker will be the controller, and therefore only one broker will be writing to this logger. The information includes topic creation and modification, broker status changes, and cluster activities such as preferred replica elections and partition moves. The other logger to separate is kafka.server.ClientQuotaManager, also at the INFO level. This logger is used to show messages related to produce and consume quota activities. While this is useful information, it is better to not have it in the main broker log file.

It is also helpful to log information regarding the status of the log compaction threads. There is no single metric to show the health of these threads, and it is possible for failure in compaction of a single partition to halt the log compaction threads entirely, and silently. Enabling the kafka.log.LogCleaner, kafka.log.Cleaner, and kafka.log.LogCleanerManager loggers at the DEBUG level will output information about the status of these threads. This will include information about each partition being compacted, including the size and number of messages in each. Under normal operations, this is not a lot of logging, which means that it can be enabled by default without overwhelming you.

There is also some logging that may be useful to turn on when debugging issues with Kafka. One such logger is kafka.request.logger, turned on at either DEBUG or TRACE levels. This logs information about every request sent to the broker. At DEBUG level, the log includes connection end points, request timings, and summary information. At the TRACE level, it will also include topic and partition information—nearly all request information short of the message payload itself. At either level, this logger generates a significant amount of data, and it is not recommended to enable it unless necessary for debugging.

Client Monitoring

All applications need monitoring. Those that instantiate a Kafka client, either a producer or consumer, have metrics specific to the client that should be captured. This section covers the official Java client libraries, though other implementations should have their own measurements available.

Producer Metrics

The new Kafka producer client has greatly compacted the metrics available by making them available as attributes on a small number of mbeans. In contrast, the previous version of the producer client (which is no longer supported) used a larger number of mbeans but had more detail in many of the metrics (providing a greater number of percentile measurements and different moving averages). As a result, the overall number of metrics provided covers a wider surface area, but it can be more difficult to track outliers.

All of the producer metrics have the client ID of the producer client in the bean names. In the examples provided, this has been replaced with *CLIENTID*. Where a bean name contains a broker ID, this has been replaced with *BROKERID*. Topic names have been replaced with *TOPICNAME*. See Table 10-15 for an example.

Table 10-15. Kafka Producer Metric MBeans

Name	JMX MBean
Overall Producer	`kafka.producer:type=producer-metrics,client-id=`*CLIENTID*
Per-Broker	`kafka.producer:type=producer-node-metrics,client-id=`*CLIENTID*`,node-id=node-`*BROKERID*
Per-Topic	`kafka.producer:type=producer-topic-metrics,client-id=`*CLIENTID*`,topic=`*TOPICNAME*

Each of the metric beans in Table 10-15 have multiple attributes available to describe the state of the producer. The particular attributes that are of the most use are described in "Overall producer metrics" on page 236. Before proceeding, be sure you understand the semantics of how the producer works, as described in Chapter 3.

Overall producer metrics

The overall producer metrics bean provides attributes describing everything from the sizes of the message batches to the memory buffer utilization. While all of these measurements have their place in debugging, there are only a handful needed on a regular basis, and only a couple of those that should be monitored and have alerts. Note that while we will discuss several metrics that are averages (ending in `-avg`), there are also maximum values for each metric (ending in -max) that have limited usefulness.

The record-error-rate is one attribute that you will definitely want to set an alert for. This metric should always be zero, and if it is anything greater than that, the producer is dropping messages it is trying to send to the Kafka brokers. The producer has a configured number of retries and a backoff between those, and once that has been exhausted, the messages (called records here) will be dropped. There is also a record-retry-rate attribute that can be tracked, but it is less critical than the error rate because retries are normal.

The other metric to alert on is the request-latency-avg. This is the average amount of time a produce request sent to the brokers takes. You should be able to establish a baseline value for what this number should be in normal operations, and set an alert threshold above that. An increase in the request latency means that produce requests are getting slower. This could be due to networking issues, or it could indicate problems on the brokers. Either way, it's a performance issue that will cause back-pressure and other problems in your producing application.

In addition to these critical metrics, it is always good to know how much message traffic your producer is sending. Three attributes will provide three different views of this. The outgoing-byte-rate describes the messages in absolute size in bytes per second. The record-send-rate describes the traffic in terms of the number of messages produced per second. Finally, the request-rate provides the number of produce requests sent to the brokers per second. A single request contains one or more batches. A single batch contains one or more messages. And, of course, each message is made up of some number of bytes. These metrics are all useful to have on an application dashboard.

Why Not ProducerRequestMetrics?

There is a producer metric bean called ProducerRequestMetrics that provides both percentiles for request latency as well as several moving averages for the request rate. So why is it not one of the recommended metrics to use? The problem is that this metric is provided separately for each producer thread. In applications where there are multiple threads used for performance reasons it will be difficult to reconcile these metrics. It is normally sufficient to use the attributes provided by the single overall producer bean.

There are also metrics that describe the size of both records, requests, and batches. The request-size-avg metric provides the average size of the produce requests being sent to the brokers in bytes. The batch-size-avg provides the average size of a single message batch (which, by definition, is comprised of messages for a single topic partition) in bytes. The `record-size-avg` shows the average size of a single record in bytes. For a single-topic producer, this provides useful information about the messages being produced. For multiple-topic producers, such as Mirror Maker, it is less informative. Besides these three metrics, there is a `records-per-request-avg` metric that describes the average number of messages that are in a single produce request.

The last overall producer metric attribute that is recommended is `record-queue-time-avg`. This measurement is the average amount of time, in milliseconds, that a single message waits in the producer, after the application sends it, before it is actually produced to Kafka. After an application calls the producer client to send a message (by calling the `send` method), the producer waits until one of two things happens:

- It has enough messages to fill a batch based on the `max.partition.bytes` configuration
- It has been long enough since the last batch was sent based on the `linger.ms` configuration

Either of these two will cause the producer client to close the current batch it is building and send it to the brokers. The easiest way to understand it is that for busy topics the first condition will apply, whereas for slow topics the second will apply. The `record-queue-time-avg` measurement will indicate how long messages take to be produced, and therefore is helpful when tuning these two configurations to meet the latency requirements for your application.

Per-broker and per-topic metrics

In addition to the overall producer metrics, there are metric beans that provide a limited set of attributes for the connection to each Kafka broker, as well as for each topic that is being produced. These measurements are useful for debugging problems in some cases, but they are not metrics that you are going to want to review on an ongoing basis. All of the attributes on these beans are the same as the attributes for the overall producer beans described previously, and have the same meaning as described previously (except that they apply either to a specific broker or a specific topic).

The most useful metric that is provided by the per-broker producer metrics is the `request-latency-avg` measurement. This is because this metric will be mostly stable (given stable batching of messages) and can still show a problem with connections to a specific broker. The other attributes, such as `outgoing-byte-rate` and `request-latency-avg`, tend to vary depending on what partitions each broker is leading. This means that what these measurements "should" be at any point in time can quickly change, depending on the state of the Kafka cluster.

The topic metrics are a little more interesting than the per-broker metrics, but they will only be useful for producers that are working with more than one topic. They will also only be useable on a regular basis if the producer is not working with a lot of topics. For example, a MirrorMaker could be producing hundreds, or thousands, of topics. It is difficult to review all of those metrics, and nearly impossible to set reasonable alert thresholds on them. As with the per-broker metrics, the per-topic measurements are best used when investigating a specific problem. The `record-send-rate` and `record-error-rate` attributes, for example, can be used to isolate dropped messages to a specific topic (or validated to be across all topics). In addition, there is a `byte-rate` metric that provides the overall messages rate in bytes per second for the topic.

Consumer Metrics

Similar to the new producer client, the new consumer in Kafka consolidates many of the metrics into attributes on just a few metric beans. These metrics have also eliminated the percentiles for latencies and the moving averages for rates, similar to the producer client. In the consumer, because the logic around consuming messages is a little more complex than just firing messages into the Kafka brokers, there are a few more metrics to deal with as well. See Table 10-16.

Table 10-16. Kafka Consumer Metric MBeans

Name	JMX MBean
Overall Consumer	`kafka.consumer:type=consumer-metrics,client-id=CLIENTID`
Fetch Manager	`kafka.consumer:type=consumer-fetch-manager-metrics,client-id=CLIENTID`
Per-Topic	`kafka.consumer:type=consumer-fetch-manager-metrics,client-id=CLIENTID,topic=TOPICNAME`
Per-Broker	`kafka.consumer:type=consumer-node-metrics,client-id=CLIENTID,node-id=node-BROKERID`
Coordinator	`kafka.consumer:type=consumer-coordinator-metrics,client-id=CLIENTID`

Fetch manager metrics

In the consumer client, the overall consumer metric bean is less useful for us because the metrics of interest are located in the fetch manager beans instead. The overall consumer bean has metrics regarding the lower-level network operations, but the fetch manager bean has metrics regarding bytes, request, and record rates. Unlike the producer client, the metrics provided by the consumer are useful to look at but not useful for setting up alerts on.

For the fetch manager, the one attribute you may want to set up monitoring and alerts for is `fetch-latency-avg`. As with the equivalent `request-latency-avg` in the producer client, this metric tells us how long fetch requests to the brokers take. The problem with alerting on this metric is that the latency is governed by the consumer configurations `fetch.min.bytes` and `fetch.max.wait.ms`. A slow topic will have erratic latencies, as sometimes the broker will respond quickly (when there are messages available), and sometimes it will not respond for `fetch.max.wait.ms` (when there are no messages available). When consuming topics that have more regular, and abundant, message traffic, this metric may be more useful to look at.

Wait! No Lag?

The best advice for all consumers is that you must monitor the consumer lag. So why do we not recommend monitoring the `records-lag-max` attribute on the fetch manager bean? This metric shows the current lag (number of messages behind the broker) for the partition that is the most behind.

The problem with this is twofold: it only shows the lag for one partition, and it relies on proper functioning of the consumer. If you have no other option, use this attribute for lag and set up alerting for it. But the best practice is to use external lag monitoring, as will be described in "Lag Monitoring" on page 243.

In order to know how much message traffic your consumer client is handling, you should capture the `bytes-consumed-rate` or the `records-consumed-rate`, or preferably both. These metrics describe the message traffic consumed by this client instance in bytes per second and messages per second, respectively. Some users set minimum thresholds on these metrics for alerting, so that they are notified if the consumer is not doing enough work. You should be careful when doing this, however. Kafka is intended to decouple the consumer and producer clients, allowing them to operate independently. The rate at which the consumer is able to consume messages is often dependent on whether or not the producer is working correctly, so monitoring these metrics on the consumer makes assumptions about the state of the producer. This can lead to false alerts on the consumer clients.

It is also good to understand the relationship between bytes, messages, and requests, and the fetch manager provides metrics to help with this. The `fetch-rate` measurement tells us the number of fetch requests per second that the consumer is performing. The `fetch-size-avg` metric gives the average size of those fetch requests in bytes. Finally, the `records-per-request-avg` metric gives us the average number of messages in each fetch request. Note that the consumer does not provide an equivalent to the producer `record-size-avg` metric to let us know what the average size of a message is. If this is important, you will need to infer it from the other metrics available, or capture it in your application after receiving messages from the consumer client library.

Per-broker and per-topic metrics

The metrics that are provided by the consumer client for each of the broker connections and each of the topics being consumed, as with the producer client, are useful for debugging issues with consumption, but will probably not be measurements that you review daily. As with the fetch manager, the request-latency-avg attribute provided by the per-broker metrics bean has limited usefulness, depending on the message traffic in the topics you are consuming. The incoming-byte-rate and request-rate metrics break down the consumed message metrics provided by the fetch manager into per-broker bytes per second and requests per second measurements, respectively. These can be used to help isolate problems that the consumer is having with the connection to a specific broker.

Per-topic metrics provided by the consumer client are useful if more than one topic is being consumed. Otherwise, these metrics will be the same as the fetch manager's metrics and redundant to collect. On the other end of the spectrum, if the client is consuming many topics (Kafka MirrorMaker, for example) these metrics will be difficult to review. If you plan on collecting them, the most important metrics to gather are the bytes-consumed-rate, the records-consumed-rate, and the fetch-size-avg. The bytes-consumed-rate shows the absolute size in bytes consumed per second for the specific topic, while the records-consumed-rate shows the same information in terms of the number of messages. The fetch-size-avg provides the average size of each fetch request for the topic in bytes.

Consumer coordinator metrics

As described in Chapter 4, consumer clients generally work together as part of a consumer group. This group has coordination activities, such as group members joining and heartbeat messages to the brokers to maintain group membership. The consumer coordinator is the part of the consumer client that is responsible for handling this work, and it maintains its own set of metrics. As with all metrics, there are many numbers provided, but only a few key ones that you should monitor regularly.

The biggest problem that consumers can run into due to coordinator activities is a pause in consumption while the consumer group synchronizes. This is when the consumer instances in a group negotiate which partitions will be consumed by which individual client instances. Depending on the number of partitions that are being consumed, this can take some time. The coordinator provides the metric attribute sync-time-avg, which is the average amount of time, in milliseconds, that the sync activity takes. It is also useful to capture the sync-rate attribute, which is the number of group syncs that happen every second. For a stable consumer group, this number should be zero most of the time.

The consumer needs to commit offsets to checkpoint its progress in consuming messages, either automatically on a regular interval, or by manual checkpoints triggered in the application code. These commits are essentially just produce requests (though they have their own request type), in that the offset commit is a message produced to a special topic. The consumer coordinator provides the `commit-latency-avg` attribute, which measures the average amount of time that offset commits take. You should monitor this value just as you would the request latency in the producer. It should be possible to establish a baseline expected value for this metric, and set reasonable thresholds for alerting above that value.

One final coordinator metric that can be useful to collect is `assigned-partitions`. This is a count of the number of partitions that the consumer client (as a single instance in the consumer group) has been assigned to consume. This is helpful because, when compared to this metric from other consumer clients in the group, it is possible to see the balance of load across the entire consumer group. We can use this to identify imbalances that might be caused by problems in the algorithm used by the consumer coordinator for distributing partitions to group members.

Quotas

Apache Kafka has the ability to throttle client requests in order to prevent one client from overwhelming the entire cluster. This is configurable for both producer and consumer clients, and is expressed in terms of the permitted amount of traffic from an individual client ID to an individual broker in bytes per second. There is a broker configuration, which sets a default value for all clients, as well as per-client overrides that can be dynamically set. When the broker calculates that a client has exceeded its quota, it slows the client down by holding the response back to the client for enough time to keep the client under the quota.

The Kafka broker does not use error codes in the response to indicate that the client is being throttled. This means that it is not obvious to the application that throttling is happening without monitoring the metrics that are provided to show the amount of time that the client is being throttled. The metrics that must be monitored are shown in Table 10-17.

Table 10-17. Metrics to monitor

Client	Bean name
Consumer	bean `kafka.consumer:type=consumer-fetch-manager-metrics,client-id=CLIENTID`, attribute `fetch-throttle-time-avg`
Producer	bean `kafka.producer:type=producer-metrics,client-id=CLIENTID`, attribute `produce-throttle-time-avg`

Quotas are not enabled by default on the Kafka brokers, but it is safe to monitor these metrics irrespective of whether or not you are currently using quotas. Monitoring them is a good practice as they may be enabled at some point in the future, and it's easier to start with monitoring them as opposed to adding metrics later.

Lag Monitoring

For Kafka consumers, the most important thing to monitor is the consumer lag. Measured in number of messages, this is the difference between the last message produced in a specific partition and the last message processed by the consumer. While this topic would normally be covered in the previous section on consumer client monitoring, it is one of the cases where external monitoring far surpasses what is available from the client itself. As mentioned previously, there is a lag metric in the consumer client, but using it is problematic. It only represents a single partition, the one that has the most lag, so it does not accurately show how far behind the consumer is. In addition, it requires proper operation of the consumer, because the metric is calculated by the consumer on each fetch request. If the consumer is broken or offline, the metric is either inaccurate or not available.

The preferred method of consumer lag monitoring is to have an external process that can watch both the state of the partition on the broker, tracking the offset of the most recently produced message, and the state of the consumer, tracking the last offset the consumer group has committed for the partition. This provides an objective view that can be updated regardless of the status of the consumer itself. This checking must be performed for every partition that the consumer group consumes. For a large consumer, like MirrorMaker, this may mean tens of thousands of partitions.

Chapter 9 provided information on using the command-line utilities to get consumer group information, including committed offsets and lag. Monitoring lag like this, however, presents its own problems. First, you must understand for each partition what is a reasonable amount of lag. A topic that receives 100 messages an hour will need a different threshold than a topic that receives 100,000 messages per second. Then, you must be able to consume all of the lag metrics into a monitoring system and set alerts on them. If you have a consumer group that consumes 100,000 partitions over 1,500 topics, you may find this to be a daunting task.

One way to monitor consumer groups in order to reduce this complexity is to use Burrow (*https://github.com/linkedin/Burrow*). This is an open source application, originally developed by LinkedIn, which provides consumer status monitoring by gathering lag information for all consumer groups in a cluster and calculating a single status for each group saying whether the consumer group is working properly, falling behind, or is stalled or stopped entirely. It does this without requiring thresholds by monitoring the progress that the consumer group is making on processing messages, though you can also get the message lag as an absolute number. There is an in-depth discussion of the reasoning and methodology behind how Burrow works on the LinkedIn Engineering Blog (*http://bit.ly/2sanKZb*). Deploying Burrow can be an easy way to provide monitoring for all consumers in a cluster, as well as in multiple clusters, and it can be easily integrated with your existing monitoring and alerting system.

If there is no other option, the `records-lag-max` metric from the consumer client will provide at least a partial view of the consumer status. It is strongly suggested, however, that you utilize an external monitoring system like Burrow.

End-to-End Monitoring

Another type of external monitoring that is recommended to determine if your Kafka clusters are working properly is an end-to-end monitoring system that provides a client point of view on the health of the Kafka cluster. Consumer and producer clients have metrics that can indicate that there might be a problem with the Kafka cluster, but this can be a guessing game as to whether increased latency is due to a problem with the client, the network, or Kafka itself. In addition, it means that if you are responsible for running the Kafka cluster, and not the clients, you would now have to monitor all of the clients as well. What you really need to know is:

- Can I produce messages to the Kafka cluster?
- Can I consume messages from the Kafka cluster?

In an ideal world, you would be able to monitor this for every topic individually. However, in most situations it is not reasonable to inject synthetic traffic into every topic in order to do this. We can, however, at least provide those answers for every broker in the cluster, and that is what Kafka Monitor (*https://github.com/linkedin/kafka-monitor*) does. This tool, open sourced by the Kafka team at LinkedIn, continually produces and consumes data from a topic that is spread across all brokers in a cluster. It measures the availability of both produce and consume requests on each broker, as well as the total produce to consume latency. This type of monitoring is invaluable to be able to externally verify that the Kafka cluster is operating as intended, since just like consumer lag monitoring, the Kafka broker cannot report whether or not clients are able to use the cluster properly.

Summary

Monitoring is a key aspect of running Apache Kafka properly, which explains why so many teams spend a significant amount of their time perfecting that part of operations. Many organizations use Kafka to handle petabyte-scale data flows. Assuring that the data does not stop, and that messages are not lost, is a critical business requirement. It is also our responsibility to assist users with monitoring how their applications use Kafka by providing the metrics that they need to do this.

In this chapter we covered the basics of how to monitor Java applications, and specifically the Kafka applications. We reviewed a subset of the numerous metrics available in the Kafka broker, also touching on Java and OS monitoring, as well as logging. We then detailed the monitoring available in the Kafka client libraries, including quota monitoring. Finally, we discussed the use of external monitoring systems for consumer lag monitoring and end-to-end cluster availability. While certainly not an exhaustive list of the metrics that are available, this chapter has reviewed the most critical ones to keep an eye on.

## CHAPTER 11

Stream Processing

Kafka was traditionally seen as a powerful message bus, capable of delivering streams of events but without processing or transformation capabilities. Kafka's reliable stream delivery capabilities make it a perfect source of data for stream-processing systems. Apache Storm, Apache Spark Streaming, Apache Flink, Apache Samza, and many more stream-processing systems were built with Kafka often being their only reliable data source.

Industry analysts sometimes claim that all those stream-processing systems are just like the complex event processing (CEP) systems that have been around for 20 years. We think stream processing became more popular because it was created after Kafka and therefore could use Kafka as a reliable source of event streams to process. With the increased popularity of Apache Kafka, first as a simple message bus and later as a data integration system, many companies had a system containing many streams of interesting data, stored for long amounts of time and perfectly ordered, just waiting for some stream-processing framework to show up and process them. In other words, in the same way that data processing was significantly more difficult before databases were invented, stream processing was held back by lack of a stream-processing platform.

Starting from version 0.10.0, Kafka does more than provide a reliable source of data streams to every popular stream-processing framework. Now Kafka includes a powerful stream-processing library as part of its collection of client libraries. This allows developers to consume, process, and produce events in their own apps, without relying on an external processing framework.

We'll begin the chapter by explaining what we mean by stream processing (since this term is frequently misunderstood), then discuss some of the basic concepts of stream processing and the design patterns that are common to all stream-processing systems. We'll then dive into Apache Kafka's stream-processing library—its goals and architecture. We'll give a small example of how to use Kafka Streams to calculate a moving average of stock prices. We'll then discuss other examples for good stream-processing use cases and finish off the chapter by providing a few criteria you can use when choosing which stream-processing framework (if any) to use with Apache Kafka. This chapter is intended as a brief introduction to stream processing and will not cover every Kafka Streams feature or attempt to discuss and compare every stream-processing framework in existence—those topics deserve entire books on their own, possibly several.

What Is Stream Processing?

There is a lot of confusion about what stream processing means. Many definitions mix up implementation details, performance requirements, data models, and many other aspects of software engineering. I've seen the same thing play out in the world of relational databases—the abstract definitions of the relational model are getting forever entangled in the implementation details and specific limitations of the popular database engines.

The world of stream processing is still evolving, and just because a specific popular implementation does things in specific ways or has specific limitations doesn't mean that those details are an inherent part of processing streams of data.

Let's start at the beginning: What is a data stream (also called an *event stream* or *streaming data*)? First and foremost, a *data stream* is an abstraction representing an unbounded dataset. *Unbounded* means infinite and ever growing. The dataset is unbounded because over time, new records keep arriving. This definition is used by Google (*http://oreil.ly/1p1AKux*), Amazon (*http://amzn.to/2sfc334*), and pretty much everyone else.

Note that this simple model (a stream of events) can be used to represent pretty much every business activity we care to analyze. We can look at a stream of credit card transactions, stock trades, package deliveries, network events going through a switch, events reported by sensors in manufacturing equipment, emails sent, moves in a game, etc. The list of examples is endless because pretty much everything can be seen as a sequence of events.

There are few other attributes of event streams model, in addition to their unbounded nature:

Event streams are ordered
> There is an inherent notion of which events occur before or after other events. This is clearest when looking at financial events. A sequence in which I first put money in my account and later spend the money is very different from a sequence at which I first spend the money and later cover my debt by depositing money back. The latter will incur overdraft charges while the former will not.

Note that this is one of the differences between an event stream and a database table—records in a table are always considered unordered and the "order by" clause of SQL is not part of the relational model; it was added to assist in reporting.

Immutable data records

Events, once occured, can never be modified. A financial transaction that is cancelled does not disapear. Instead, an additional event is written to the stream, recording a cancellation of previous transaction. When a customer returns merchandise to a shop, we don't delete the fact that the merchandise was sold to him earlier, rather we record the return as an additional event. This is another difference between a data stream and a database table—we can delete or update records in a table, but those are all additional transactions that occur in the database, and as such can be recorded in a stream of events that records all transactions. If you are familiar with binlogs, WALs, or redo logs in databases you can see that if we insert a record into a table and later delete it, the table will no longer contain the record, but the redo log will contain two transactions—the insert and the delete.

Event streams are replayable

This is a desirable property. While it is easy to imagine nonreplayable streams (TCP packets streaming through a socket are generally nonreplayable), for most business applications, it is critical to be able to replay a raw stream of events that occured months (and sometimes years) earlier. This is required in order to correct errors, try new methods of analysis, or perform audits. This is the reason we believe Kafka made stream processing so successful in modern businesses—it allows capturing and replaying a stream of events. Without this capability, stream processing would not be more than a lab toy for data scientists.

It is worth noting that neither the definition of event streams nor the attributes we later listed say anything about the data contained in the events or the number of events per second. The data differs from system to system—events can be tiny (sometimes only a few bytes) or very large (XML messages with many headers); they can also be completely unstructured, key-value pairs, semi-structured JSON, or structured Avro or Protobuf messages. While it is often assumed that data streams are "big data" and involve millions of events per second, the same techniques we'll discuss apply equally well (and often better) to smaller streams of events with only a few events per second or minute.

Now that we know what event streams are, it's time to make sure we understand stream processing. Stream processing refers to the ongoing processing of one or more event streams. Stream processing is a programming paradigm—just like request-response and batch processing. Let's look at how different programming paradigms compare to get a better understanding of how stream processing fits into software architectures:

Request-response

This is the lowest latency paradigm, with response times ranging from submilliseconds to a few milliseconds, usually with the expectation that response times will be highly consistent. The mode of processing is usually blocking—an app sends a request and waits for the processing system to respond. In the database world, this paradigm is known as *online transaction processing* (OLTP). Point-of-sale systems, credit card processing, and time-tracking systems typically work in this paradigm.

Batch processing

This is the high-latency/high-throughput option. The processing system wakes up at set times—every day at 2:00 A.M., every hour on the hour, etc. It reads all required input (either all data available since last execution, all data from beginning of month, etc.), writes all required output, and goes away until the next time it is scheduled to run. Processing times range from minutes to hours and users expect to read stale data when they are looking at results. In the database world, these are the data warehouse and business intelligence systems—data is loaded in huge batches once a day, reports are generated, and users look at the same reports until the next data load occurs. This paradigm often has great efficiency and economy of scale, but in recent years, businesses need the data available in shorter timeframes in order to make decision-making more timely and efficient. This puts huge pressure on systems that were written to exploit economy of scale —not to provide low-latency reporting.

Stream processing

This is a contentious and nonblocking option. Filling the gap between the request-response world where we wait for events that take two milliseconds to process and the batch processing world where data is processed once a day and takes eight hours to complete. Most business processes don't require an immediate response within milliseconds but can't wait for the next day either. Most business processes happen continuously, and as long as the business reports are updated continuously and the line of business apps can continuously respond, the processing can proceed without anyone waiting for a specific response within milliseconds. Business processes like alerting on suspicious credit transactions or network activity, adjusting prices in real-time based on supply and demand, or tracking deliveries of packages are all natural fit for continuous but nonblocking processing.

It is important to note that the definition doesn't mandate any specific framework, API, or feature. As long as you are continuously reading data from an unbounded dataset, doing something to it, and emitting output, you are doing stream processing.

But the processing has to be continuous and ongoing. A process that starts every day at 2:00 A.M., reads 500 records from the stream, outputs a result, and goes away doesn't quite cut it as far as stream processing goes.

Stream-Processing Concepts

Stream processing is very similar to any type of data processing—you write code that receives data, does something with the data—a few transformations, aggregates, enrichments, etc.—and then place the result somewhere. However, there are some key concepts that are unique to stream processing and often cause confusion when someone who has data processing experience first attempts to write stream-processing applications. Let's take a look at a few of those concepts.

Time

Time is probably the most important concept in stream processing and often the most confusing. For an idea of how complex time can get when discussing distributed systems, we recommend Justin Sheehy's excellent "There is No Now" (*http://bit.ly/ 2rXXdLr*) paper. In the context of stream processing, having a common notion of time is critical because most stream applications perform operations on time windows. For example, our stream application might calculate a moving five-minute average of stock prices. In that case, we need to know what to do when one of our producers goes offline for two hours due to network issues and returns with two hours worth of data—most of the data will be relevant for five-minute time windows that have long passed and for which the result was already calculated and stored.

Stream-processing systems typically refer to the following notions of time:

Event time
> This is the time the events we are tracking occurred and the record was created—the time a measurement was taken, an item at was sold at a shop, a user viewed a page on our website, etc. In versions 0.10.0 and later, Kafka automatically adds the current time to producer records at the time they are created. If this does not match your application's notion of *event time*, such as in cases where the Kafka record is created based on a database record some time after the event occurred, you should add the event time as a field in the record itself. Event time is usually the time that matters most when processing stream data.

Log append time
> This is the time the event arrived to the Kafka broker and was stored there. In versions 0.10.0 and higher, Kafka brokers will automatically add this time to records they receive if Kafka is configured to do so or if the records arrive from older producers and contain no timestamps. This notion of time is typically less relevant for stream processing, since we are usually interested in the times the

events occurred. For example, if we calculate number of devices produced per day, we want to count devices that were actually produced on that day, even if there were network issues and the event only arrived to Kafka the following day. However, in cases where the real event time was not recorded, log append time can still be used consistently because it does not change after the record was created.

Processing time

This is the time at which a stream-processing application received the event in order to perform some calculation. This time can be milliseconds, hours, or days after the event occurred. This notion of time assigns different timestamps to the same event depending on exactly when each stream processing application happened to read the event. It can even differ for two threads in the same application! Therefore, this notion of time is highly unreliable and best avoided.

Mind the Time Zone

When working with time, it is important to be mindful of time zones. The entire data pipeline should standardize on a single time zones; otherwise, results of stream operations will be confusing and often meaningless. If you must handle data streams with different time zones, you need to make sure you can convert events to a single time zone before performing operations on time windows. Often this means storing the time zone in the record itself.

State

As long as you only need to process each event individually, stream processing is a very simple activity. For example, if all you need to do is read a stream of online shopping transactions from Kafka, find the transactions over $10,000 and email the relevant salesperson, you can probably write this in just few lines of code using a Kafka consumer and SMTP library.

Stream processing becomes really interesting when you have operations that involve multiple events: counting the number of events by type, moving averages, joining two streams to create an enriched stream of information, etc. In those cases, it is not enough to look at each event by itself; you need to keep track of more information—how many events of each type did we see this hour, all events that require joining, sums, averages, etc. We call the information that is stored between events a *state*.

It is often tempting to store the state in variables that are local to the stream-processing app, such as a simple hash-table to store moving counts. In fact, we did just that in many examples in this book. However, this is not a reliable approach for managing state in stream processing because when the stream-processing application is stopped, the state is lost, which changes the results. This is usually not the desired outcome, so care should be taken to persist the most recent state and recover it when starting the application.

Stream processing refers to several types of state:

Local or internal state

State that is accessible only by a specific instance of the stream-processing application. This state is usually maintained and managed with an embedded, in-memory database running within the application. The advantage of local state is that it is extremely fast. The disadvantage is that you are limited to the amount of memory available. As a result, many of the design patterns in stream processing focus on ways to partition the data into substreams that can be processed using a limited amount of local state.

External state

State that is maintained in an external datastore, often a NoSQL system like Cassandra. The advantages of an external state are its virtually unlimited size and the fact that it can be accessed from multiple instances of the application or even from different applications. The downside is the extra latency and complexity introduced with an additional system. Most stream-processing apps try to avoid having to deal with an external store, or at least limit the latency overhead by caching information in the local state and communicating with the external store as rarely as possible. This usually introduces challenges with maintaining consistency between the internal and external state.

Stream-Table Duality

We are all familiar with database tables. A table is a collection of records, each identified by its primary key and containing a set of attributes as defined by a schema. Table records are mutable (i.e., tables allow update and delete operations). Querying a table allows checking the state of the data at a specific point in time. For example, by querying the CUSTOMERS_CONTACTS table in a database, we expect to find current contact details for all our customers. Unless the table was specifically designed to include history, we will not find their past contacts in the table.

Unlike tables, streams contain a history of changes. Streams are a string of events wherein each event caused a change. A table contains a current state of the world, which is the result of many changes. From this description, it is clear that streams and tables are two sides of the same coin—the world always changes, and sometimes we are interested in the events that caused those changes, whereas other times we are interested in the current state of the world. Systems that allow you to transition back and forth between the two ways of looking at data are more powerful than systems that support just one.

In order to convert a table to a stream, we need to capture the changes that modify the table. Take all those `insert`, `update`, and `delete` events and store them in a stream. Most databases offer change data capture (CDC) solutions for capturing these changes and there are many Kafka connectors that can pipe those changes into Kafka where they will be available for stream processing.

In order to convert a stream to a table, we need to apply all the changes that the stream contains. This is also called *materializing* the stream. We create a table, either in memory, in an internal state store, or in an external database, and start going over all the events in the stream from beginning to end, changing the state as we go. When we finish, we have a table representing a state at a specific time that we can use.

Suppose we have a store selling shoes. A stream representation of our retail activity can be a stream of events:

"Shipment arrived with red, blue, and green shoes"

"Blue shoes sold"

"Red shoes sold"

"Blue shoes returned"

"Green shoes sold"

If we want to know what our inventory contains right now or how much money we made until now, we need to materialize the view. Figure 11-1 shows that we currently have blue and yellow shoes and $170 in the bank. If we want to know how busy the store is, we can look at the entire stream and see that there were five transactions. We may also want to investigate why the blue shoes were returned.

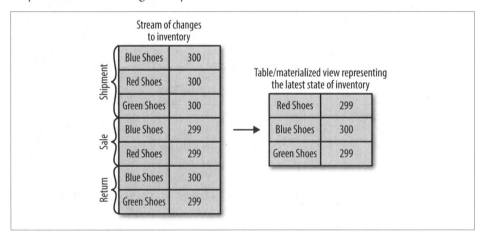

Figure 11-1. Materializing inventory changes

Time Windows

Most operations on streams are windowed operations—operating on slices of time: moving averages, top products sold this week, 99th percentile load on the system, etc. Join operations on two streams are also windowed—we join events that occurred at the same slice of time. Very few people stop and think about the type of window they want for their operations. For example, when calculating moving averages, we want to know:

- Size of the window: do we want to calculate the average of all events in every five-minute window? Every 15-minute window? Or the entire day? Larger windows are smoother but they lag more—if price increases, it will take longer to notice than with a smaller window.

- How often the window moves (*advance interval*): five-minute averages can update every minute, second, or every time there is a new event. When the *advance interval* is equal to the window size, this is sometimes called a *tumbling window*. When the window moves on every record, this is sometimes called a *sliding window*.

- How long the window remains updatable: our five-minute moving average calculated the average for 00:00-00:05 window. Now an hour later, we are getting a few more results with their *event time* showing 00:02. Do we update the result for the 00:00-00:05 period? Or do we let bygones be bygones? Ideally, we'll be able to define a certain time period during which events will get added to their respective time-slice. For example, if the events were up to four hours late, we should recalculate the results and update. If events arrive later than that, we can ignore them.

Windows can be aligned to clock time—i.e., a five-minute window that moves every minute will have the first slice as 00:00-00:05 and the second as 00:01-00:06. Or it can be unaligned and simply start whenever the app started and then the first slice can be 03:17-03:22. Sliding windows are never aligned because they move whenever there is a new record. See Figure 11-2 for the difference between two types of these windows.

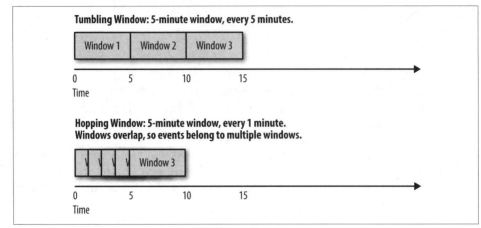

Figure 11-2. Tumbling window versus Hopping window

Stream-Processing Design Patterns

Every stream-processing system is different—from the basic combination of a con‐sumer, processing logic, and producer to involved clusters like Spark Streaming with its machine learning libraries, and much in between. But there are some basic design patterns, which are known solutions to common requirements of stream-processing architectures. We'll review a few of those well-known patterns and show how they are used with a few examples.

Single-Event Processing

The most basic pattern of stream processing is the processing of each event in isola‐tion. This is also known as a map/filter pattern because it is commonly used to filter unnecessary events from the stream or transform each event. (The term "map" is based on the map/reduce pattern in which the map stage transforms events and the reduce stage aggregates them.)

In this pattern, the stream-processing app consumes events from the stream, modifies each event, and then produces the events to another stream. An example is an app that reads log messages from a stream and writes ERROR events into a high-priority stream and the rest of the events into a low-priority stream. Another example is an application that reads events from a stream and modifies them from JSON to Avro. Such applications need to maintain state within the application because each event can be handled independently. This means that recovering from app failures or load-balancing is incredibly easy as there is no need to recover state; you can simply hand off the events to another instance of the app to process.

This pattern can be easily handled with a simple producer and consumer, as seen in Figure 11-3.

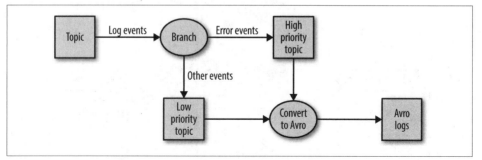

Figure 11-3. Single-event processing topology

Processing with Local State

Most stream-processing applications are concerned with aggregating information, especially time-window aggregation. An example of this is finding the minimum and maximum stock prices for each day of trading and calculating a moving average.

These aggregations require maintaining a *state* for the stream. In our example, in order to calculate the minimum and average price each day, we need to store the minimum and maximum values we've seen up until the current time and compare each new value in the stream to the stored minimum and maximum.

All these can be done using *local* state (rather than a shared state) because each operation in our example is a *group by* aggregate. That is, we perform the aggregation per stock symbol, not on the entire stock market in general. We use a Kafka partitioner to make sure that all events with the same stock symbol are written to the same partition. Then, each instance of the application will get all the events from the partitions that are assigned to it (this is a Kafka consumer guarantee). This means that each instance of the application can maintain state for the subset of stock symbols that are written to the partitions that are assigned to it. See Figure 11-4.

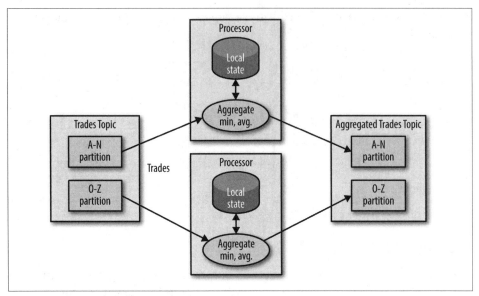

Figure 11-4. Topology for event processing with local state

Stream-processing applications become significantly more complicated when the application has local state and there are several issues a stream-processing application must address:

Memory usage

The local state must fit into the memory available to the application instance.

Persistence

We need to make sure the state is not lost when an application instance shuts down, and that the state can be recovered when the instance starts again or is replaced by a different instance. This is something that Kafka Streams handles very well—local state is stored in-memory using embedded RocksDB, which also persists the data to disk for quick recovery after restarts. But all the changes to the local state are also sent to a Kafka topic. If a stream's node goes down, the local state is not lost—it can be easily recreated by rereading the events from the Kafka topic. For example, if the local state contains "current minimum for IBM=167.19," we store this in Kafka, so that later we can repopulate the local cache from this data. Kafka uses log compaction for these topics to make sure they don't grow endlessly and that recreating the state is always feasible.

Rebalancing

Partitions sometimes get reassigned to a different consumer. When this happens, the instance that loses the partition must store the last good state, and the instance that receives the partition must know to recover the correct state.

Stream-processing frameworks differ in how much they help the developer manage the local state they need. If your application requires maintaining local state, be sure to check the framework and its guarantees. We'll include a short comparison guide at the end of the chapter, but as we all know, software changes quickly and stream-processing frameworks doubly so.

Multiphase Processing/Repartitioning

Local state is great if you need a *group by* type of aggregate. But what if you need a result that uses all available information? For example, suppose we want to publish the top 10 stocks each day—the 10 stocks that gained the most from opening to closing during each day of trading. Obviously, nothing we do locally on each application instance is enough because all the top 10 stocks could be in partitions assigned to other instances. What we need is a two-phase approach. First, we calculate the daily gain/loss for each stock symbol. We can do this on each instance with a local state. Then we write the results to a new topic with a single partition. This partition will be read by a single application instance that can then find the top 10 stocks for the day. The second topic, which contains just the daily summary for each stock symbol, is obviously much smaller with significantly less traffic than the topics that contain the trades themselves, and therefore it can be processed by a single instance of the application. Sometimes more steps are needed to produce the result. See Figure 11-5.

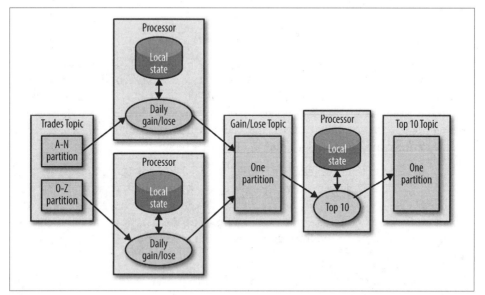

Figure 11-5. Topology that includes both local state and repartitioning steps

This type of multiphase processing is very familiar to those who write map-reduce code, where you often have to resort to multiple reduce phases. If you've ever written map-reduce code, you'll remember that you needed a separate app for each reduce step. Unlike MapReduce, most stream-processing frameworks allow including all steps in a single app, with the framework handling the details of which application instance (or worker) will run reach step.

Processing with External Lookup: Stream-Table Join

Sometimes stream processing requires integration with data external to the stream— validating transactions against a set of rules stored in a database, or enriching click-stream information with data about the users who clicked.

The obvious idea on how to perform an external lookup for data enrichment is something like this: for every click event in the stream, look up the user in the profile database and write an event that includes the original click plus the user age and gender to another topic. See Figure 11-6.

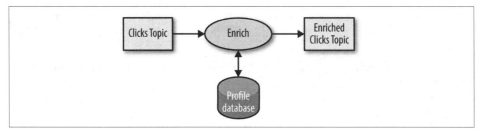

Figure 11-6. Stream processing that includes an external data source

The problem with this obvious idea is that an external lookup adds significant latency to the processing of every record—usually between 5-15 milliseconds. In many cases, this is not feasible. Often the additional load this places on the external datastore is also not acceptable—stream-processing systems can often handle 100K-500K events per second, but the database can only handle perhaps 10K events per second at reasonable performance. We want a solution that scales better.

In order to get good performance and scale, we need to cache the information from the database in our stream-processing application. Managing this cache can be challenging though—how do we prevent the information in the cache from getting stale? If we refresh events too often, we are still hammering the database and the cache isn't helping much. If we wait too long to get new events, we are doing stream processing with stale information.

But if we can capture all the changes that happen to the database table in a stream of events, we can have our stream-processing job listen to this stream and update the cache based on database change events. Capturing changes to the database as events in a stream is known as CDC, and if you use Kafka Connect you will find multiple connectors capable of performing CDC and converting database tables to a stream of change events. This allows you to keep your own private copy of the table, and you will be notified whenever there is a database change event so you can update your own copy accordingly. See Figure 11-7.

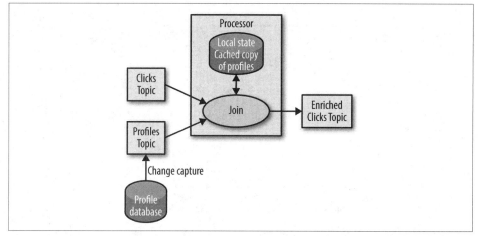

Figure 11-7. Topology joining a table and a stream of events, removing the need to involve an external data source in stream processing

Then, when you get click events, you can look up the user_id at your local cache and enrich the event. And because you are using a local cache, this scales a lot better and will not affect the database and other apps using it.

We refer to this as a *stream-table join* because one of the streams represents changes to a locally cached table.

Streaming Join

Sometimes you want to join two real event streams rather than a stream with a table. What makes a stream "real"? If you recall the discussion at the beginning of the chapter, streams are unbounded. When you use a stream to represent a table, you can ignore most of the history in the stream because you only care about the current state in the table. But when you join two streams, you are joining the entire history, trying to match events in one stream with events in the other stream that have the same key and happened in the same time-windows. This is why a streaming-join is also called a *windowed-join*.

For example, let's say that we have one stream with search queries that people entered into our website and another stream with clicks, which include clicks on search results. We want to match search queries with the results they clicked on so that we will know which result is most popular for which query. Obviously we want to match results based on the search term but only match them within a certain time-window.

We assume the result is clicked seconds after the query was entered into our search engine. So we keep a small, few-seconds-long window on each stream and match the results from each window. See Figure 11-8.

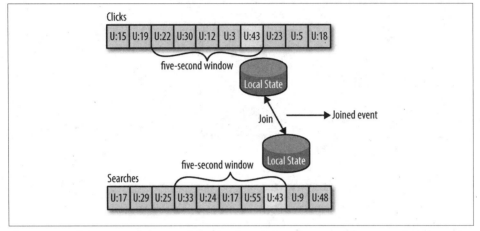

Figure 11-8. Joining two streams of events; these joins always involve a moving time window

The way this works in Kafka Streams is that both streams, queries and clicks, are partitioned on the same keys, which are also the join keys. This way, all the click events from user_id:42 end up in partition 5 of the clicks topic, and all the search events for user_id:42 end up in partition 5 of the search topic. Kafka Streams then makes sure that partition 5 of both topics is assigned to the same task. So this task sees all the relevant events for user_id:42. It maintains the join-window for both topics in its embedded RocksDB cache, and this is how it can perform the join.

Out-of-Sequence Events

Handling events that arrive at the stream at the wrong time is a challenge not just in stream processing but also in traditional ETL systems. Out-of-sequence events happen quite frequently and expectedly in IoT (Internet of Things) scenarios (Figure 11-9). For example, a mobile device loses WiFi signal for a few hours and sends a few hours' worth of events when it reconnects. This also happens when monitoring network equipment (a faulty switch doesn't send diagnostics signals until it is repaired) or manufacturing (network connectivity in plants is notoriously unreliable, especially in developing countries).

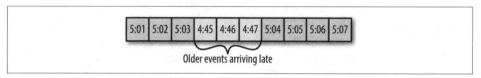

Figure 11-9. Out of sequence events

Our streams applications need to be able to handle those scenarios. This typically means the application has to do the following:

- Recognize that an event is out of sequence—this requires that the application examine the event time and discover that it is older than the current time.

- Define a time period during which it will attempt to reconcile out-of-sequence events. Perhaps a three-hour delay should be reconciled and events over three weeks old can be thrown away.

- Have an in-band capability to reconcile this event. This is the main difference between streaming apps and batch jobs. If we have a daily batch job and a few events arrived after the job completed, we can usually just rerun yesterday's job and update the events. With stream processing, there is no "rerun yesterday's job" —the same continuous process needs to handle both old and new events at any given moment.

- Be able to update results. If the results of the stream processing are written into a database, a *put* or *update* is enough to update the results. If the stream app sends results by email, updates may be trickier.

Several stream-processing frameworks, including Google's Dataflow and Kafka Streams, have built-in support for the notion of event time independent of the processing time and the ability to handle events with event times that are older or newer than the current processing time. This is typically done by maintaining multiple aggregation windows available for update in the local state and giving developers the ability to configure how long to keep those window aggregates available for updates. Of course, the longer the aggregation windows are kept available for updates, the more memory is required to maintain the local state.

The Kafka's Streams API always writes aggregation results to result topics. Those are usually `compacted topics`, which means that only the latest value for each key is preserved. In case the results of an aggregation window need to be updated as a result of a late event, Kafka Streams will simply write a new result for this aggregation window, which will overwrite the previous result.

Reprocessing

The last important pattern is processing events. There are two variants of this pattern:

- We have an improved version of our stream-processing application. We want to run the new version of the application on the same event stream as the old, produce a new stream of results that does not replace the first version, compare the results between the two versions, and at some point move clients to use the new results instead of the existing ones.

- The existing stream-processing app is buggy. We fix the bug and we want to reprocess the event stream and recalculate our results

The first use case is made simple by the fact that Apache Kafka stores the event streams in their entirety for long periods of time in a scalable datastore. This means that having two versions of a stream processing-application writing two result streams only requires the following:

- Spinning up the new version of the application as a new consumer group

- Configuring the new version to start processing from the first offset of the input topics (so it will get its own copy of all events in the input streams)

- Letting the new application continue processing and switching the client applications to the new result stream when the new version of the processing job has caught up

The second use case is more challenging—it requires "resetting" an existing app to start processing back at the beginning of the input streams, resetting the local state (so we won't mix results from the two versions of the app), and possibly cleaning the previous output stream. While Kafka Streams has a tool for resetting the state for a stream-processing app, our recommendation is to try to use the first method whenever sufficient capacity exists to run two copies of the app and generate two result streams. The first method is much safer—it allows switching back and forth between multiple versions and comparing results between versions, and doesn't risk losing critical data or introducing errors during the cleanup process.

Kafka Streams by Example

In order to demonstrate how these patterns are implemented in practice, we'll show a few examples using Apache Kafka's Streams API. We are using this specific API because it is relatively simple to use and it ships with Apache Kafka, which you already have access to. It is important to remember that the patterns can be implemented in any stream-processing framework and library—the patterns are universal but the examples are specific.

Apache Kafka has two streams APIs—a low-level Processor API and a high-level Streams DSL. We will use Kafka Streams DSL in our examples. The DSL allows you to define the stream-processing application by defining a chain of transformations to events in the streams. Transformations can be as simple as a filter or as complex as a stream-to-stream join. The lower level API allows you to create your own transformations, but as you'll see, this is rarely required.

An application that uses the DSL API always starts with using the StreamBuilder to create a processing *topology*—a directed graph (DAG) of transformations that are applied to the events in the streams. Then you create a KafkaStreams execution object from the topology. Starting the KafkaStreams object will start multiple threads, each applying the processing topology to events in the stream. The processing will conclude when you close the KafkaStreams object.

We'll look at few examples that use Kafka Streams to implement some of the design patterns we just discussed. A simple word count example will be used to demonstrate the map/filter pattern and simple aggregates. Then we'll move to an example where we calculate different statistics on stock market trades, which will allow us to demonstrate window aggregations. Finally we'll use ClickStream Enrichment as an example to demonstrate streaming joins.

Word Count

Let's walk through an abbreviated word count example for Kafka Streams. You can find the full example on GitHub (*http://bit.ly/2ri00gj*).

The first thing you do when creating a stream-processing app is configure Kafka Streams. Kafka Streams has a large number of possible configurations, which we won't discuss here, but you can find them in the documentation (*http://bit.ly/2t7obPU*). In addition, you can also configure the producer and consumer embedded in Kafka Streams by adding any producer or consumer config to the Properties object:

```
public class WordCountExample {

    public static void main(String[] args) throws Exception{

        Properties props = new Properties();
        props.put(StreamsConfig.APPLICATION_ID_CONFIG,
          "wordcount"); ❶
        props.put(StreamsConfig.BOOTSTRAP_SERVERS_CONFIG,
          "localhost:9092"); ❷
        props.put(StreamsConfig.KEY_SERDE_CLASS_CONFIG,
          Serdes.String().getClass().getName()); ❸
        props.put(StreamsConfig.VALUE_SERDE_CLASS_CONFIG,
          Serdes.String().getClass().getName());
```

❶ Every Kafka Streams application must have an application ID. This is used to coordinate the instances of the application and also when naming the internal local stores and the topics related to them. This name must be unique for each Kafka Streams application working with the same Kafka cluster.

❷ The Kafka Streams application always reads data from Kafka topics and writes its output to Kafka topics. As we'll discuss later, Kafka Streams applications also use Kafka for coordination. So we had better tell our app where to find Kafka.

❸ When reading and writing data, our app will need to serialize and deserialize, so we provide default Serde classes. If needed, we can override these defaults later when building the streams topology.

Now that we have the configuration, let's build our streams topology:

```
KStreamBuilder builder = new KStreamBuilder(); ❶

KStream<String, String> source =
  builder.stream("wordcount-input");


final Pattern pattern = Pattern.compile("\\W+");

KStream counts  = source.flatMapValues(value->
  Arrays.asList(pattern.split(value.toLowerCase())))) ❷
        .map((key, value) -> new KeyValue<Object,
          Object>(value, value))
        .filter((key, value) -> (!value.equals("the"))) ❸
        .groupByKey() ❹
        .count("CountStore").mapValues(value->
          Long.toString(value)).toStream();❺
counts.to("wordcount-output"); ❻
```

❶ We create a `KStreamBuilder` object and start defining a stream by pointing at the topic we'll use as our input.

❷ Each event we read from the source topic is a line of words; we split it up using a regular expression into a series of individual words. Then we take each word (currently a value of the event record) and put it in the event record key so it can be used in a group-by operation.

❸ We filter out the word "the," just to show how easy filtering is.

❹ And we group by key, so we now have a collection of events for each unique word.

❺ We count how many events we have in each collection. The result of counting is a `Long` data type. We convert it to a `String` so it will be easier for humans to read the results.

❻ Only one thing left–write the results back to Kafka.

Now that we have defined the flow of transformations that our application will run, we just need to... run it:

```
KafkaStreams streams = new KafkaStreams(builder, props); ❶

streams.start(); ❷

// usually the stream application would be running
    forever,
// in this example we just let it run for some time and
    stop since the input data is finite.
Thread.sleep(5000L);

streams.close(); ❸

    }
}
```

❶ Define a `KafkaStreams` object based on our topology and the properties we defined.

❷ Start Kafka Streams.

❸ After a while, stop it.

Thats it! In just a few short lines, we demonstrated how easy it is to implement a single event processing pattern (we applied a map and a filter on the events). We repartitioned the data by adding a group-by operator and then maintained simple local state when we counted the number of records that have each word as a key. Then we maintained simple local state when we counted the number of times each word appeared.

At this point, we recommend running the full example. The README in the GitHub repository (*http://bit.ly/2sOXzUN*) contains instructions on how to run the example.

One thing you'll notice is that you can run the entire example on your machine without installing anything except Apache Kafka. This is similar to the experience you may have seen when using Spark in something like *Local Mode*. The main difference is that if your input topic contains multiple partitions, you can run multiple instances of the `WordCount` application (just run the app in several different terminal tabs) and you have your first Kafka Streams processing cluster. The instances of the `WordCount` application talk to each other and coordinate the work. One of the biggest barriers to entry with Spark is that local mode is very easy to use, but then to run a production cluster, you need to install YARN or Mesos and then install Spark on all those machines, and then learn how to submit your app to the cluster. With the Kafka's Streams API, you just start multiple instances of your app—and you have a cluster. The exact same app is running on your development machine and in production.

Stock Market Statistics

The next example is more involved—we will read a stream of stock market trading events that include the stock ticker, ask price, and ask size. In stock market trades, *ask price* is what a seller is asking for whereas *bid price* is what the buyer is suggesting to pay. *Ask size* is the number of shares the seller is willing to sell at that price. For simplicity of the example, we'll ignore bids completely. We also won't include a timestamp in our data; instead, we'll rely on event time populated by our Kafka producer.

We will then create output streams that contains a few windowed statistics:

- Best (i.e., minimum) ask price for every five-second window
- Number of trades for every five-second window
- Average ask price for every five-second window

All statistics will be updated every second.

For simplicity, we'll assume our exchange only has 10 stock tickers trading in it. The setup and configuration are very similar to those we used in the "Word Count" on page 265:

```
Properties props = new Properties();
props.put(StreamsConfig.APPLICATION_ID_CONFIG, "stockstat");
props.put(StreamsConfig.BOOTSTRAP_SERVERS_CONFIG,
Constants.BROKER);
props.put(StreamsConfig.KEY_SERDE_CLASS_CONFIG,
Serdes.String().getClass().getName());
props.put(StreamsConfig.VALUE_SERDE_CLASS_CONFIG,
TradeSerde.class.getName());
```

The main difference is the Serde classes used. In the "Word Count" on page 265, we used strings for both key and value and therefore used the Serdes.String() class as a serializer and deserializer for both. In this example, the key is still a string, but the value is a Trade object that contains the ticker symbol, ask price, and ask size. In order to serialize and deserialize this object (and a few other objects we used in this small app), we used the Gson library from Google to generate a JSon serializer and deserializer from our Java object. Then created a small wrapper that created a Serde object from those. Here is how we created the Serde:

```
static public final class TradeSerde extends WrapperSerde<Trade> {
    public TradeSerde() {
        super(new JsonSerializer<Trade>(),
          new JsonDeserializer<Trade>(Trade.class));
    }
}
```

Nothing fancy, but you need to remember to provide a Serde object for every object you want to store in Kafka—input, output, and in some cases, also intermediate results. To make this easier, we recommend generating these Serdes through projects like GSon, Avro, Protobufs, or similar.

Now that we have everything configured, it's time to build our topology:

```
KStream<TickerWindow, TradeStats> stats = source.groupByKey() ❶
        .aggregate(TradeStats::new, ❷
            (k, v, tradestats) -> tradestats.add(v), ❸
            TimeWindows.of(5000).advanceBy(1000), ❹
            new TradeStatsSerde(), ❺
            "trade-stats-store") ❻
        .toStream((key, value) -> new TickerWindow(key.key(),
            key.window().start())) ❼
        .mapValues((trade) -> trade.computeAvgPrice()); ❽

        stats.to(new TickerWindowSerde(), new TradeStatsSerde(),
            "stockstats-output"); ❾
```

❶ We start by reading events from the input topic and performing a groupByKey() operation. Despite its name, this operation does not do any grouping. Rather, it ensures that the stream of events is partitioned based on the record key. Since we wrote the data into a topic with a key and didn't modify the key before calling groupByKey(), the data is still partitioned by its key—so this method does nothing in this case.

❷ After we ensure correct partitioning, we start the windowed aggregation. The "aggregate" method will split the stream into overlapping windows (a five-second window every second), and then apply an aggregate method on all the events in the window. The first parameter this method takes is a new object that will contain the results of the aggregation—Tradestats in our case. This is an object we created to contain all the statistics we are interested in for each time window—minimum price, average price, and number of trades.

❸ We then supply a method for actually aggregating the records—in this case, an add method of the Tradestats object is used to update the minimum price, number of trades, and total prices in the window with the new record.

❹ We define the window—in this case, a window of five seconds (5,000 ms), advancing every second.

❺ Then we provide a Serde object for serializing and deserializing the results of the aggregation (the Tradestats object).

❻ As mentioned in "Stream-Processing Design Patterns" on page 256, windowing aggregation requires maintaining a state and a local store in which the state will be maintained. The last parameter of the aggregate method is the name of the state store. This can be any unique name.

❼ The results of the aggregation is a *table* with the ticker and the time window as the primary key and the aggregation result as the value. We are turning the table back into a stream of events and replacing the key that contains the entire time window definition with our own key that contains just the ticker and the start time of the window. This toStream method converts the table into a stream and also converts the key into my TickerWindow object.

❽ The last step is to update the average price—right now the aggregation results include the sum of prices and number of trades. We go over these records and use the existing statistics to calculate average price so we can include it in the output stream.

❾ And finally, we write the results back to the stockstats-output stream.

After we define the flow, we use it to generate a KafkaStreams object and run it, just like we did in the "Word Count" on page 265.

This example shows how to perform windowed aggregation on a stream—probably the most popular use case of stream processing. One thing to notice is how little work was needed to maintain the local state of the aggregation—just provide a Serde and name the state store. Yet this application will scale to multiple instances and automatically recover from a failure of each instance by shifting processing of some partitions to one of the surviving instances. We will see more on how it is done in "Kafka Streams: Architecture Overview" on page 272.

As usual, you can find the complete example including instructions for running it on GitHub (*http://bit.ly/2r6BLm1*).

Click Stream Enrichment

The last example will demonstrate streaming joins by enriching a stream of clicks on a website. We will generate a stream of simulated clicks, a stream of updates to a fictional profile database table, and a stream of web searches. We will then join all three streams to get a 360-view into each user activity. What did the users search for? What did they click as a result? Did they change their "interests" in their user profile? These kinds of joins provide a rich data collection for analytics. Product recommendations are often based on this kind of information—user searched for bikes, clicked on links for "Trek," and is interested in travel, so we can advertise bikes from Trek, helmets, and bike tours to exotic locations like Nebraska.

Since configuring the app is similar to the previous examples, let's skip this part and take a look at the topology for joining multiple streams:

```
KStream<Integer, PageView> views =
builder.stream(Serdes.Integer(),
new PageViewSerde(), Constants.PAGE_VIEW_TOPIC); ❶
KStream<Integer, Search> searches =
builder.stream(Serdes.Integer(), new SearchSerde(),
Constants.SEARCH_TOPIC);
KTable<Integer, UserProfile> profiles =
builder.table(Serdes.Integer(), new ProfileSerde(),
Constants.USER_PROFILE_TOPIC, "profile-store"); ❷

KStream<Integer, UserActivity> viewsWithProfile = views.leftJoin(profiles, ❸
    (page, profile) -> new UserActivity(profile.getUserID(),
    profile.getUserName(), profile.getZipcode(),
    profile.getInterests(), "", page.getPage())); ❹

KStream<Integer, UserActivity> userActivityKStream =
viewsWithProfile.leftJoin(searches, ❺
    (userActivity, search) ->
    userActivity.updateSearch(search.getSearchTerms()), ❻
    JoinWindows.of(1000), Serdes.Integer(),
    new UserActivitySerde(), new SearchSerde()); ❼
```

❶ First, we create a streams objects for the two streams we want to join—clicks and searches.

❷ We also define a KTable for the user profiles. A KTable is a local cache that is updated through a stream of changes.

❸ Then we enrich the stream of clicks with user-profile information by joining the stream of events with the profile table. In a stream-table join, each event in the stream receives information from the cached copy of the profile table. We are doing a left-join, so clicks without a known user will be preserved.

❹ This is the join method—it takes two values, one from the stream and one from the record, and returns a third value. Unlike in databases, you get to decide how to combine the two values into one result. In this case, we created one activity object that contains both the user details and the page viewed.

⑤ Next, we want to `join` the click information with searches performed by the same user. This is still a left `join`, but now we are joining two streams, not streaming to a table.

⑥ This is the `join` method—we simply add the search terms to all the matching page views.

⑦ This is the interesting part—a *stream-to-stream join* is a join with a time window. Joining all clicks and searches for each user doesn't make much sense—we want to join each search with clicks that are related to it—that is, click that occurred a short period of time after the search. So we define a join window of one second. Clicks that happen within one second of the search are considered relevant, and the search terms will be included in the activity record that contains the click and the user profile. This will allow a full analysis of searches and their results.

After we define the flow, we use it to generate a `KafkaStreams` object and run it, just like we did in the "Word Count" on page 265.

This example shows two different join patterns possible in stream processing. One joins a stream with a table to enrich all streaming events with information in the table. This is similar to joining a fact table with a dimension when running queries on a data warehouse. The second example joins two streams based on a time window. This operation is unique to stream processing.

As usual, you can find the complete example including instructions for running it on GitHub (*http://bit.ly/2sq096i*).

Kafka Streams: Architecture Overview

The examples in the previous section demonstrated how to use the Kafka Streams API to implement a few well-known stream-processing design patterns. But to understand better how Kafka's Streams library actually works and scales, we need to peek under the covers and understand some of the design principles behind the API.

Building a Topology

Every streams application implements and executes at least one *topology*. Topology (also called DAG, or directed acyclic graph, in other stream-processing frameworks) is a set of operations and transitions that every event moves through from input to output. Figure 11-10 shows the topology in the "Word Count" on page 265.

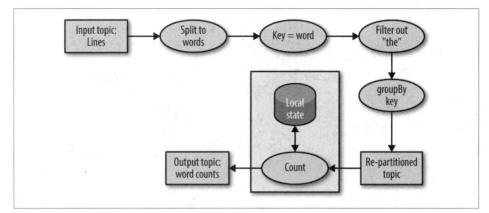

Figure 11-10. Topology for the word-count stream processing example

Even a simple app has a nontrivial topology. The topology is made up of processors—those are the nodes in the topology graph (represented by circles in our diagram). Most processors implement an operation of the data—filter, map, aggregate, etc. There are also source processors, which consume data from a topic and pass it on, and sink processors, which take data from earlier processors and produce it to a topic. A topology always starts with one or more source processors and finishes with one or more sink processors.

Scaling the Topology

Kafka Streams scales by allowing multiple threads of executions within one instance of the application and by supporting load balancing between distributed instances of the application. You can run the Streams application on one machine with multiple threads or on multiple machines; in either case, all active threads in the application will balance the work involved in data processing.

The Streams engine parallelizes execution of a topology by splitting it into tasks. The number of tasks is determined by the Streams engine and depends on the number of partitions in the topics that the application processes. Each task is responsible for a subset of the partitions: the task will subscribe to those partitions and consume events from them. For every event it consumes, the task will execute all the processing steps that apply to this partition in order before eventually writing the result to the sink. Those tasks are the basic unit of parallelism in Kafka Streams, because each task can execute independently of others. See Figure 11-11.

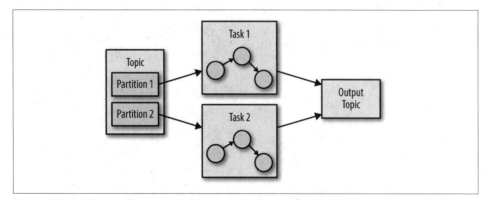

Figure 11-11. Two tasks running the same topology—one for each partition in the input topic

The developer of the application can choose the number of threads each application instance will execute. If multiple threads are available, every thread will execute a subset of the tasks that the application creates. If multiple instances of the application are running on multiple servers, different tasks will execute for each thread on each server. This is the way streaming applications scale: you will have as many tasks as you have partitions in the topics you are processing. If you want to process faster, add more threads. If you run out of resources on the server, start another instance of the application on another server. Kafka will automatically coordinate work—it will assign each task its own subset of partitions and each task will independently process events from those partitions and maintain its own local state with relevant aggregates if the topology requires this. See Figure 11-12.

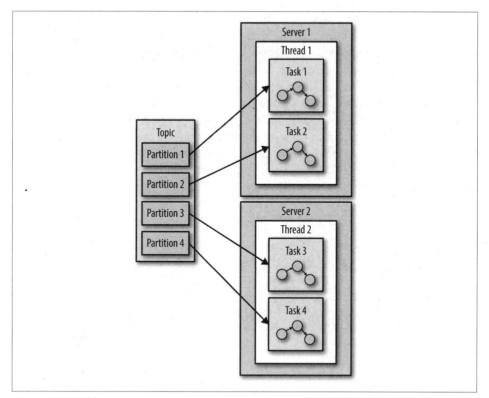

Figure 11-12. The stream processing tasks can run on multiple threads and multiple servers

You may have noticed that sometimes a processing step may require results from multiple partitions, which could create dependencies between tasks. For example, if we join two streams, as we did in the ClickStream example in "Click Stream Enrichment" on page 270, we need data from a partition in each stream before we can emit a result. Kafka Streams handles this situation by assigning all the partitions needed for one join to the same task so that the task can consume from all the relevant partitions and perform the join independently. This is why Kafka Streams currently requires that all topics that participate in a join operation will have the same number of partitions and be partitioned based on the join key.

Another example of dependencies between tasks is when our application requires repartitioning. For instance, in the ClickStream example, all our events are keyed by the user ID. But what if we want to generate statistics per page? Or per zip code? We'll need to repartition the data by the zip code and run an aggregation of the data with the new partitions. If task 1 processes the data from partition 1 and reaches a processor that repartitions the data (groupBy operation), it will need to *shuffle*, which means sending them the events—send events to other tasks to process them. Unlike other stream processor frameworks, Kafka Streams repartitions by writing the events to a new topic with new keys and partitions. Then another set of tasks reads events from the new topic and continues processing. The repartitioning steps break our topology into two subtopologies, each with its own tasks. The second set of tasks depends on the first, because it processes the results of the first subtopology. However, the first and second sets of tasks can still run independently and in parallel because the first set of tasks writes data into a topic at its own rate and the second set consumes from the topic and processes the events on its own. There is no communication and no shared resources between the tasks and they don't need to run on the same threads or servers. This is one of the more useful things Kafka does—reduce dependencies between different parts of a pipeline. See Figure 11-13.

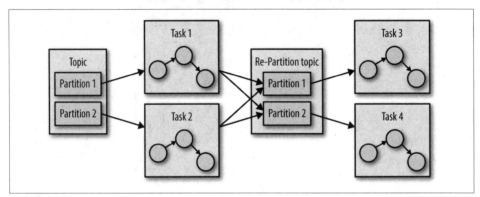

Figure 11-13. Two sets of tasks processing events with a topic for re-partitioning events between them

Surviving Failures

The same model that allows us to scale our application also allows us to gracefully handle failures. First, Kafka is highly available, and therefore the data we persist to Kafka is also highly available. So if the application fails and needs to restart, it can look up its last position in the stream from Kafka and continue its processing from the last offset it committed before failing. Note that if the local state store is lost (e.g., because we needed to replace the server it was stored on), the streams application can always re-create it from the change log it stores in Kafka.

Kafka Streams also leverages Kafka's consumer coordination to provide high availability for tasks. If a task failed but there are threads or other instances of the streams application that are active, the task will restart on one of the available threads. This is similar to how consumer groups handle the failure of one of the consumers in the group by assigning partitions to one of the remaining consumers.

Stream Processing Use Cases

Throughout this chapter we've learned how to do stream processing—from general concepts and patterns to specific examples in Kafka Streams. At this point it may be worth looking at the common stream processing use cases. As explained in the beginning of the chapter, stream processing—or continuous processing—is useful in cases where you want your events to be processed in quick order rather than wait for hours until the next batch, but also where you are not expecting a response to arrive in milliseconds. This is all true but also very abstract. Let's look at a few real scenarios that can be solved with stream processing:

Customer Service

Suppose that you just reserved a room at a large hotel chain and you expect an email confirmation and receipt. A few minutes after reserving, when the confirmation still hasn't arrived, you call customer service to confirm your reservation. Suppose the customer service desk tells you "I don't see the order in our system, but the batch job that loads the data from the reservation system to the hotels and the customer service desk only runs once a day, so please call back tomorrow. You should see the email within 2-3 business days." This doesn't sound like very good service, yet I've had this conversation more than once with a large hotel chain. What we really want is every system in the hotel chain to get an update about a new reservations seconds or minutes after the reservation is made, including the customer service center, the hotel, the system that sends email confirmations, the website, etc. You also want the customer service center to be able to immediately pull up all the details about any of your past visits to any of the hotels in the chain, and the reception desk at the hotel to know that you are a loyal customer so they can give you an upgrade. Building all those systems using stream-processing applications allows them to receive and process updates in near real time, which makes for a better customer experience. With such a system, I'd receive a confirmation email within minutes, my credit card would be charged on time, the receipt would be sent, and the service desk could immediately answer my questions regarding the reservation.

Internet of Things

Internet of Things can mean many things—from a home device for adjusting temperature and ordering refills of laundry detergent to real-time quality control of pharmaceutical manufacturing. A very common use case when applying stream processing to sensors and devices is to try to predict when preventive maintenance is needed. This is similar to application monitoring but applied to hardware and is common in many industries, including manufacturing, telecommunications (identifying faulty cellphone towers), cable TV (identifying faulty box-top devices before users complain), and many more. Every case has its own pattern, but the goal is similar: process events arriving from devices at a large scale and identify patterns that signal that a device requires maintenance. These patterns can be dropped packets for a switch, more force required to tighten screws in manufacturing, or users restarting the box more frequently for cable TV.

- **Fraud Detection**: Also known as anomaly detection, is a very wide field that focuses on catching "cheaters" or bad actors in the system. Examples of fraud-detection applications include detecting credit card fraud, stock trading fraud, video-game cheaters, and cybersecurity risks. In all these fields, there are large benefits to catching fraud as early as possible, so a near real-time system that is capable of responding to events quickly—perhaps stopping a bad transaction before it is even approved—is much preferred to a batch job that detects fraud three days after the fact when cleanup is much more complicated. This is again a problem of identifying patterns in a large-scale stream of events.

In cyber security, there is a method known as *beaconing*. When the hacker plants malware inside the organization, it will occasionally reach outside to receive commands. It can be difficult to detect this activity since it can happen at any time and any frequency. Typically, networks are well defended against external attacks but more vulnerable to someone inside the organization reaching out. By processing the large stream of network connection events and recognizing a pattern of communication as abnormal (for example, detecting that this host typically doesn't access those specific IPs), the security organization can be alerted early, before more harm is done.

How to Choose a Stream-Processing Framework

When choosing a stream-processing framework, it is important to consider the type of application you are planning on writing. Different types of applications call for different stream-processing solutions:

Ingest
Where the goal is to get data from one system to another, with some modification to the data on how it will make it conform to the target system.

Low milliseconds actions
Any application that requires almost immediate response. Some fraud detection use cases fall within this bucket.

Asynchronous microservices
These microservices perform a simple action on behalf of a larger business process, such as updating the inventory of a store. These applications may need to maintain a local state caching events as a way to improve performance.

Near real-time data analytics
> These streaming applications perform complex aggregations and joins in order to slice and dice the data and generate interesting business-relevant insights.

The stream-processing system you will choose will depend a lot on the problem you are solving.

- If you are trying to solve an ingest problem, you should reconsider whether you want a stream processing system or a simpler ingest-focused system like Kafka Connect. If you are sure you want a stream processing system, you need to make sure it has both a good selection of connectors and high-quality connectors for the systems you are targeting.

- If you are trying to solve a problem that requires low milliseconds actions, you should also reconsider your choice of streams. Request-response patterns are often better suited to this task. If you are sure you want a stream-processing system, then you need to opt for one that supports an event-by-event low-latency model rather than one that focuses on microbatches.

- If you are building asynchronous microservices, you need a stream processing system that integrates well with your message bus of choice (Kafka, hopefully), has change capture capabilities that easily deliver upstream changes to the microservice local caches, and has the good support of a local store that can serve as a cache or materialized view of the microservice data.

- If you are building a complex analytics engine, you also need a stream-processing system with great support for a local store—this time, not for maintenance of local caches and materialized views but rather to support advanced aggregations, windows, and joins that are otherwise difficult to implement. The APIs should include support for custom aggregations, window operations, and multiple join types.

In addition to use-case specific considerations, there are a few global considerations you should take into account:

Operability of the system
> Is it easy to deploy to production? Is it easy to monitor and troubleshoot? Is it easy to scale up and down when needed? Does it integrate well with your existing infrastructure? What if there is a mistake and you need to reprocess data?

Usability of APIs and ease of debugging
> I've seen orders of magnitude differences in the time it takes to write a high-quality application among different versions of the same framework. Development time and time-to-market is important so you need to choose a system that makes you efficient.

Makes hard things easy

Almost every system will claim they can do advanced windowed aggregations and maintain local caches, but the question is: do they make it easy for you? Do they handle gritty details around scale and recovery, or do they supply leaky abstractions and make you handle most of the mess? The more a system exposes clean APIs and abstractions and handles the gritty details on its own, the more productive developers will be.

Community

Most stream processing applications you consider are going to be open source, and there's no replacement for a vibrant and active community. Good community means you get new and exciting features on a regular basis, the quality is relatively good (no one wants to work on bad software), bugs get fixed quickly, and user questions get answers in timely manner. It also means that if you get a strange error and Google it, you will find information about it because other people are using this system and seeing the same issues.

Summary

We started the chapter by explaining stream processing. We gave a formal definition and discussed the common attributes of the stream-processing paradigm. We also compared it to other programming paradigms.

We then discussed important stream-processing concepts. Those concepts were demonstrated with three example applications written with Kafka Streams.

After going over all the details of these example applications, we gave an overview of the Kafka Streams architecture and explained how it works under the covers. We conclude the chapter, and the book, with several examples of stream-processing use cases and advice on how to compare different stream-processing frameworks.

Installing Kafka on Other Operating Systems

Apache Kafka is primarily a Java application, and therefore should be able to run on any system where you are able to install a JRE. It has, however, been optimized for Linux-based operating systems so that is where it will perform best. Running on other operating systems may result in bugs specific to the OS. For this reason, when using Kafka for development or test purposes on a common desktop OS, it is a good idea to consider running in a virtual machine that matches your eventual production environment.

Installing on Windows

As of Microsoft Windows 10, there are now two ways that you can run Kafka. The traditional way is using a native Java installation. Windows 10 users also have the option to use the Windows Subsystem for Linux. The latter method is highly preferred because it provides a much simpler setup that more closely matches the typical production environment, so we will review it first.

Using Windows Subsystem for Linux

If you are running Windows 10, you can install native Ubuntu support under Windows using Windows Subsystem for Linux (WSL). At the time of publication, Microsoft still considers WSL to be an experimental feature. Though it acts similar to a virtual machine, it does not require the resources of a full VM and provides richer integration with the Windows OS.

In order to install WSL, you should follow the instructions available from the Microsoft Developer Network at the Bash on Ubuntu on Windows (*http://bit.ly/2r6HnN7*) page. Once that is done, you will need to install a JDK using `apt-get`:

```
$ sudo apt-get install openjdk-7-jre-headless
[sudo] password for username:
Reading package lists... Done
Building dependency tree
Reading state information... Done
[...]
done.
$
```

Once you have installed the JDK, you can proceed to install Apache Kafka using the instructions in Chapter 2.

Using Native Java

For older versions of Windows, or if you prefer not to use the WSL environment, you can run Kafka natively with a Java environment for Windows. Be aware, however, that this can introduce bugs specific to the Windows environment. These bugs may not get the attention in the Apache Kafka development community as similar problems on Linux might.

Before installing Zookeeper and Kafka, you must have a Java environment set up. You should install the latest version of Oracle Java 8, which can be found on the Oracle Java SE Download page (*http://bit.ly/TEA7iC*). Download a full JDK package, so that you have all the Java tools available, and follow the instructions for installation.

Be Careful with Paths

When installing Java and Kafka, it is highly recommended that you stick to installation paths that do not contain spaces. While Windows allows spaces in paths, applications that are designed to run in Unix environments are not set up this way and specifying paths will be difficult. When installing Java, make sure to set the installation path with this in mind. For example, if installing JDK 1.8 update 121, a good choice would be to use the path `C:\Java\jdk1.8.0_121`.

Once Java is installed, you should set up the environment variables so that it can be used. This is done in the Control Panel for Windows, though the exact location will depend on your version of the OS. In Windows 10, you must select System and Security, then System, and then click Change settings under the Computer name, domain, and workgroup settings section. This will open the System Properties window, where you can select the Advanced tab and then finally click the Environment Variables...

button. Use this section to add a new user variable named JAVA_HOME (Figure A-1) and set to the path where you installed Java. Then edit the system variable named Path and add a new entry which is **%JAVA_HOME%\bin**. Save these settings and exit out of the Control Panel.

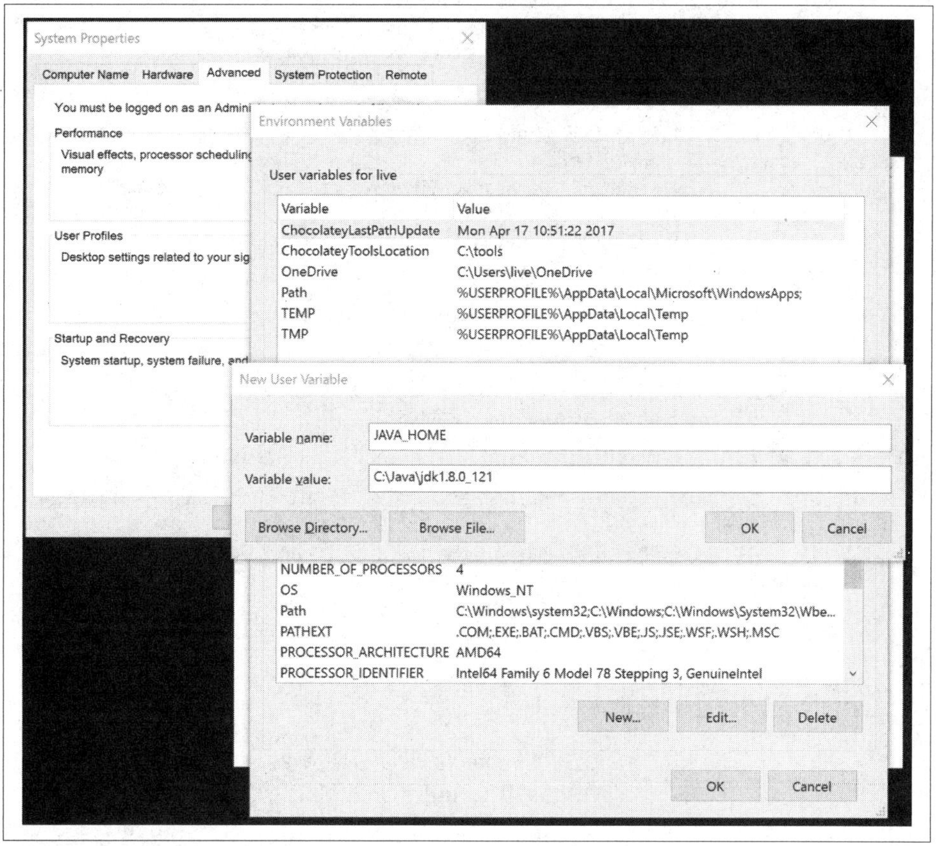

Figure A-1. Adding the JAVA_HOME variable

Now you can proceed to install Apache Kafka. The installation includes Zookeeper, so you do not have to install it separately. The current release of Kafka can be downloaded (*http://kafka.apache.org/downloads.html*). At publication time, that version is 0.10.1.0 running under Scala version 2.11.0. The downloaded file will be GZip compressed and packaged with the tar utility, so you will need to use a Windows application such as 8Zip to uncompress it. Similar to installing on Linux, you must choose a directory to extract Kafka into. For this example, we will assume Kafka is extracted into C:\kafka_2.11-0.10.1.0.

Running Zookeeper and Kafka under Windows is a little different, as you must use the batch files designed for Windows rather than the shell scripts for other platforms.

These batch files also do not support backgrounding the application, so you will need a separate shell for each application. First, start Zookeeper:

```
PS C:\> cd kafka_2.11-0.10.2.0
PS C:\kafka_2.11-0.10.2.0> bin/windows/zookeeper-server-start.bat C:
\kafka_2.11-0.10.2.0\config\zookeeper.properties
[2017-04-26 16:41:51,529] INFO Reading configuration from: C:
\kafka_2.11-0.10.2.0\config\zookeeper.properties (org.apache.zoo
keeper.server.quorum.QuorumPeerConfig)
[...]
[2017-04-26 16:41:51,595] INFO minSessionTimeout set to -1 (org.apache.zoo
keeper.server.ZooKeeperServer)
[2017-04-26 16:41:51,596] INFO maxSessionTimeout set to -1 (org.apache.zoo
keeper.server.ZooKeeperServer)
[2017-04-26 16:41:51,673] INFO binding to port 0.0.0.0/0.0.0.0:2181
(org.apache.zookeeper.server.NIOServerCnxnFactory)
```

Once Zookeeper is running, you can open another window to start Kafka:

```
PS C:\> cd kafka_2.11-0.10.2.0
PS C:\kafka_2.11-0.10.2.0> .\bin\windows\kafka-server-start.bat C:
\kafka_2.11-0.10.2.0\config\server.properties
[2017-04-26 16:45:19,804] INFO KafkaConfig values:
[...]
[2017-04-26 16:45:20,697] INFO Kafka version : 0.10.2.0 (org.apache.kafka.com
mon.utils.AppInfoParser)
[2017-04-26 16:45:20,706] INFO Kafka commitId : 576d93a8dc0cf421
(org.apache.kafka.common.utils.AppInfoParser)
[2017-04-26 16:45:20,717] INFO [Kafka Server 0], started (kafka.server.Kafka
Server)
```

Installing on MacOS

MacOS runs on Darwin, a Unix OS that is derived, in part, from FreeBSD. This means that many of the expectations of running on a Unix OS hold true, and installing applications designed for Unix, like Apache Kafka, is not too difficult. You can either keep the installation simple by using a package manager (like Homebrew), or you can install Java and Kafka manually for greater control over versions.

Using Homebrew

If you have already installed Homebrew (*https://brew.sh/*) for MacOS, you can use it to install Kafka in one step. This will assure that you have Java installed first, and it will then install Apache Kafka 0.10.2.0 (as the time of writing).

If you have not yet installed Homebrew, do that first by following the directions on the installation page (*http://docs.brew.sh/Installation.html*). Then you can install Kafka itself. The Homebrew package manager will ensure that you have all the dependencies installed first, including Java:

```
$ brew install kafka
==> Installing kafka dependency: zookeeper
[...]
==> Summary
/usr/local/Cellar/kafka/0.10.2.0: 132 files, 37.2MB
$
```

Homebrew will install Kafka under */usr/local/Cellar*, but the files will be linked into other directories:

- Binaries and scripts will be in /usr/local/bin
- Kafka configurations will be in /usr/local/etc/kafka
- Zookeeper configuration will be in /usr/local/etc/zookeeper
- The log.dirs config (the location for Kafka data) will be set to /usr/local/var/lib/kafka-logs

After installation is complete, you can start Zookeeper and Kafka (this example starts Kafka in the foreground):

```
$ /usr/local/bin/zkServer start
JMX enabled by default
Using config: /usr/local/etc/zookeeper/zoo.cfg
Starting zookeeper ... STARTED
$ kafka-server-start.sh /usr/local/etc/kafka/server.properties
[...]
[2017-02-09 20:48:22,485] INFO [Kafka Server 0], started (kafka.server.Kafka
Server)
```

Installing Manually

Similar to a manual installation for the Windows OS, when installing Kafka on MacOS you must first install a JDK. The same Oracle Java SE Download page (*http://bit.ly/TEA7iC*) can be used to get the proper version for MacOS. You can then download Apache Kafka, similar to Windows again. For this example, we will assume that the Kafka download is expanded into the /usr/local/kafka_2.11-0.10.2.0 directory.

Starting Zookeeper and Kafka looks just like starting them when using Linux, though you will need to make sure your JAVA_HOME directory is set first:

```
$ export JAVA_HOME=`/usr/libexec/java_home`
$ echo $JAVA_HOME
/Library/Java/JavaVirtualMachines/jdk1.8.0._131.jdk/Contents/Home
$ /usr/local/kafka_2.11-0.10.2.0/bin/zookeeper-server-start.sh -daemon /usr/
local/kafka_2.11-0.10.2.0/config/zookeeper.properties
$ /usr/local/kafka_2.11-0.10.2.0/bin/kafka-server-start.sh /usr/local/etc/kafka/
server.properties
[2017-04-26 16:45:19,804] INFO KafkaConfig values:
```

```
[...]
[2017-04-26 16:45:20,697] INFO Kafka version : 0.10.2.0 (org.apache.kafka.com
mon.utils.AppInfoParser)
[2017-04-26 16:45:20,706] INFO Kafka commitId : 576d93a8dc0cf421
(org.apache.kafka.common.utils.AppInfoParser)
[2017-04-26 16:45:20,717] INFO [Kafka Server 0], started (kafka.server.Kafka
Server)
```

Index

D

data ecosystem, Kafka, 11-13
    activity tracking, 12
    commit log, 13
    messaging, 12
    metrics and logging, 13
    stream processing, 13
    use cases, 12
data formats, data pipelines and, 138
data mirroring (see cross-cluster data mirroring)
data pipelines, 135-156
    considerations when building, 136-141
    coupling and agility, 140
    data formats, 138
    failure handling, 140
    high/varying throughput, 137
    Kafka Connect vs. traditional producer/
        consumer, 141
    reliability, 137
    security, 139
    timeliness requirements, 136
    transformations, 139
data stream, 248
data, reading from Kafka (see consumers)
data-lake architecture, 139
datacenter failure, stretch clusters and, 169
decoupling
    data formats and, 5
    data pipelines, 140
deleted events, 112
deletions
    consumer groups, 188
    topics, 184, 209
deserializers, 88-92
    custom, 89-91
    using Avro deserialization with Kafka consumer, 91
dirty pages, 33
dirty records, 110, 112
disaster recovery (DR), 158, 164
disk
    filesystem choice, 34
    HDD vs. SSD, 29
    monitoring usage of, 234
    performance when using time-based log
        segment limits, 28
disk capacity, 29
disk failures, effects of, 218
disk throughput, 29
disk-based retention, 10
distributed commit log, 4
distributed streaming platform, 4
dynamic configuration changes
    overriding client configuration defaults, 192
    overriding topic defaults, 190
    removing configuration overrides, 193

E

Elasticsearch, loading MySQL table into,
    146-151
ELT (Extract-Load-Transform), 139
enable.auto.commit parameter, 74, 126
end-to-end monitoring, 244
ensemble (Zookeeper), 19
error messages
    for nonexistent topics, 184
    retries, 50
error-rate per record, 132
ETL (Extract-Transform-Load), 139
event stream, 248
event time, stream processing and, 251
events, deleted, 112
exactly-once delivery, 129, 137
EXT4 (fourth extended file system), 34
Extents File System (XFS), 34
external metrics
    end-to-end monitoring, 244
    internal metrics vs., 212
external offset mapping, 167
external state, 253

F

failure handling
    in data pipelines, 140
    Kafka Streams API, 276
fetch manager metrics, 239
fetch requests, 102
fetch.max.wait.ms parameter, 72
fetch.message.max.bytes parameter, 28
fetch.min.bytes parameter, 72
file management, 107
filesystem, 34
fire-and-forget, 45
follower replicas, 97
fraud detection (use case), 278

G

garbage collection (GC)
    monitoring, 231
    options, 36
Garbage First (G1) collector, 36
group coordinator, 67
group leader, 68
group.id, 69, 126, 142
guarantees, reliable data delivery, 116

H

hard drives, HDD vs. SSD, 29
hardware
    CPU, 30
    disk capacity, 29
    disk throughput, 29
    memory, 29
    networking, 30
    selection, 28-30
health checks, 213
heap memory, 30
heartbeats, 67
high-fidelity pipelines, 139
Homebrew, Kafka installation on OS X using,
    284
hub-and-spokes architecture, 160

I

idempotent writes, 129
in-sync replicas, 98
    and unclean leader election, 119
    minimum, 121
    topics and, 117
indexes, 109
installation (Kafka), 17-39
    broker installation, 20
    cloud computing environments, 30
    cluster configuration, 31-35
    colocating applications on Zookeeper, 37
    datacenter layout, 37
    disk capacity, 29
    disk throughput, 29
    garbage collector options, 36
    hardware selection, 28-30
    installation on OS other than Linux,
        281-285
    Java installation, 17
    OS choice, 17

OS X, 284
    production concerns, 36-38
    using WSL, 281
    Windows, 281-284
    Zookeeper installation, 18-20
instance configuration, 30
internal metrics, 212
internal state, 253
internals, 95-113
    cluster membership, 95
    controller, 96
    physical storage, 105-113
    replication, 97-99
    request processing, 99-105
Internet of Things (use case), 277
IO threads, 100

J

Java
    garbage collector tuning, 36
    installation, 17
    Kafka installation on Windows, 282
Java Management Extensions (JMX), 211
JMX (Java Management Extensions), 132, 211,
    212
JVM (Java Virtual Machine)
    garbage collection monitoring, 231
    heap memory, 30
    monitoring, 231
    OS monitoring, 232

K

Kafka (basics), 1-16
    batches, 4
    birth of, 15
    brokers and clusters, 7
    data ecosystem, 11-13
    first release, 15
    installation on OS other than Linux,
        281-285
    installation on OS X, 284
    installation on Windows, 281-284
    internals (see internals)
    LinkedIn and, 14
    manual installation on OS X, 285
    messages, 4
    multiple clusters, 8
    name's origin, 16
    origins, 14-16

producers and consumers, 6
publish-subscribe messaging before Kafka,
    1-4
publish-subscribe messaging with, 4-9
reasons to use, 10
scalability of, 10
schemas, 5
topics and partitions, 5
Kafka Connect (see Connect)
Kafka Streams API
    architecture overview, 272-276
    building a topology, 272
    ClickStream enrichment example, 270-272
    examples, 264-272
    scaling a topology, 273-276
    stock market statistics example, 268-270
    surviving failures, 276
    word count example, 265-268
kafka-acls.sh, 207
kafka-console-consumer.sh tool, 202-205
    consuming the offsets topic, 205
    message formatter options, 204
kafka.console.producer.sh tool, 205-207
KafkaConsumer, 68
    (see also consumers)
KafkaProducer (see producers)
key-value pairs, 59
key.serializer class, 44
keyed topics, partitions and, 183
keys
    mapping to partitions, 60
    purposes of, 59
Kreps, Jay, 15

L
lag monitoring, 173, 243
leader count metric, 225
leaders
    automatic rebalancing, 194
    controller and, 96
    leader count metric, 225
    no leader error, 47
    preferred, 98
    replicas, 97
    unclean leader election, 119-121, 119
line-reader options, 205, 207
linger.ms parameter, 50
LinkedIn, 14
Linux

networking configuration, 35, 176
    swappiness, 33
    tuning, 32
    Windows subsystem for, 281
listeners, rebalancing, 82-83
livelock, 67
local state
    defined, 253
    stream processing with, 257
log append time, 251
log compacted topics, 8
log segments, dumping, 199
log, clean/dirty portions of, 110
log.dirs parameter, 23
log.retention.bytes parameter, 26
log.retention.ms parameter, 26
log.segment.bytes parameter, 27
log.segment.ms parameter, 27
logging
    and data ecosystem, 13
    monitoring and, 235

M
map-filter pattern, 256
max.block.ms parameter, 51
max.in.flight.requests.per.connection parame-
    ter, 51
max.partition.fetch.bytes parameter, 72
max.poll.records parameter, 75
max.request.size parameter, 51
membership, cluster, 95
memory, hardware considerations, 29
message retention (see retention)
message size configurations, 28
message.max.bytes parameter, 28
messages, 4
    (see also producers)
    acks parameter, 48
    asynchronous transmission, 47
    file format, 108
    ordering guarantees, 52
    primary methods of sending, 45
    sending, 46-48
    synchronous transmission, 47
    topics and partitions, 5
messages in per second, 224
messaging (use case), 12
metadata requests, 100
metadata.fetch.timeout.ms parameter, 51

deleting topics manually, 209
killing a partition move, 208
moving the cluster controller, 208
removing topics to be deleted, 209
uReplicator, 178

V

value.serializer class, 44
virtual memory, 33
vm.swappiness, 33

W

windowed operations, 255
windowed-join, 261
Windows, Kafka installation, 281-284
    using native Java, 282
    using WSL, 281
wire protocol, 42
word count, 265-268

workers
    Connect, 152
    key configurations for, 142
wrapper message, 108
writers, 6
    (see also producers)

Z

Zookeeper
    broker list of cluster members, 95
    chroot path, 22
    colocating applications on, 37
    consumers and, 38
    ensemble, 19
    for standalone server, 18
    installation, 18-20
zookeeper.connect parameter, 22
ZookeeperConsumerConnector, 93

About the Authors

Neha Narkhede is cofounder and head of engineering at Confluent, a company backing the popular Apache Kafka messaging system. Prior to founding Confluent, Neha led streams infrastructure at LinkedIn, where she was responsible for LinkedIn's petabyte scale-streaming infrastructure built on top of Apache Kafka and Apache Samza. Neha specializes in building and scaling large distributed systems and is one of the initial authors of Apache Kafka. In the past she has worked on searching within the database at Oracle and holds a masters in computer science from Georgia Tech.

Gwen Shapira is a product manager at Confluent. She is a PMC member of the Apache Kafka project, has contributed Kafka integration to Apache Flume, and is a committer on Apache Sqoop. Gwen has 15 years of experience working with customers to design scalable data architectures. Formerly a software engineer at Cloudera, senior consultant at Pythian, Oracle ACE Director, and board member at NoCOUG. Gwen is a frequent speaker at industry conferences and contributes to multiple industry blogs including O'Reilly Radar.

Todd Palino is a senior staff site reliability engineer at LinkedIn, tasked with keeping the largest deployment of Apache Kafka, Zookeeper, and Samza fed and watered. He is responsible for architecture, day-to-day operations, and tools development, including the creation of an advanced monitoring and notification system. Todd is the developer of the open source project Burrow, a Kafka consumer monitoring tool, and can be found sharing his experience with Apache Kafka at industry conferences and tech talks. Todd has spent more than 20 years in the technology industry running infrastructure services, most recently as a systems engineer at Verisign, developing service management automation for DNS, networking, and hardware management, as well as managing hardware and software standards across the company.

Colophon

The animal on the cover of *Kafka: The Definitive Guide* is a blue-winged kookaburra (*Dacelo leachii*). It is part of the Alcedinidae family and can be found in southern New Guinea and the less dry area of northern Australia. They are considered to be river kingfisher birds.

The male kookaburra has a colorful look. The lower wing and tail feathers are blue, hence its name, but tails of females are reddish-brown with black bars. Both sexes have cream colored undersides with streaks of brown, and white irises in their eyes. Adult kookaburras are smaller than other kingfishers at just 15 to 17 inches in length and, on average, weigh about 260 to 330 grams.

The diet of the blue-winged kookaburra is heavily carnivorous, with prey varying slightly given changing seasons. For example, in the summer months there is a larger abundance of lizards, insects, and frogs that this bird feeds on, but drier months introduce more crayfish, fish, rodents, and even smaller birds into their diet. They're not alone in eating other birds, however, as red goshawks and rufous owls have the blue-winged kookaburra on their menu when in season.

Breeding for the blue-winged kookaburra occurs in the months of September through December. Nests are hollows in the high parts of trees. Raising young is a community effort, as there is at least one helper bird to help mom and dad. Three to four eggs are laid and incubated for about 26 days. Chicks will fledge around 36 days after hatching—if they survive. Older siblings have been known to kill the younger ones in their aggressive and competitive first week of life. Those who aren't victims of fratricide or other causes of death will be trained by their parents to hunt for 6 to 10 weeks before heading off on their own.

Learn from experts.
Find the answers you need.

Sign up for a **10-day free trial** to get **unlimited access** to all of the content on Safari, including Learning Paths, interactive tutorials, and curated playlists that draw from thousands of ebooks and training videos on a wide range of topics, including data, design, DevOps, management, business—and much more.

Start your free trial at:
oreilly.com/safari

(No credit card required.)